Boom and Bust:
The Politics of the California Budget

Boom and Bust:
The Politics of the California Budget

Jeff Cummins

Berkeley Public Policy Press
Institute of Governmental Studies
University of California, Berkeley
2015

Library of Congress Cataloging-in-Publication Data

Cummins, Jeff (Economist)
  Boom and bust : the politics of the California budget / Jeff Cummins.
    pages cm
Includes bibliographical references and index.
ISBN 978-0-87772-447-6
1. Budget process—California. 2. California—Appropriations and expenditures. I. Title.
HJ2053.C3C86 2015
352.4'809794—dc23

                                                                    2014039656

Contents

Preface

In September 2001, I began working as an analyst at the Legislative Analyst's Office (LAO) in Sacramento. At the time, the state of California was at the tail end of a prosperous period that was jumpstarted by the dot.com boom of the late 1990s. Unemployment at the state and national levels was the lowest it had been in recent memory and government coffers had enjoyed a windfall of revenues since the mid-1990s. However, only two months later in November 2001, the LAO issued its *Fiscal Outlook* that drastically changed the budget environment in the capital and ushered in what I refer to as California's second crisis budgeting era (the 1930s was the first). Instead of policymakers ruminating over surpluses as far as the eye could see, severe deficits were forecast. To assist legislators with the gargantuan task of aligning expenditures with revenues, the LAO issued a report, *Addressing the State's Fiscal Problem*, which provided options for cutting expenditures and generating revenue. To assemble this options list, the office turned to previous lists it had published in the early 1990s and '80s, many of which made it onto the new list. What struck me about this exercise was its cyclical nature and the rather predictable response to crisis.

Fast forward to 2005 when I was asked to put together a course on public budgeting at California State University, Fresno. I thought the natural focus of the course should be on the state budget since it dominated the state political scene since I first arrived at the LAO. As I searched for materials for the course, there was no current comprehensive book that explained the California budget process or system. As other instructors did, I selected a common budget textbook that focused on the federal level and heavily supplemented it with California-specific materials. In the meantime, the idea for a comprehensive book about the California budget was born. As I continued to teach budgeting courses, many students were employees of the state, counties, cities and non-profit organizations. Because of the state's precarious financial situation and its effects on their place of employment, students were particularly interested in how budgeting worked in California.

The purpose of this book is to provide a comprehensive examination of the California budget and to explore many of the fiscal issues that the state has confronted in recent decades. Through an historical, theoretical, and political context, I hope to increase our understanding of how state and local policymakers, as well as voters, make budgetary decisions that have wide-ranging impacts on the state's nearly 40 million residents.

One aspect of California budgeting that I focus on is the boom-and-bust budget cycles that the title alludes to, including why the system is prone to these cycles. In the boom phases of the cycle, when revenues are flowing into the state treasury and policymakers are eager to convince others of the merits of their pet projects, little attention is paid to the inner workings of the budget process and how the system is set up for the eventual fall. The good times only mask the underlying structural problems with the system. During the bust phase, when revenues decline, usually precipitously, a new budgeting mindset for policymakers emerges—what I have termed crisis budgeting—that is distinctly different from the boom phase. Previous budgetary perspectives commonly favored by budget scholars, such as incrementalism, are ill-equipped to explain policymakers' behavior in such times. This is when underlying structural issues rear their head, but policymakers are in no position to address them on a more permanent basis as they scramble to pay the bills. There is a routine—almost predictable—response to these crisis periods.

In the course of writing this book, I received support and assistance from many people. California State University, Fresno and the College of Social Sciences both provided funding support for much of the book. Several colleagues reviewed one or more chapters and greatly enhanced its accuracy, clarified concepts, or offered new angles. This included Steve Boilard, Michael Thom, Nicole Winger, and Jonathan Clay. I contacted numerous state agencies in the process of writing this book, but information and reports provided by the Department of Finance and Legislative Analyst's Office were indispensable. Current and former LAO staff provided information on various topics, including Anthony Simbol and Jason Sisney. Leighanna Mixter, Christopher Veira, Orry Hamilton, and Alex Andrade-Lozano all provided invaluable research assistance. Fresno State librarians Carol Doyle, Allison Cowgill, and Arturo Mendoza helped me track down old speeches, documents, and newspaper articles, among other requests.

I was lucky to have an editor, Ethan Rarick, who was enthusiastic and supportive of the project from the start and thought it should join the long line of fine books focusing on California politics that have been published by the Institute of Governmental Studies. I also need to thank Maria Wolf, who copyedited, designed the cover, finalized all of the graphics, and always answered all of my tedious formatting questions quickly.

Lastly, the book is dedicated to my wife, Natasha, who patiently and thoughtfully listened to and responded to my ideas, concerns, and complaints from the beginning of the idea to its final publication. That's no small task when the subject is the California budget.

Jeff Cummins
California State University, Fresno
2014

Chapter 1

Understanding California Budgeting

An examination of our financial condition irresistibly forces upon us the conviction that we have been progressing rapidly towards a condition of bankruptcy and ruin, and seemingly without making an effort to arrest the downward progress of events.
—Governor Neely Johnson, *State of the State Address, January 7, 1857*[1]

In 2011, newly elected Governor Jerry Brown (D) found California in the condition he left it in 1983—a fiscal wreck, only more so. Like many of his predecessors, he entered office facing an enormous budget deficit, leaving some observers scratching their heads as to why anyone would want the job in the first place. Between his first and second stint as the chief executive, the state underwent fundamental changes that altered its potential "governability." Term limits, numerous ballot measures, high levels of party polarization, and an increasingly circumscribed budget process all contributed to a perception of dysfunction from Californians and the rest of the country. Since Brown's first go-round, the California budget became the embodiment of this dysfunction. Perennially late, unbalanced, and in a condition of perpetual crisis, the budget became an annual reminder of how the California political system was not working.

Although the crisis budgeting environment was the dominant issue of the 2000s, it was really the culmination of a decades-long march towards fiscal dysfunction. An economy in transition, an outdated tax system, short-sighted policy decisions, and politicians' proclivities toward higher government spending led the state to the brink of insolvency. Students of California history may have seen

---

[1] California Assembly, "Assembly Journal, 8th Session" (Sacramento: California Assembly, 1957), accessed January 8, 2014 at http://192.234.213.35/clerkarchive/, 20.

the signs of these fiscal problems surface from time to time in what have been commonly called "boom-and-bust cycles." Fiscal conditions in the early years of the 1970s, 1980s, and 1990s highlighted the cyclical nature of the state's finances. But this pattern changed in the 2000s. The eventual boom that appeared in the earlier decades never really materialized. Instead, the fiscal crisis ran into its second decade and did not let up until 2013.

This book examines California's recent budget experience and public budgeting in California more generally through an historical, theoretical, and political perspective. In the process, we hope to provide a better understanding of an essential function of California government—how it manages the public purse. It is important to focus on the state budget because much of the state's fortunes rest on its back. It facilitates the growth of one of the top 10 economies in the world, provides a significant portion of local government funding, and extends the safety net and public education to tens of millions of Californians. Although the budget plays a pivotal role in the functioning of the state, the general public is commonly misinformed about the budget and lacks a basic understanding of the process.

To help gain an understanding of the California budget, it is necessary to explain the basic concepts of budgeting that underlie the process and discuss some of the theoretical perspectives that scholars have used to explain public budgeting. In addition to the common perspectives, we also offer a new perspective, *crisis budgeting*, through which to view California budgeting in particular, although it seems increasingly applicable to other states and the federal government as well. Indeed, California's budget experience may be a harbinger of what is to come at the national level for a decade or longer.

This and subsequent chapters (Chapters 1–6) serve as the foundation and building blocks for understanding the state budget process, its political environment, the phenomenon of ballot-box budgeting, and the voluminous fiscal challenges that policymakers face. Chapter 7 examines the state's performance on balancing the budget and the various "tools" at its disposal to accomplish this balancing act. Chapter 8 familiarizes readers with budgeting at the county and city level and how these local governments grapple with a state-dominant fiscal relationship. Chapter 9, the last chapter, discusses and analyzes California's experience with budgetary reform and various policy vehicles for improving the budget system.

Budgeting Basics

In its simplest form, a budget is a plan of where and how to spend money. A more formal definition of government budgeting would characterize it as the authoritative decision-making regarding the acquisition, allocation, and use of public resources. Although we typically assume that budgeting authority rests solely with our elected policymakers, and for the bulk of decisions it does, California is unusual in that the electorate often plays a central role in this decision-making as well when it votes on budget-related ballot measures. The acquisition of public resources is the most politically charged aspect of budgeting because it extracts money from individuals and businesses in the form of taxes and fees. The allocation of this tax revenue can be controversial too, particularly when it is directed toward social welfare programs that the public has come to view more dubiously. As we will examine in Chapter 4, the overall level of government spending has also become a hot-button issue, especially since the conservative movement gained traction with the election of Ronald Reagan as president in 1980.

Beyond purely administrative functions, budgeting is also important in many other ways. Aside from the constitution, the document itself is probably the most important product that a government can develop. Embodied within it are societal values, public priorities, choices about whom and how to tax, compromises over long-term and newly emerging conflicts and issues, and decisions over how the government should improve the living conditions of its residents. Noted scholar Irene Rubin summarizes budgeting this way: "Budgets reflect choices about what government will and will not do. They reflect the public consensus about what kinds of services governments should provide and what citizens are entitled to as members of society."[2] Long-standing decisions about the importance of education, for example, have far-ranging implications for future generations and lay the foundation for economic prosperity. About 92 percent of K-12 education in California is provided by public schools and the vast majority of this funding comes from state and local sources.[3] This funding priority reflects a conscious decision by generations of policymakers and the public to value education over all other public services (it receives the highest level of state and local funding). Of those high school graduates who attend college, most of them attend state colleges and universities, which, in turn, prepare them to fill jobs in a dynamic economy. This pipeline of workers would not be possible without the initial decision to invest vast sums of funding in our state's school systems.

While the budget may contain thousands of pages of innocuous line items and dollar figures, it belies the fact that budgeting is fundamentally a political process. The governor, legislative leaders, committee chairs, and other legislators all participate in the budget process with their own pet priorities and projects in mind. There is never enough revenue to satisfy all requests for spending, so the final dollar figures represent the consensus and tradeoffs around each of their priorities. The final numbers are also greatly influenced by over a thousand lobbyists and interest groups that descend upon the capitol during the budget session, each seeking to secure a piece of the pie for their clients and membership. And, of course, public opinion and preferences permeate the process, setting the broad outlines for the level of taxation and spending priorities. What

---

[2] Irene Rubin, *The Politics of Public Budgeting,* 7th ed. (Washington, DC: CQ Press, 2014), 1.

[3] California Department of Education, "Private School Enrollment – CalEdFacts," accessed August 26, 2014 at http://www.cde.ca.gov/sp/ps/rs/cefprivinstr.asp.

comes out of this process is an aggregation of the wins and losses of these participants with some of the victors enjoying more of the spoils.

One particularly important purpose of budgeting is public accountability. Budgets document how much money the government will take in and how this money will be distributed. This seems like a basic observation, but the historical record is replete with examples of governments abusing their fiscal responsibilities, so a transparent budget is essential to maintaining the integrity of government. In centuries past, it was not uncommon for emperors and monarchs to inflict heavy tax burdens on peasants or their political enemies. Our nation was born in the crucible of similar such abuses. In present times, the tax revolt movement that began in the late 1970s has led to much closer scrutiny of changes in the tax code. Concerns about government waste and excessive spending have risen in recent decades and provide popular stories for media outlets. The intense scrutiny of taxes and spending that is at the heart of public accountability would not be possible without the budget and public access to its contents.

Norms of Budgeting

Scholars who study public budgeting often identify budgeting norms, or criteria, for evaluating a budget process. In the next chapter, we provide a more detailed discussion of budget norms, but here we introduce them as a way to further elaborate on the concept of budgeting. Three of the more common norms are annularity, balance, and comprehensiveness. *Annularity* refers to the timeline for creating and adopting a budget and the common belief that budgets should operate on a one-year calendar (fiscal year). California and many cities within the state use an annual process, while others use a biennial cycle. This periodicity, as it is sometimes called, is important because it provides stability to a process and facilitates the accounting procedures for financial management. Without an endpoint, it is difficult to track spending and revenue and determine the second norm of balance. Closing the books at the end of the fiscal year (or biennium) allows the government entity to evaluate how well actual revenue and spending match up against what was budgeted.

Spending that exceeds revenue overall or funding for a particular department or program indicates that the norm of *balance* has been violated. One main goal of budgeting in the first place is to prevent overspending. A *surplus*, or excess revenues, at the end of the fiscal year indicates whether this goal has been met. When overspending happens frequently, as it has for the state of California, it indicates a larger budgeting problem that necessitates corrective action. In some limited cases, such as at the national level, a balanced budget is not always of paramount concern because the government and economy can operate smoothly under such circumstances. One could even argue that it might be preferable for states, such as California, to run deficits during economic downturns, but the norm of balance at the state level is reinforced with constitutional requirements to balance the budget. Even with these restrictions, California has faced three different types of deficits. *Operational deficits* are imbalances that occur in one year and have been fairly common in the last several decades. *Cyclical deficits* have occurred less frequently and coincide with the economic business cycle. *Structural deficits*, which are ongoing mismatches between spending and revenue, are the most severe and emerged, most notably, during the tumultuous fiscal environment of the 2000s.

One last common norm is *comprehensiveness*. This refers to whether there is centralized accounting of revenue and spending. In other words, is there one account for all types of revenue and spending? This norm makes it easier to track fiscal patterns. If certain types of spending or revenue are "off-budget," or do not flow through the main account, then spending or revenue may not be adequately measured. In modern budgeting, it is quite common for government entities to maintain a main general fund account and other more specialized accounts. However, this also makes it easier for "slush funds" to flourish and may encourage creative accounting to ensure the norm of balance in the state's main general fund account.

General Approaches to Budgeting

For much of the post-World War II time period, governments in the United States engaged in *pro-growth budgeting*. Pro-growth budgeting characterizes a process that revolves around decisions of where and how to increase spending. We introduce a few factors behind this pro-growth environment here and return to a fuller discussion in Chapter 7. First, the rapid economic expansion in the wake of World War II catalyzed government revenue growth at all levels. For California, annual revenue growth of 10 percent or more was common and provided the fiscal capacity to support rapid government growth. Second, there was general consensus among the public and policymakers, even Republicans, for spending growth on education, infrastructure, and social programs, although the latter has always had the least support. When it appeared that the state did not have enough revenue to match its spending levels, governors and legislators routinely turned to higher taxes instead of spending cuts to fill the gaps. Decision-making centered around *how much* to increase spending on various priorities rather than *whether* to increase spending.

This pro-growth approach began to deteriorate in the 1970s and culminated in the passage of Proposition 13 in 1978. Support for spending growth, and especially for social welfare, began to wane as the public questioned whether their tax dollars were being spent wisely. There was also growing momentum embodied in the tax revolt movement to lower the overall level of taxation. This emerging mindset ushered in the *austerity budgeting* approach. Austerity budgeting is where decision-making centers around where and how much to cut spending. It also involves a conscious effort to downsize government and reduce revenue levels either through lower tax rates or tax breaks. This approach generally characterized California budgeting from the early 1980s on, with a few temporary respites (e.g., late 1990s). Revenue growth during this period was markedly different than under pro-growth budgeting. Annual growth was consistently below 10 percent a year and, for some stretches, hovered around 5 percent, barely enough to keep up with population growth and inflation. The slower revenue growth was somewhat self-inflicted because of the tax revolt efforts to lower the tax burden, but, as we discuss in later chapters, other factors, such as an outdated tax system, have contributed to the slower growth as well.

Theoretical Perspectives of Budgeting

Although we might assume that it is easy to decide how to spend other people's money, it is generally believed that only those who participate in the budget process or observe it on a regular basis have a decent understanding of the political machinations and outcomes. With enormous sums of money at stake, budgeting is the focal point of powerful forces, all clamoring for their interests under time constraints and arcane procedures. It is often difficult to see how all the pieces fit together and what the likely outcomes will be. Scholars have proposed various theories, or simplified explanations, of the process to identify key players, principles, and factors that explicate the outcomes. Some theories present a picture of how public budgeting *should* work in an ideal world, while others seek to capture the essence of how budgeting *actually works* in practice. Here we review several of the more common theories of public budgeting as they apply to the California case and introduce a new one that is particularly relevant to California's experience.

Incrementalism

The most widely recognized, and perhaps powerful, theory of public budgeting is incrementalism. Originally developed and refined by political scientist Aaron Wildavsky, it suggests and somewhat predicts that last year's budget for a government entity or agency will grow in small increases, or increments, each year. "The largest determining factor of this year's budget is last year's. Most of each budget is a product of previous decisions. The budget may be conceived of as an iceberg; by far the largest part lies below the surface, outside the control of anyone."[4] This happens because budget makers do not have the time, energy, or resources to evaluate previous decisions and often cannot agree on large-scale changes anyway. Conflicting demands pull spending in different directions so that consensus can only be reached on these incremental changes. In what Wildavsky refers to as satisficing, no one is completely happy, but no one is completely unhappy either. Under this explanation and practice, budget makers only consider the proposals each year for *new* spending.

Wildavsky intended incrementalism to be a theory of how budgeting should work *and* one that explains actual practice. Its track record is strong as certain years of any public agency's budget can attest (See Figure 1.1). However, incre-

---

[4] Aaron Wildavskey and Naomi Caiden, *The New Politics of the Budgetary Process*, 5th ed. (Montreal: Pearson, 2004), 46.

Figure 1.1. California State Spending, 1995–2013

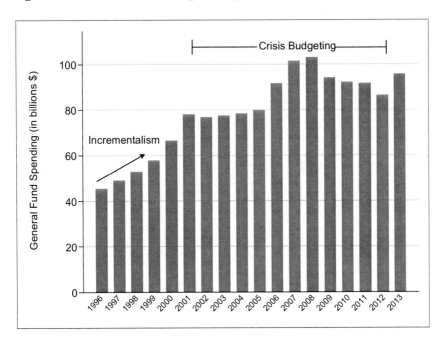

Source: Department of Finance, Chart A.
Note: 1996=1995–96 fiscal year.

mentalism also has its flaws, and its explanatory power began to deteriorate in the austerity budget environment of the 1980s. For California in the 2000s, it does little to explain the crisis that engulfed Sacramento. Most observers agree that it is particularly suited for the pro-growth budgeting environment when revenues are consistently moving upward. As a model of budgeting, critics also point out that it is wasteful because it does not scrutinize previous spending that may be ineffective, inefficient, or no longer necessary. Moreover, incrementalism does not speak to more dramatic changes in spending levels, or punctuations, that occur from time to time. To capture such large-scale fluctuations, scholars proposed *punctuated equilibrium* as a modification to incrementalism. It suggests that incrementalism explains a good portion of spending behavior, but that pressures build over time to eventually force a spike in spending. Incremental increases then move upward from this new equilibrium point.

Rational Decision-Making

Another normative theory that posits how budgeting should work is rational decision-making. Adapted from the field of economics, it assumes policymakers act as consumers would in a private marketplace. Using a series of logical steps, budget makers would rank order their goals, evaluate the options for meeting the top goals using a cost-benefit analysis, and decide accordingly on a course of action. This decision-making process is intended to allocate public resources where they are most needed and offer the "biggest bang for the buck." It assumes that decision-makers have complete information on their options and it is just a matter of figuring out how to efficiently allocate those dollars. Rational decision-making suffers from its share of shortcomings. It assumes decisions are made in a vacuum or one at a time, ignoring the larger budgeting environment. It also ignores the influence of public opinion and interest groups who exert pressure on policymakers and distort the criteria for spending decisions. As we will see in the next chapter, budget negotiations among state leaders typically yield "deals" that represent tradeoffs between competing priorities and do not necessarily allocate funding to the most in need.

Budget-Maximizing Bureaucrats

Since bureaucracies are the beneficiaries of government budgeting, budget-maximizing theory was developed to capture the motivations of public administrators. Proponents of this perspective argue that bureaucracies and their staff proactively seek to expand their budgets for several reasons. First, budget expansion reaps personal rewards for these bureaucrats as it increases agency capacity to grant salary increases and promotions. Second, larger budgets typically entail more power, authority, and responsibilities. This can increase the prestige and reputation of the agency and its employees. Third, elected officials who oversee these agencies do not have strong incentives to monitor and scrutinize spending, particularly if it benefits their constituents. Taken together, these factors promote the agency's survival through demand for its services and, in an austerity budgeting environment, protect its staff from government downsizing. Some empirical evidence supports the central tenet that agencies seek larger budgets, but other research suggests that employee salaries do not track appropriation increases and that bureaucrats may only seek to expand discretionary components of their budget.[5] Like rational decision-making, this perspective does not consider the larger context that policy actors operate in, a factor that is of overarching concern in the next perspective.

---

[5] André Blais and Stéphane Dion, *The Budget-Maximizing Bureaucrat: Appraisals and Evidence* (Pittsburgh: University of Pittsburg Press, 1991).

Crisis Budgeting

Crisis budgeting is a concept and perspective we introduce here to describe and explain the budgeting environment when the normal budgeting procedures and process break down. It is particularly relevant for examining California budgeting in the 2000s and earlier, less frequent periods in the decades before. The central premise is that the pursuit of a balanced budget is the preeminent concern of policymakers. However, true balance is illusory and not all budget players share the same concern with balance.

What Conditions Trigger Crisis Budgeting?

There are several fiscal conditions that set crisis budgeting in motion. The first indicator is a budget projection that indicates a deficit is imminent and that structural deficits will continue for the foreseeable future. In the 2000s, the trigger point occurred in November 2001, when California's legislative analyst issued a report projecting $10 billion annual general fund deficits for years to come. At this point, policymakers may consider, although they do not usually immediately adopt, more routine belt-tightening measures, such as across-the-board cuts or hiring freezes. However, even if eventually approved, they are insufficient to address the scale of the problem (see Figure 1.2).

Aside from projected deficits, other financial conditions are also present. Perhaps the most telling indicator of crisis budgeting is cash-flow problems, which affect the state's ability to pay its bills, a routine function of government. Although cash flow is an ongoing issue throughout any budget crisis, it reaches its peak when the state controller is forced to issue IOUs to vendors, as controllers have done three times in state history. Another condition present is budget gridlock, or the inability of policymakers to approve a budget plan. From the 1970s on, gridlock was a regular feature of the budget process in Sacramento, to the point that in the 2000s budgets were late more than 80 percent of the time. This condition of crisis budgeting should become more rare, as the threshold for budget approval was shifted to a simple majority with the passage of Proposition 25 in 2010.

Yet another financial condition of crisis budgeting is the ticking time bomb of long-term financial commitments. These issues are not as urgent as budget deficits or cash-flow problems, but they all relate to one another. With budget deficits present, policymakers avoid making payments on long-term commitments, such as state employee pensions or retiree health care, and pass the burden, and eventual catastrophe, on to future policymakers and taxpayers. As the contributions to these long-term issues and others, such as the state's mounting infrastructure needs, are avoided, it increases the magnitude of solutions necessary to address them later. It is analogous to the "boiling frog syndrome" where the frog, initially in a pot of cold water, does not realize the heat being turned up to the boiling point.

Figure 1.2. Crisis Budgeting Components

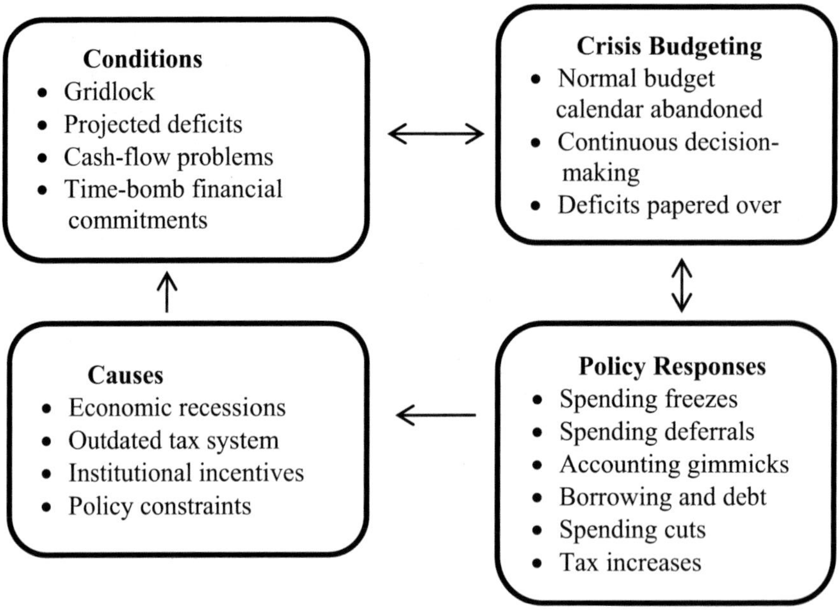

Conditions • Gridlock • Projected deficits • Cash-flow problems • Time-bomb financial commitments	⟷	**Crisis Budgeting** • Normal budget calendar abandoned • Continuous decision-making • Deficits papered over
Causes • Economic recessions • Outdated tax system • Institutional incentives • Policy constraints	⟵	**Policy Responses** • Spending freezes • Spending deferrals • Accounting gimmicks • Borrowing and debt • Spending cuts • Tax increases

Characteristics

In "normal" budgeting times, the process is subject to a predictable calendar where executive and legislative actions are statutorily or constitutionally stipulated. For example, the budget session usually runs from January, when the governor introduces the budget for the coming year, to July 1, when the fiscal year begins. During crisis budgeting, consideration and approval of budget items is continuous throughout the year as one of the norms of budgeting, annularity, is discarded. As policymakers tread fiscal water, frequent decision points to avert cash-flow issues or end-of-year deficits become common. Unlike many other states and the federal government, policymakers in California also have to contend with restrictions imposed by ballot-box budgeting (see Chapter 5). Thus, some crucial budget decisions, requiring voter approval, may be deferred until a special election can be held or until the next regularly scheduled election.

While decisions in this chaotic environment need to be made, budget players are motivated by their own self-interests. For the governor and legislators, the ultimate decision-makers, the overarching concern is balance, but to varying degrees. As the face of the state, governors seem the most concerned with balance, probably because research suggests they are the targets of voter wrath for fiscal mismanagement.[6] On the other hand, legislators must project a concern for

---

[6] Robert C. Lowry, James E. Alt, and Karen E. Ferree, "Fiscal Policy Outcomes and Electoral Accountability in American States," *American Political Science Review* 92, no.

balance, but also need to claim credit for program creations that entail higher spending or for tax cuts that reduce revenue to please voters. The general public also has conflicting interests, as opinion polls usually show preferences for a balanced budget and safeguarding certain types of spending, such as education. The remaining budget players, interest groups and bureaucracies, are motivated by the same goal: protect their program area. For these participants, their goal may conflict with the pursuit of a balanced budget. They are interested in maintaining the jobs of their staff and members.

California's experience with crisis budgeting can be divided into two categories based on their length and severity. *Crisis budgeting periods* are shorter in length, usually about three or four years, and typically end with a robust economic expansion that pulls the state out of the budget trough. Policymakers can enact enough measures to mitigate the more severe effects until an economic boom comes to the rescue. Fiscal conditions in the early parts of three consecutive decades, the 1970s, 1980s, and 1990s, are examples of these periods. *Crisis budgeting eras* last about a decade or longer and are not erased with an economic recovery. Underlying structural fiscal problems are made worse by severe economic recessions. Common budgeting tactics are not enough to paper over structural deficits. More fundamental structural changes are necessary to place the state on stronger fiscal ground. California has encountered two crisis budgeting eras. The first occurred in the 1930s with the Great Depression. Fundamental changes in the tax structure, namely the advent of the sales and income tax, and the economic surge from World War II spending helped end the first era. The second era began in 2001 with a mild recession and was exacerbated in the late 2000s by the Great Recession. For the most part, it ended in 2013, although certain conditions of crisis budgeting still exist and suggest it may only be a temporary respite. We discuss this further at the end of the chapter.

Causes and Policy Responses

In Chapter 7, we trace in more detail the roots of the most recent crisis budgeting era so here we limit our discussion to the overriding factors common to all crises. First, economic recessions play a central role in the occurrence of crisis. The more severe the recession, the more severe the budget crisis. Second, an evolving economy renders the tax system outdated and insufficient for raising adequate revenue. The deterioration of the current sales tax base for tangible goods is but one example of this factor. Increasingly, services, rather than goods, are a larger share of the economy, but most are not subject to taxation. Third, the budget process is too constrained to allow flexibility for crisis responses. The process in each successive encounter with crisis is more constrained than the last. Many of these constraints are a result of the semiconstitutional laws imposed by ballot initiatives because only voters can modify previously approved measures. But legislators themselves are to blame for some of the constraints that initially arose out of the legislature through the constitutional amendment process.

Fourth, institutional factors and trends also contribute to these crises. Term limits reduce policy expertise and negotiation experience and encourage short-sighted perspectives that could otherwise help address recurring budget problems. Increasing levels of partisanship have also made it more difficult for policymakers to fashion compromises. Lastly, previous policy decisions, or the outcomes of the three aforementioned factors, on the revenue and spending side have exacerbated existing structural problems or provided patchwork solutions. Generous pension and retiree health care benefits for state workers are examples of these spending decisions, while an expanding number of tax breaks bleed revenue sources.

We should note that not all of these factors play a role in every crisis budgeting occurrence. Term limits and partisanship were not factors in the first crisis budgeting era of the 1930s, while there was a perfect storm of all of these factors in the second era of the 2000s.

Crisis budgeting produces responses from policymakers built on several assumptions. First, options that inflict the least harm on the politically powerful are chosen first. Second, the option that is most unpopular with the public is usually chosen last. Finally, similar to punctuated equilibrium, initial decisions are incremental in nature, but pressure eventually builds for more dramatic action.

Based on these assumptions, policy responses are somewhat predictable. Spending freezes on hiring and travel are immediately imposed, although hiring exemptions usually undermine any real savings. Spending deferrals, revenue accelerations, and other accounting gimmicks are employed to stave off actual year-end deficits. Pushing major spending items into the next fiscal year may buy some time to see if the economy yields more revenue next year. Special fund borrowing is the norm in such crisis situations and, in some cases, these loans may not have to be paid back if some legal nexus can be justified between the spending and the source.[7] As these options become exhausted, policymakers then turn to actual spending cuts, starting with the low hanging fruit and moving on to cutting around the margins of departments and programs. When the urgency of the situation dictates it, the last option is tax increases on major sources, such as sales or income (see Cartoon 1.1).

---

[7] Robert Bifulco, William Duncombe, Beverly Bunch, Mark Robbins, and William Simonsen, "Debt and Deception: How States Avoid Making Hard Fiscal Decisions," *Public Administration Review* 72, no. 5 (2012): 659–67.

Cartoon 1.1. Budget Medicine

Source: Tom Meyer.

Impact on Functioning of State and Local Government

Crisis budgeting severely hampers the functioning of state and local government. Since the 2000s, budgeting has become the dominant issue for state and local government. Because Proposition 13 (1978) decimated the main source of revenue, property taxes, for local government, local funding decisions have been centralized in Sacramento and depend on the contents of the annual state budget. In the decades of perpetual gridlock, cities and counties passed two budgets—one before the state budget was finalized and another once it was adopted. State departments and agencies and local governments do not know how much funding support to expect from one year to the next and thus must avoid any long-term planning that may improve their effectiveness and efficiency.

Just as budgeting is continuous for policymakers in the capitol, it is also for the budget and program staff in numerous state departments and local government entities. Staff must constantly monitor income and outgo with an eye on the year-end condition of their budgets. Budget "drills" that produce quick estimates of various cut options become routine as department directors, county executives, and city managers game out potential scenarios to reduce spending.

School districts are required by state law to send potential layoff notices to teachers by March 15 who may lose their job in the upcoming school year. Because of the uncertainty of school funding, thousands of teachers statewide are pink-slipped each March, but only two or three out of 10 actually lose their jobs.[8] Instead of elected officials and public administrators working on how to better serve the needs of the public, during crisis budgeting, the primary concern is financial survival.

Conclusion: The Easing of Crisis or Calm before the Storm?

Budgeting is perhaps the single most important function that government performs. Laws that are passed but have no funding to implement them are impotent. An unstable budgeting environment reveals the scope and depth that public services touch in our everyday lives. Only when our favorite services are cut or crisis budgeting disrupts our daily lives does the public begin to pay attention to fiscal policy. Since the early 2000s, Californians in every corner of the state have experienced the detrimental effects of crisis budgeting—from dilapidated roads and highways to exponentially higher college tuition rates to the gutting of social service programs.

The big question is whether the state is pulling out of its fiscal doldrums on a more permanent basis or whether the improving conditions in the mid-2010s are a temporary respite from the budget chaos of the previous decade. Governor Brown announced the end of budget deficits in 2013 and vowed not to return to the dire conditions of crisis budgeting. "So I want to avoid the boom and the bust, the borrow and the spend, where we make the promise and then we take it back."[9] The end of crisis budgeting yielded once again to incrementalism as policymakers quickly sought to restore programs to their prerecession levels. Yet, while California appears to be pulling away from crisis budgeting, some of its conditions remain. Cash-flow problems, debt overhang, and "time-bomb" financial commitments still point towards a state in poor financial shape. The pivotal factor in the state's budget outlook is Proposition 30, which temporarily raises sales and income taxes through 2018. Without it, the state would still be mired in structural deficits. If policymakers can set enough savings aside in budget reserves or enact major tax reform, the state may avoid the budget convulsions of the past. However, if Proposition 30 expires without taking these remedial steps, crisis budgeting, in full force, is likely to rear its head once more.

---

[8] Legislative Analyst's Office, *A Review of the Teacher Layoff Process in California* (Sacramento: Legislative Analyst's Office, 2012), accessed at http://www.lao.ca.gov/reports/2012/edu/teacher-layoffs/teacher-layoffs-032212.pdf.

[9] Quoted in Kevin Yamamura, "California Gov. Jerry Brown Says Budget Deficit has Disappeared," *Sacramento Bee*, January 11, 2013.

Review Questions

1. Why is public budgeting an important government function?

2. What theoretical perspectives are most applicable to budgeting in your local city or county?

3. What is the likelihood of crisis budgeting within the next decade?

Additional Resources

California Budget website: http://www.dof.ca.gov/budget/

This website, maintained by the Department of Finance, is the comprehensive source for the California budget. It has the governor's budget going back a decade and extensive supplementary materials on expenditures, revenues, economic data, and demographics.

Chapter 2

The Budget Dance: The Politics of Process

I'm going to express enough flexibility so that the other side will know that, as for me, if they express flexibility on those things that I think are important, I'm going to express flexibility on those things that they think are important.

—Assemblyman Roger Niello
Republican Vice Chair of Budget Committee, January 22, 2009

It has been called the "Budget Dance" and "Budget Kabuki."[1] These nicknames are alluding to the ritualistic movement and posturing that occurs annually between the governor and state legislature to develop and adopt a state spending plan. In recent decades, the dance has more often been a standstill than a graceful waltz across the capitol stage. Budgeting in California has not always been plagued by partisan gridlock, questions about the state's financial stability, and negative press coverage. Although the state, like many other states and the federal government, underwent fiscal stress in the 1930s during the Great Depression, the ongoing challenge to produce a balanced budget before the start of the fiscal year did not emerge and become routine until the early 1980s. Before this, the budget process managed to produce an on-time, balanced budget each year more often than not. Moreover, the process also established consistent funding support for a robust social safety net, one of the top university systems in the world, and a network of roads and highways that moved an increasing number of both goods and people.

---

[1] Richard Krolak, *California's Budget Dance* (Sacramento: California Journal Press, 1994); George Skelton, "'Dance of Death' Would Revive Budget Process," *The Los Angeles Times*, August 4, 2008.

In this chapter, we describe and explain the development of the current budget process and the various stages that a typical budget goes through in order to reach the governor's desk. Although there is a commonly understood "text-book" set of stages that the annual budget must move through, this textbook version was jettisoned during the crisis budgeting era and only in the last few years has the process returned to its more predictable routine. The chapter then turns to a brief review of California's history with budget gridlock since it dominated state politics for four decades. Finally, we discuss budgeting norms that have been identified by scholars and evaluate the state's process against these standards.

Origins of the Current Structure

Like much of budgeting in the United States, the central components of the current structure in California did not take shape until the 1920s. Prior to that period, the Hiram Johnson (R) administration made some attempts to bring order to budget management in 1911. However, before the Johnson administration, budgeting in California was decentralized, unorganized, and haphazard. Governor-elect C. C. Young (R) would later reflect on this pre-1911 budget environment in a 1926 speech:

> When I first entered the Legislature in 1909, there was little short of chaos as far as any orderly provisions for State expenditures were concerned. There had been no audit of State finances for over twenty years. The finance committees of the two houses were scenes of a blind scramble on the part of the various institutions and departments of the State in an endeavor to secure as large a portion as possible of whatever money might happen to be in the treasury.[2]

In contrast to present day budgeting, the executive was not responsible for the budget and played little role in the process. There were multiple appropriations bills passed each year, and the total amount authorized was not clear until all bills reached the governor. The heads of state agencies made their funding requests directly to fiscal committees in each chamber. Department heads were required to attend committee hearings every day and did not know which day their request would be heard. Legislators were also known to request favors from department heads and steer state contracts in the direction of their campaign supporters.[3]

In 1911, Governor Johnson sought to instill procedural norms into the appropriation of state funding through the creation of a budget review board that

---

[2] A. E. Buck, *Public Budgeting: A Discussion of Budgetary Practice in the National, State and Local Governments of the United States* (New York: Harper and Brothers, 1929), 11–12.

[3] "Development of Modern Budgeting," Department of Finance, accessed May 30, 2014 at http://www.dof.ca.gov/fisa/bag/history.htm; Douglas Jay Doubleday, *Legislative Review of the Budget* (Berkeley: Institute of Governmental Studies, 1967), 13.

consisted of the governor, state controller, and the Board of Control, which was comprised of three members appointed by the governor. The budget board held hearings on departmental funding requests, required justification for these requests, and made recommendations to the legislature. This process was never formally adopted in law so there was no obligation on the part of Johnson's successors to follow it.[4]

The basic foundation for the current process was laid in 1922 when several key reforms were adopted through an initiative constitutional amendment (Proposition 12). The most important reform to emerge was the assignment of primary responsibility for the budget to the executive. By the time California voters considered this reform, 22 other states had already adopted an executive budget process and, with the passage of the Budget and Accounting Act of 1921, the federal government was also converting to a similar format. This change created a single point of accountability for the budget since the governor would be responsible for proposing the initial budget and for implementing it once the legislature passed it.

Several other important budgeting changes were contained in Proposition 12. Instead of the previous practice of enacting multiple appropriations bills, the governor was required to submit a unified, balanced budget that encompassed all appropriation amounts. If total proposed expenditures for the biennium period (the state adopted an annual process in 1946) exceeded the revenue available, "the governor shall recommend the sources from which the additional revenue should be provided."[5] Of course, submitting a balanced budget on paper is much different than a requirement to sign a balanced budget, but it still represented a substantial improvement to the previous chaos that was endemic to the legislature. Another reform stipulated that the budget bill should be introduced in each chamber by the chairmen of the committees with jurisdiction over the budget. This established a dual-track process that made it easier to record modifications to the budget bill in each chamber and eventually led to the routine use of two-house conference committees that are responsible for reconciling differences between the budget bill emerging from each house.[6]

Finally, Proposition 12 authorized line-item reduction veto powers for the governor. Prior to this new authority, the governor retained line-item veto authority, which only allowed him to veto entire appropriation amounts. According to the 1922 Ballot Statement, this new power would allow the governor to modify appropriations so that they could "meet the condition of the treasury."[7]

---

[4] Doubleday, *Legislative Review.*

[5] California Constitution, Article IV, Section 12a.

[6] Doubleday (1967) notes that from 1937–1961 conference committees were regularly appointed to resolve budget issues, except for five occasions.

[7] *General Election Ballot Pamphlet,* California Secretary of State. (Sacramento: California State Printing Office, 1922), http://library.uchastings.edu/research/online-research/ballots.php.

Evolution of the Budget Process

Although the basic structure and procedures for the state budget were established in 1922, there have been a number of developments since that have either significantly altered procedures, added new agencies to the process (e.g., Department of Finance), or substantially changed the institutional environment of the legislature. Table 2.1 provides a timeline of these developments, starting with the adoption of the executive budget in 1922. Although in some cases these developments had much broader implications for state government in general, some of which will be discussed in subsequent chapters, we limit the discussion here specifically to the effects on the budget process.

Department of Finance (1927)

There was one missing element of the executive budget model when it was initially adopted in California: professional experts that would assist the governor in the development and execution of the budget. At the national level, the Bureau of the Budget was created to support the president in this role. Although the Board of Control continued to fill this role, it became apparent that their capacity and resources were not adequate to manage the growing size and responsibilities of the state budget. In 1927, the Department of Finance (DOF) was created to assist the governor with budget preparation and execution. It has become the central clearinghouse for all budget-related activity and one of the most powerful agencies in state government. With this central clearing process, all departmental budgets are reviewed and "cleared" by DOF staff before they reach the governor for consideration.

The Department of Finance is led by the Director of Finance, who is appointed by the governor. Although the director is a political appointee, governors normally appoint individuals who have considerable experience and expertise on the state budget. These individuals have either worked their way up through the Department of Finance, or in the case of Schwarzenegger's first director, Donna Arduin, had experience leading other large states (New York and Florida). One notable exception was the appointment of former long-time legislator Steve Peace by Governor Gray Davis in 2003, but even he had chaired the Senate Budget and Fiscal Review Committee and was intricately familiar with state finances. Although the director may change from one administration to the other, the rest of DOF staff do not.

Riley-Stewart Amendment (1933)

The next significant development was the adoption of the Riley-Stewart amendment in 1933, which resulted in an overhaul of the tax system, more state

Table 2.1. Timeline of Significant Developments in the Budget Process

Year	Development
1922	Executive budget adopted
	• Governor required to propose unified, balanced budget
	• Budget bill introduced in each chamber by budget committee chairs
	• Authorized line-item reduction authority
1927	Department of Finance created
	• Oversees development and implementation of budget
	• Functions as a central clearing agency
1933	Riley-Stewart Amendment adopted
	• Requires 2/3 vote in legislature to pass budget if spending will increase by 5% over previous year
1941	Legislative Analyst Office (LAO) created
	• Reviews and analyzes governor's budget proposal and legislation with a fiscal impact
1962	Proposition 16 adopted
	• Subjects all budget acts, regardless of spending level, to 2/3 vote
1966	Professional legislature adopted
	• Legislature is full-time
	• Sessions are lengthened
1978	Proposition 13 adopted
	• Limits property tax rate and growth rates in assessment values
	• Requires 2/3 vote in legislature to pass tax increases
1988	Proposition 98 adopted
	• Guarantees a minimum level of funding for K-14 education
1990	Term Limits adopted
	• Assembly members limited to 3 2-year terms
	• Senators and governor limited to 2 4-year terms
2004	Proposition 58 adopted
	• Limits ability of state to borrow money to support operational deficits
	• Requires governor to sign balanced budget
	• Triggers fiscal emergency and mid-year cut process if budget falls out of balance

- Established budget reserve up to 5% of general fund

2010   Proposition 25 adopted
- Lowers vote requirement to pass budget to simple majority
- Eliminates legislative pay if legislature does not pass budget by constitutional deadline of June 15

---

funding support for K-12 education, and limitations on state and local spending. While the amendment played a central role in the transformation of the state's fiscal system during the Great Depression (this is discussed further in Chapter 3), it also sought to control state expenditures by requiring a two-thirds vote in the legislature to approve a budget when expenditures would grow by more than five percent.[8] At the time, it was considered one of the more minor provisions of the measure, but it eventually led to the two-thirds vote requirement to pass *any* budget when the five percent condition was removed in 1962.[9] This supermajoritarian vote requirement to pass the budget was considered one of the main, if not the primary, factors in the gridlock that gripped Sacramento for four decades until 2011.

Legislative Analyst's Office (1941)

Since DOF operated under the direction of the governor, the agency acted in his interests, which, at times, meant not assisting the legislature in good faith. In 1941, the legislature adopted a resolution establishing the Joint Legislative Budget Committee (JLBC) and the Office of the Legislative Analyst seeking to "secure more objective, more accurate, and more complete information on state finances" and "to tighten legislative control over expenditures."[10] Although the legislative and executive branches were intended to be relatively equal in power, the creation of the DOF, not to mention the increasing number of state agencies under the governor's purview, placed the legislature at a disadvantage *vis-à-vis* the executive branch. The legislative analyst came to serve as a counterweight against the resources and expertise of the DOF by providing objective information, analysis, and recommendations to the legislature on the governor's proposed budget and other fiscal matters.

---

[8] James Hartley, Steven H. Sheffrin, and J. David Vasche. "Reform During Crisis: The Transformation of California's Fiscal System During the Great Depression," *The Journal of Economic History* 56 (1996): 657–78.

[9] Proposition 16 in 1962 sought to eliminate obsolete and superfluous provisions of the state constitution. Ironically, the conditional five percent threshold provision was packaged with other "obsolete" provisions.

[10] Doubleday, *Legislative Review of the Budget*, 36–37.

Professional Legislature (1966)

Another pivotal development affecting the process was the transition to a full-time, professional legislature spawned by the adoption of Proposition 1A in 1966. The proposition made a number of substantive revisions to the constitution covering several different topics that had been carefully studied and recommended by the Constitution Revision Commission established by the legislature in 1963. Among the legislative changes were provisions to provide a full-time salary to legislators and an unlimited length of session. These were important changes to the budget environment in particular because they gave the legislature more power in negotiations with the governor. Governor Pat Brown (D) was originally reluctant to call a special session for the legislature to consider Proposition 1A. "The revision would set up a full-time legislature and the two-thirds vote for budget approval had been retained—both of these would restrict executive influence over the legislative process."[11] For budget negotiations, with increased financial independence and longer sessions, this meant that legislators would not be eager to return to their occupations to earn a living and would expect to spend a longer time dealing with legislative business in Sacramento. Governor Brown's concern was validated just three years later when California experienced its first budget delay in 1969, as Governor Ronald Reagan signed the Budget Act on July 3, two days after the start of the fiscal year. In addition, recent multistate studies suggest that longer sessions and higher pay reduce the governor's influence over the size of the budget and lead to protracted delays in passage of the budget, indicating that the transition to a professional legislature in California played an important role in the evolution of the budget process.[12]

Proposition 13 (1978)

Yet another substantial development was the passage of Proposition 13 in 1978. Perhaps no other California initiative has reverberated across the nation as much as Proposition 13. It spawned numerous antitax measures in other states and is believed to be a crucial precursor to the conservative, antitax movement that swept the nation in the 1980s and exists to the present day. Its impact in California cannot be overstated. It changed the fundamental relationship between the state and local government. Its main purpose was to limit property taxes for homeowners, who struggled to pay them when assessed values of their homes increased rapidly in the 1970s. One of the major consequences was a

---

[11]Bernard L. Hyink, "California Revises its Constitution," *The Western Political Quarterly* 22 (1969): 637–54. Hyink served as a member of the commission.

[12]Thad Kousser and Justin H. Phillips, "Who Blinks First? Legislative Patience and Bargaining with Governors," *Legislative Studies Quarterly* 304 (2009): 55–86; Carl E. Klarner, Justin H. Phillips, and Matt Muckler, "Overcoming Fiscal Gridlock: Institutions and Budget Bargaining," *Journal of Politics* 74, no. 4 (2010): 992–1009.

drastic decrease in property tax revenues, which served as the primary revenue source for local government and K-14 education. We refrain from a full analysis of its impact because Proposition 13 is discussed further in several other chapters. For now, we wish to introduce its effects on the procedures and negotiations of the process.

With regard to budgetary procedures, one provision of Proposition 13 instituted a two-thirds vote requirement in the legislature to pass tax increases. Since passage of the budget was already contingent upon a two-thirds vote, this new requirement did not have much effect on budget adoption. However, it also meant that taxes could not be raised outside the budget process either. Prior to this change, taxes could be raised with an ordinary bill that was approved by a majority vote and signed by the governor. This path was no longer an option which put more emphasis on the annual budget bill and increased the leverage of the minority party in the legislature, usually Republicans by this time. Not only would the governor need to secure Republican votes to pass the budget without revenue increases, if he wished to include tax increases, he would need to convince some normally antitax Republicans to support them. Given their ideological predisposition against taxes, Republicans used this leverage to extract more concessions, either in the form of increased spending or tax cuts, from the process, which contributed to the state's fiscal problems.

In addition to the new vote threshold, Governor Jerry Brown (D) and the legislature dealt with the significant loss of property tax revenue by backfilling the funding holes for local government, the K-12 education system, and community colleges with state revenue. At the time of Proposition 13's passage, the state was sitting on a sizeable reserve, which in part contributed to the antitax fervor, and therefore had the resources to ease the transition process for local government and school districts. However, sending a larger share of state revenue to lower levels also had the effect of reducing the pool of funding available for state programs and services. Since local government and school districts were now more reliant on state funding, debates and lobbying efforts at the local level over the allocation of dollars were transplanted to Sacramento. Along with state agencies and interest groups already forced to squabble over a shrinking pot of state funding, the addition of more local hands in the pot further complicated and hamstrung the annual appropriation process.

Proposition 98 (1988)

The annual fight over spending allocations in the state capital exacerbated by Proposition 13 precipitated the practice of earmarking. *Earmarking* occurs when an appropriation amount or percentage of spending is dedicated to a particular program or service. With the adoption of Proposition 98 in 1988, a minimum level of funding was secured for K-12 schools and community colleges. More specifically, it guaranteed that at least 40 percent of state funding would be allocated to K-14 education and that this level would be based on growth rates for personal income and the general fund. While the obvious effect is that it protected funding for education, its larger impact has had repercussions for the entire budgeting process. Again, we leave a more detailed analysis for subsequent chapters, but for now it is important to consider its implications for budget negotiations.

First, while one might think an earmark makes budgeting easier because fewer decisions need to be made, this is not true for Proposition 98.[13] Because of the structure of Proposition 98, it produces two decisions that need to be made by the governor and legislature each year. One provision allows the legislature to suspend the requirements of the measure with a two-thirds vote. In poor economic climates, this is frequently a subject of negotiations. One example of this occurred in 1991 when Republican Governor Pete Wilson wanted to suspend it and legislative Democrats did not. It became one of the central sticking points in budget talks. However, while it is discussed, the governor and legislature are reluctant to utilize this provision because they fear that it will signal to voters that education is a lower priority. For an issue that is frequently identified as one of the top priorities in statewide public opinion polls, such a maneuver would not play well at election time.

Second, once the suspension option is abandoned, the funding level must be determined, which can also be contentious since Democrats, pressured by unions in the education community, typically seek higher levels of education spending than Republicans want. Proposition 98 sets a floor for spending, but the state can exceed that floor as much as it wants, although that new level sets a higher baseline for future years and can further tie the state's hands. Had the initiative set aside a predetermined percentage of funding for education, it would have preempted these discussions each year.

The other ways that Proposition 98 affects budget negotiations is that it produces spillover effects in the other non-Proposition 98 policy areas and has spawned a series of earmarking ballot initiatives. State and local agencies and interest groups in these other areas must fight for a piece of the pie leftover after funding has already been apportioned to education. In poor economic conditions, battles intensify over the shrinking level of revenues. To protect their funding levels, program advocates and interest groups have also sponsored initiatives that seek to carve out dedicated funding for their programs and services. For example, the Mental Health Association in California and the California Nurses Association sponsored Proposition 63 in 2004 which dedicates $1.8 billion annually to mental health programs. Since Proposition 98 was one of the first to do this, earmark initiatives have become an increasingly attractive policy option for those advocacy groups who have the resources to qualify them and support a campaign to pass them. With each one that voters adopt, there is less flexibility for the legislature and governor in the options that they can pursue to balance the budget each year.[14]

---

[13] Jeff Cummins, "An Empirical Analysis of California Budget Gridlock," *State Politics and Policy Quarterly* 12, no. 1 (2012): 23–42.

[14] John Matsusaka, "A Case Study on Direct Democracy: Direct Democracy and Fis-

Term Limits (1990)

Similar to the adoption of a professional legislature, the advent of term limits significantly changed the legislative environment and resulted in a number of effects that hamper the budget situation. Placed on the ballot in 1990, Proposition 140 was a response to growing mistrust of politicians in Sacramento who were perceived as currying favor with lobbyists and interest groups and shirking the concerns of the average citizen. It did not help matters that an FBI investigation led to corruption convictions for several legislators in the late 1980s. The main provisions of Proposition 140 limited assemblymembers to three two-year terms and senators and the governor to two four-year terms. It also reduced the legislature's budget and cut pensions for state elected officials. Whereas the creation of the professional legislature balanced the powers between the executive and legislative branches, term limits swung the balance back in the governor's favor.[15] Post-term limits legislators come to office with virtually no legislative experience (unless they move from one chamber to the other), are ill-suited to negotiate with the governor, and, with a smaller legislative budget, lack the staff resources that their predecessors had that could serve to compensate for the other shortcomings.

Term limits also seem to have influenced the political and fiscal outlook of legislative members.[16] Gone are the days when a legislator could get elected to a seat and hold it for 10 to 16 years because of incumbency advantages such as name recognition and a healthy campaign account. Instead, to continue a career in elected office, newly elected assemblymembers or senators must begin to consider their next electoral opportunity in either the other legislative chamber, Congress, or a local office. This myopic perspective influences their approach to budgetary and fiscal matters. Legislators who wish to position themselves for a competitive campaign will avoid votes to increase taxes and cut popular programs and services that may provide fodder for a wily opponent. However, often it is these tough budget votes that help maintain balance and a decent reserve. Voters are more likely to tolerate these tough votes if their incumbent legislator has a longer relationship with them rather than if they are running for a new office. Moreover, term-limited legislators are more likely to support short-term budget solutions that have a deleterious long-term fiscal impact because these legislators may have moved on to another office or been termed out when the full impact of these decisions materializes. In recent years, the legislature has

---

cal Gridlock" in *The Book of the States* (Lexington: The Council of State Governments, 2010). Although some observers believe that up to 80 percent of the state budget is tied up in dedicated funding, Matsusaka conducts the most thorough analysis and estimates that only about 30 percent is earmarked, but he only looks at *initiative* earmarks.

[15] Bruce Cain, Thad Kousser, and Karl Kurtz, "California: A Professional Legislature after Term Limits" in *Governing California: Politics, Government, and Public Policy in the Golden State*, ed. Gerald C. Lubenow (Berkeley: Institute of Governmental Studies Press, 2006), 39–65.

[16] Cummins, "An Empirical Analysis," 29.

often voted to move certain expenditures to the next fiscal year, take out temporary loans from special funds, skip state contributions to pension funds, and purposely overestimate revenues, all of which allow a budget to be balanced on paper, but only for a few months. In 2012, voters approved a new term-limits law, Proposition 28, which allows legislators to serve up to 12 years in the legislature, regardless of the chamber. This modification should ameliorate some of the effects of the previous law.

Proposition 58 (2004)

California voters adopted Proposition 58, tabbed the California Balanced Budget Act, in the aftermath of several years of severe budget deficits, the first gubernatorial recall in state history (Gray Davis), and the first replacement, Governor Arnold Schwarzenegger (R), of a recalled governor. Once in office Governor Schwarzenegger immediately set out to campaign for two ballot measures (Propositions 57 and 58) that were intended to address the state's dire budget situation and were part of the budget package adopted by Governor Davis and the legislature in 2003. Proposition 57 authorized $15 billion in bonds to support the state's general fund deficit, which was originally estimated at $35 billion by the Davis administration in January 2003.[17] Its companion measure, Proposition 58, contained several important provisions that were intended to help the state avoid future deficits. These provisions included the following:
1. required the governor to sign a balanced budget;
2. if the state faced revenue shortfalls or projected deficits, the governor could declare a fiscal emergency that called the legislature into special session and prohibited other legislative business if the legislature did not send the governor a bill to address the budget problem in 45 days;
3. established a special reserve fund to stabilize state finances during economic downturns; and
4. prohibited future borrowing (like Proposition 57) to cover budget deficits.

With the exception of the fiscal emergency provision, Proposition 58 did little to avert chronic budget problems. The provision for the governor to sign a balanced budget has not made much difference because there is no audit or enforcement mechanism to ensure that a signed budget is indeed balanced. California's fiscal condition was never strong enough to set money aside in a reserve account. The state continued to borrow from local government, schools, internally from special funds, and externally on a short-term basis to cover cash-flow needs.

---

[17] The Legislative Analyst's Office reported that the $35 billion deficit was an overstatement of the "true" deficit. In their January 2003 report on the governor's budget, they pegged the deficit at $26 billion plus. A total deficit of $28 billion was commonly referred to at the time.

The fiscal emergency provision has probably had the most impact of any on the budget process. Prior to its adoption, the legislature had considered mid-year proposals to address deficits, but there was no legally prescribed format for doing so. With ongoing budget problems from 2008 to 2011, fiscal emergencies were declared five times. In December 2008, two were declared in the same month after Schwarzenegger vetoed a bill that contained various budget solutions that responded to the first declaration. While fiscal emergencies have not prevented budget deficits, they have vaulted the budget problem to the top of the legislature's agenda each time they have been declared. As opposed to pre-Proposition 58 mid-year efforts, there is a sense of urgency and responsibility in the legislature that was not present prior to its passage. Nonbudget issues have taken a backseat to pushing legislation to address the budget problem. In addition, although the state issued $2.6 billion in IOUs temporarily in 2009 because of cash shortages, the declaration of fiscal emergencies accelerated budget negotiations between the governor and legislature and probably prevented a longer and more frequent use of IOUs.

Proposition 25 (2010)

After multiple attempts to lower the two-thirds voting requirement to pass the annual budget, voters approved Proposition 25 in 2010, which reduced the threshold to a simple majority. The initiative was particularly popular because it eliminated legislative pay for each day that the legislature failed to enact a state budget by the constitutional deadline of June 15. In effect, the measure allowed majority Democrats in the legislature to adopt a spending plan on their own without the support of Republicans. However, noticeably missing from the proposition was a provision to allow taxes to be raised by a simple majority. In years with declining revenue, this means that Democrats are still precluded from raising taxes on their own to fill in these revenue gaps. Thus, the governor and majority party in the legislature can approve the allocation of spending on their own, which is likely to happen when revenues are growing, but, without control of two-thirds of the seats, Democrats still need the support of Republicans if they wish to pursue tax changes.[18] Despite a rough beginning for Democrats in 2011 under the new majority vote requirement (legislators temporarily forfeited their pay), the legislature managed to pass on-time budgets in the first four years it was effective, perhaps signaling that the prolonged stalemates of the past will be a rare occurrence.

---

[18] On the same 2010 ballot, voters also approved Proposition 26, which tightened restrictions on fee and tax increases. A two-thirds legislative vote is now required for *any tax increases*, even if they are revenue neutral overall. Previously, a two-thirds vote was required only if overall revenue increased.

The Current Structure and Process

Although the latter stages of the budget process deviated from the norm in the crisis budgeting era, the main elements of the current structure and process have roughly been in place since at least the 1960s.[19] There are three general stages to the process: (1) the internal process in the executive branch that leads to the submission of the budget bill; (2) legislative review and modification of the governor's budget through public hearings; and (3) finalization of the budget by the governor with the signing and issuance of vetoes.[20] The first stage, internal executive preparation, begins in individual departments about 18 months prior to the start of the fiscal year.[21] In California, for both state and local government, the fiscal year begins on July 1 and ends on June 30. The second stage, legislative and public review, begins with the release of the budget in January and concludes with final passage in both chambers anywhere from mid-June to as late as October. The last stage, the gubernatorial signing and vetoes, lasts several days once the legislature adopts a final bill. While legislators and the governor may announce their positions or take actions on the budget, it is important to note that budget decisions are not final until the bill has been passed by the legislature and signed into law by the governor.

This section outlines the major events and procedures that take place in a "typical" budget year. We begin by discussing final preparations in the departments and the subsequent review by the Department of Finance. A timeline with an overview of the steps in this process is provided in Figure 2.1.

Budget Development by Departments

Departments consider final baseline estimates and proposals approximately one year before the start of the fiscal year for which they are planning. The state uses a traditional line-item format that first divides planned expenditures by purpose into state operations and local assistance. Funding for *state operations* supports staff and operational expenses and equipment at state-level offices, while *local assistance* provides funding to local governments, mainly counties and cities, to support local administrators and staff and direct services. For developmental purposes, departments use an *incremental approach* to budgeting where last year's expenditures determine the planned expenditures for the upcoming fiscal year.[22] Departments and agencies first establish a baseline budget, which are the costs of providing services at the current level adjusted for infla-

---

[19] Doubleday, *Legislative Review.*

[20] Krolak, *California's Budget Dance,* 41.

[21] For a detailed description of the departmental process, see Krolak's *California's Budget Dance.*

[22] Aaron Wildavsky and Naomi Caiden, *The New Politics of the Budgetary Process,* (New York: Longman Classics in Political Science, 2004).

Figure 2.1. Timeline of Budget Process

July-Oct
- Departments prepare baseline budget and consider budget change proposals (BCPs)
- DOF releases Budget Guidelines

Nov
- LAO releases budget forecast in *Fiscal Outlook*
- DOF reviews department baseline budgets and BCPs

Dec
- DOF finalizes expenditure and revenue estimates
- Governor makes final decisions

Jan
- Governor delivers State of the State Address
- Governor releases budget on or before *January 10*
- Identical budget bills introduced by Budget Committee chairs in each chamber

Feb
- LAO releases analysis of the budget bill and updated forecast

Mar-Apr
- Budget subcommittees review budget and hold hearings
- DOF, LAO, Depts, interest groups, and public provide testimony

May
- Governor releases May Revise budget with updated estimates of expenditures and revenue
- Budget subcommittees continue review of budget

June
- Full Assembly and Senate consider budget bills
- Conference Committee reconciles differences between budget bills
- Legislature required to pass budget by *June 15*

July
- New fiscal year begins *July 1*
- "Big 5" or "Big 3" negotiate final budget
- Legislature passes budget with majority vote
- Governor signs budget act and issues vetoes

tion. To provide guidance on the development of baseline budgets, the Department of Finance issues Budget Letters, which provide instructions and cost-of-living adjustments that can be incorporated into department estimates. Depending on the type of department or agency, expenditure plans must be further modified based on projected caseload changes. For example, the Department of Corrections and Rehabilitation employs a sophisticated statistical model to project the number of inmates that it expects to house in its prisons. The Department's anticipated expenditures for its inmate population are augmented if it is expected to increase or reduced if the population will decline.

Once the baseline budget is established and caseload adjustments are made, departments must then consider whether to seek funding for expanded programs and/or new initiatives within their existing statutory or regulatory authority. In consultation with department directors and executive staff, budget offices within departments and agencies review requests for funding adjustments from program staff through budget change proposals (BCPs). Historically, BCPs have requested additional funding to address staff workload issues or to purchase equipment, among other items, but, during the crisis budgeting era, departments developed negative BCPs, which propose to reduce expenditures for a given program or service. In some cases, DOF may submit negative BCPs on behalf of departments who are reluctant to cut personnel or their funding levels.

LAO November Fiscal Forecast

Between the time when the budget is enacted and the release of the governor's next budget proposal in January, there is normally little budget news that attracts much public and media interest with one exception—the November fiscal forecast by the Legislative Analyst's Office. Historically, depending on the budget conditions anticipated, the release of the LAO's *Fiscal Outlook* has functioned as a bellwether for the budget environment yet to come. With the budget enacted, state government transitions into the execution phase, where departments carry out the duties and responsibilities authorized in the budget act. In good economic times, the *Fiscal Outlook* can be released with scant media attention. However, when a growing deficit is forecast by the LAO, it can generate widespread attention and concern from the media. For example, the November 2001 fiscal forecast reported that the 2001–02 budget would end the year with a $4.5 billion deficit and that a $12.4 billion deficit was expected for the 2002–03 fiscal year.[23] Not only did this report forewarn of budget troubles in the near-term, but, for the ensuing decade, it can be likened to a "canary in the coal mine." In many subsequent years, the main concern arising from the LAO forecast was not whether the analyst anticipated a deficit, but what the size of it was going to be.

---

[23] Andrew Lamar, "State Budget Short $12.4 Billion, Analyst Predicts," *Contra Costa Times*, November 14, 2001, A10.

DOF Review and Final Budget Decisions

As noted earlier, the Department of Finance heads the central clearing process and coordinates the overall development of the governor's budget. In this role, DOF, with direction from the governor, forecasts anticipated revenue levels and sets the overall level of state expenditures based on the forecasts. The Economic and Financial Research Unit is responsible for developing revenue projections several times throughout the year. The most critical estimates are those generated prior to the release of the governor's budget in January and again in May with the revised budget. In each case, revenue estimates set the parameters for upcoming budget discussions and negotiations. An optimistic revenue forecast with better than average growth means that the governor and legislature can consider new spending initiatives, while a pessimistic forecast may portend months of difficult decisions on expenditure reductions and budget manipulation with the goal of ending the year with a positive balance.

The second major responsibility for DOF is to review department baseline budgets and their BCP requests throughout the annual process. Budget staff are divided into seven major program areas where analysts under each area are assigned to specific departments and agencies. These analysts work closely with the budget units (shops) and executive team from each department. Finance staff review departmental budgets using a *zero-based budgeting* approach. This approach allows DOF to review and analyze components of the baseline budget, along with requests for additional funding (the latter is the incremental part of budgeting). Thus, department budget staff must provide justification for continuing to fund ongoing programs or equipment at their current levels. Programs whose mission is no longer as critical as it once was may have their funding reduced or eliminated altogether, particularly during poor economic times. DOF staff must also winnow BCP requests from departments so that when aggregated the overall expenditure level does not exceed available resources for the department, and, on a statewide basis, expenditures for all departments and agencies do not exceed total available resources.

Since departments are seeking to advance their budgets without alterations through executive and legislative reviews as much as possible, this places department staff in an *advocacy* role. On the other hand, since DOF staff is responsible for the bottom line of the overall budget, which often involves revising or rejecting elements of a department's budget, they frequently assume an *adversarial* role. However, DOF staff are empowered to make final decisions in accordance with the governor's priorities.

On significant issues and particularly ones that are likely to generate interest from the public, powerful interest groups, or other favored constituencies, it is quite common for the governor to make final decisions. These typically occur in December before the release of the budget in January and can even be made up until the last minute before the final drafts of the budget head to the printing presses.

Submission of Governor's Budget

The state constitution requires the governor to submit a balanced budget to the legislature "within the first 10 days of each calendar year."[24] This sets in motion the legislative review stage—the most publicly visible—of the process. Since millions of people in the state rely either directly or indirectly on funding provided in the budget, there is great interest in its contents. Newspaper headlines and stories highlight the most significant proposals and issues, while political observers opine on the likely outcome of the legislative battle. The budget is actually a set of documents that includes the *Governor's Budget Summary*, the *Governor's Budget*, and the *Salaries and Wages Supplement*. The *Summary* provides a narrative overview of revenues, expenditures, and balances for the prior, current, and budget years. It also outlines the governor's main initiatives and proposals by major program areas. The *Governor's Budget* contains detailed line-item budgets for every department, agency, board, and commission of the state and runs over 1,000 pages. The *Salaries and Wages Supplement* lists the position and salary of every department employee. Figure 2.2 provides a sample budget for the California Highway Patrol.

The governor follows the submission of the budget with the delivery of the State of the State Address to the legislature. Aside from gubernatorial inaugurations, this is the pinnacle of pomp and circumstance for state government each year. Members of the legislature attend the speech and television outlets broadcast it live statewide (most of the time). Similar to the president's State of the Union Address, governors acknowledge legislative leaders from both parties, constitutional officers, and distinguished guests before they delve into a description of their top priorities for the coming year. During the crisis budgeting era, a large portion of these speeches focused on the budget situation, proposals to address it, and reforms that should be adopted to avoid fiscal problems in the future.

Since major policy initiatives depend on stable funding support, budget conditions can limit the number and scope of these initiatives. In 2011, Governor Brown delivered one of the shortest speeches on record in recent decades. The *Los Angeles Times* observed that "his pitch was a reminder of how California's financial problems now overshadow everything the government does."[25]

For those initiatives that have made it into the speech, funding shortfalls usually lead to their demise, sometimes in an abrupt manner. Fresh off of a successful reelection in 2007, Governor Schwarzenegger sought to pass comprehensive health care reform that would have dramatically increased health insurance coverage in the state. After nearly a year of negotiations with legislative Democrats and Republicans, the Legislative Analyst's Office issued a report in January 2008 that the proposed program could add over $5 billion to the state

---

[24] California Constitution, Article IV, Section 12.

[25] Evan Harper and Anthony York, "Brown Argues for His Budget Plan in State of the State Address," *Los Angeles Times*, February 1, 2011.

Figure 2.2. 2014-15 California Highway Patrol Budget

2720 Department of the California Highway Patrol

The California Highway Patrol (CHP) ensures the safe, convenient, and efficient transportation of people and goods across the state highway system and provides the highest level of safety and security to the facilities and employees of the State of California. Since department programs drive the need for infrastructure investment, each department has a related capital outlay program to support this need. For the specifics on CHP's Capital Outlay Program see "Infrastructure Overview."

3-YR EXPENDITURES AND POSITIONS

		POSITIONS			EXPENDITURES	
	2012-13	2013-14	2014-15	2012-13	2013-14	2014-15
10	Traffic Management	8,973.3	8,606.8	8,606.8	$1,671,116	$1,783,484	$1792,216
20	Regulation and Inspection	932.3	1,031.7	1,030.9	173,629	202,548	203,650
30	Vehicle Ownership Security	180.8	230.0	230.0	33,662	43,713	46,696
40.01	Administration	721.1	1,183	1,183.0	125,338	185,650	192,575
40.02	Distributed Administration	-	-	-	-125,338	-185,650	-192,575
TOTALS, POSITIONS AND EXPENDITURES (All Programs)		10,807.5	11,051.5	11,050.7	$1,878,407	$2,029,745	$2,042,562

FUNDING		2012-13	2013-14	2014-15
0042	State Highway Account, State Transportation Fund	$54,219	$62,729	$62,780
0044	Motor Vehicle Account, State Transportation Fund	1,703,526	1,845,033	1,852,843
0293	Motor Carriers Safety Improvement Fund	2,054	2,174	2,180
0840	California Motorcyclist Safety Fund	1,900	2,351	2,341
0890	Federal Trust Fund	17,391	18,887	19,027
0942	Special Deposit Fund	1,622	2,329	2,336
0974	California Peace Officer Memorial Foundation Fund	138	300	300
0995	Reimbursements	97,557	95,942	100,755
TOTALS, EXPENDITURES, ALL FUNDS		**$1,878,407**	**$2,029,745**	**$2,042,562**

LEGAL CITATIONS AND AUTHORITY

DEPARTMENT AUTHORITY

Vehicle Code, Division 2, Chapters 2, 2.5, and 4. Division 3, Chapters 1 and 6. Division 4. Chapters 1 and 1.5. Division 6, Chapters 1 and 2. Division 11, Chapters 2 and 9. Division 13, Chapter 5. Division 14.1, Chapter 1. Division 14.7, and Division 14.8, and Education Code Section 39831.

Source: Governor's 2014–15 budget.

deficit, which effectively killed any further discussions of health care reform.[35] Thus, while governors have been eager to offer lofty policy goals in their State of the State speeches, fiscal reality can dash their ambitious hopes.

LAO Weighs In

Once the governor releases the budget, legislative budget staff, including the Legislative Analyst's Office, sequester themselves to digest and dissect the contents. Meanwhile, in nonbudget crisis times, the rest of the legislature focuses their time and energy on the regular bill process. Most close budget observers eagerly await the LAO's release of their *Analysis of the Budget Bill*. At one time, this analysis was contained in a 1,000-page book, but, in recent years, the office has released a series of reports online in each major policy area (e.g., Budget Analysis Series). Over the years, the three main components of its analysis have remained the same: (1) an updated fiscal forecast; (2) department-by-department recommendations for specific programs and line-items; and (3) analysis of major gubernatorial initiatives and "cross-cutting" issues that have wide-ranging policy implications. Figure 2.3 provides a sample LAO analysis for the Department of Health Care Services.

With more recent economic data than the governor's budget, the fiscal forecast often redefined the size of the budget "problem" during the crisis era. In budget-speak, the problem normally refers to the cumulative projected budget shortfall for the six-month period of the remaining fiscal year and the upcoming fiscal (budget) year, for a cumulative total of about 18 months. In boom times, a rosier forecast that identifies a surplus triggers calls for higher spending and tax cuts. The analysis issues identified by the LAO constitute a sizeable portion of the budget subcommittee agendas for hearings from mid-February to late May. Because of their nonpartisan orientation, as with much policy research, LAO issues are subject to political manipulation by both parties.[36] Both parties tout LAO recommendations when they suit their purposes and ignore or dismiss other recommendations they do not agree with.

Budget Subcommittee Hearings

Once the LAO issues its analysis, the hearings process in the legislature begins. The Senate Budget and Fiscal Review Committee has five budget subcom-

---

[35] Elizabeth Hill, "Health Care Reform," *Legislative Analyst's Office*, January 22, 2008. Accessed January 23, 2012 at http://www.lao.ca.gov/2008/hlth/health_reform/health_reform_012208.aspx.

[36] Carol H. Weiss, "Evaluation Decisions: Is Anybody There? Does Anybody Care?" *Evaluation Practice* 9, no.1 (1988): 5–19; Eleanor Chelimsky, "The Politics of Program Evaluation," *Society* 25 (1987): 24–32.

Figure 2.3. Sample Analysis from LAO's Analysis of the Budget Bill

---

Analyst's Recommendations
Exchange Should Report at Budget Hearings Regarding Fiscal Outlook
The Legislature should ask representatives of the Exchange to report on its fiscal outlook at budget hearings as soon as practicable after the March 31 open enrollment deadline. This will allow the Exchange sufficient time to evaluate its enrollment and financial projections after the open enrollment period ends, thereby providing a better sense of the Exchange's fiscal outlook as the Legislature nears the May Revision. We recommend that the Exchange report on the following:

Final Enrollment Numbers. The Exchange should provide updated Exchange enrollment numbers for the first open enrollment period including the number of individuals who (1) selected a health plan through the Exchange and (2) made their first premium payment. The Exchange should also report on any issues encountered by consumers in paying their premiums.

Continued Marketing and Outreach Efforts. The Exchange should report on which marketing and outreach efforts were successful, where it has identified issues, and how it plans to modify its marketing and outreach efforts to improve enrollment among hard to reach populations, including Latinos and young adults.

Integration Efforts With Counties. The Exchange should also provide an update on the status of federal approval for Medi–Cal bridge plans. The Exchange should report on any barriers or issues it has faced in working with counties to determine Medi–Cal eligibility and enroll eligible individuals.

Updated Fiscal Projections for Next Four Years at May Revision. We recommend the Exchange report at budget hearings during the May Revision on its updated fiscal forecast for 2014–15 through 2017–18. The updated fiscal forecast should include projections of enrollment, PMPM fee amounts, operating costs, and revenues.

Source: 2014–15 Analysis of the Health Budget. This analysis addresses the implementation of the Affordable Care Act.

mittees, while the Assembly Budget Committee has six. Senate subcommittees usually have three members, two Democrats and one Republican. Assembly subcommittees have five members, three Democrats and two Republicans. Each subcommittee is responsible for reviewing the departments and agencies under its jurisdiction. For instance, Assembly Budget Subcommittee 5 on public safety reviews the budgets for the Department of Corrections and Rehabilitation, the Department of Justice, California Highway Patrol, and other public safety-oriented agencies. Committees in the assembly and senate combine both the authorization and appropriations processes into one. At the national level, the authorization and appropriations processes run on separate tracks in the House and Senate where different committees are responsible for department authorization and appropriations. The *authorization process* confers legal authority to departments and agencies to operate under their statutory powers. The *appropriations process* provides the funding support to carry out the policy objectives of the departments.

The two main functions of the hearing process are to (1) conduct legislative oversight and (2) make changes to the governor's budget. To conduct oversight, the subcommittee reviews information and data from the departments and questions department administrators about their programs and services. Since departments are under the executive branch, one important concern of the subcommittees is whether departments followed legislative intent of previously authorized programs and services. When the legislature approves funding for a particular purpose, usually out of concern for the targeted population, such as special education students or low-income families, legislators want to know whether the objectives were achieved and, if not, why not. If subcommittee members believe the department has not met legislative intent or has fallen short of its goals, the line of questioning can get more tense and heated. Department administrators typically do not want to run afoul of legislators who will bring media and public attention to their agencies' shortcomings.

To modify the governor's budget, the subcommittees, and later the full committees and house, must vote to augment or delete funding for specific line-items and add budget or trailer bill language. *Budget bill language* adds provisions to the budget bill that provide directions and limitations on how a particular appropriation can be spent. *Trailer bills* are separate pieces of legislation that amend statute to implement the budget bill. Because of single subject restrictions on legislation, there is a separate trailer bill for each major service area (e.g., education, health care, etc.)

Since the budget bill serves as the primary control document, subcommittee actions are reflected as changes to line-items in the bill. Figure 2.4 provides an example of a line-item in the budget bill with a description of the line-item number. At the end of the entire budget process, these actions are recorded in the *Final Change Book*, which is developed and published by the Finance Department. If no changes are made to a program or line-item contained in the bill, the initial amount becomes law. The departments and DOF staff usually defend the governor's proposals, while LAO staff may advocate certain changes that are likely to reflect the legislature's priorities. Lobbyists also testify on behalf of their clients' views seeking to protect any benefits they might already enjoy or defeat any proposals that might harm their clients' interests. Members of the public might also testify if a proposal will negatively affect them or their family.

Figure 2.4. Sample Line-item from 2013 Budget Act – Department of Corrections and Rehabilitation

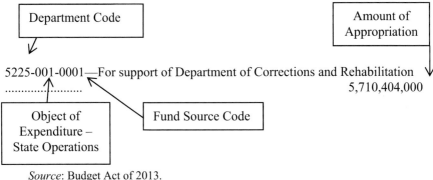

Source: Budget Act of 2013.

Subcommittee hearings at times can create unusual alliances. In some instances, if an LAO recommendation is favorable to a department, then department representatives and an LAO analyst may team up to push their case. In other instances, the governor's budget may include proposals for a department that that department opposes. This occurs because the governor has final say over department budgets even though some departments are overseen by statewide elected officials. One example occurred in 2003 with the Department of Justice (DOJ). When Governor Gray Davis was seeking to eliminate a growing deficit, the governor's budget contained a proposal to charge local law enforcement agencies for the use of state DOJ crime labs that analyze DNA samples and other crime scene evidence. Prior to the proposal, the state paid the bill for such services, so state savings would be generated by charging local governments. DOF staff pushed the proposal despite the objections of the attorney general, who oversees DOJ. The LAO recommended adoption of the fee schedule with some modifications, which led to a DOF-LAO alliance against the department. Attorney General Bill Lockyer (D) showed up to testify against the proposal even though it was part of DOJ's budget. The subcommittee eventually sided with the attorney general, since most legislators do not want to tangle with elected constitutional officers from the same party.

One frequent critique of subcommittee hearings is the limited role of the minority party in approving changes to the governor's budget. Since it only takes a majority of the committee to approve changes, the majority members of the committee, usually Democrats, run roughshod over the Republicans. If the vote threshold to pass the final budget in each chamber was a majority as well, this would not present as much of a problem to the process (although the minority party would still be frustrated). While Republicans can still ask probing questions of those who testify and attempt to influence spending priorities, their lack of inclusion and influence builds frustration for Republicans who are later need-ed to pass the budget on chamber floors. This issue is no longer a concern if the majority party seeks to pass a spending plan with no tax changes because the budget can be passed with a simple majority as a result of Proposition 25. How-ever, if tax changes are necessary or going to be considered at some point, members of the minority party may be needed to support those changes.

Research suggests that the oversight function and the quality of budget re-view have declined in recent years because of the adoption of term limits. In a study of the impact of term limits on the legislature, Cain and Kousser found that the number of certain oversight activities dropped off in the post-term limits era.[37] They examined the trend of requests for studies and information from agencies pre- and post-term limits in the annual Supplemental Report of the Budget Act. Although this report does not have the force of law, it contains spe-cific instructions on reporting requirements concerning issues that committee members are tracking. Departments are extremely reluctant to ignore the direc-tives in the report because they wish to avoid public admonishment in a hearing or putting their funding support in jeopardy the next time around. Cain and Kousser note that these requests dropped off significantly once term limits were adopted. They also show that requests for department audits from the Bureau of State Audits initially declined as well in the wake of term limits, but eventually rebounded to their previous levels. However, fewer audits are completed in time to influence legislative review of the budget, perhaps indicating that legislators are unaware of the usefulness of the audits in the budget process.

There are several reasons for this decline in oversight activities. First, be-cause term limits produce shortened time horizons, there is less incentive for legislators to track agency performance over a number of years when their stints in office will only last a few years. Second, post-term limit legislators have less experience and expertise on departmental budget issues and therefore are not familiar enough with the agency's work to make informed, analytical inquiries. Moreover, inexperienced legislators are less likely to be cognizant of available resources at their disposal to assist with the oversight function. One former as-sembly staff member summed up the oversight abilities of post-term limit legis-lators in the following manner:

> The Assembly is now talking about revamping the oversight process, but mem-bers don't know the existing process. They don't know the difference between the Legislative Analyst's Office, the California Research Bureau, the Depart-ment of Finance, and so on. They don't know when it is appropriate to ask a department, a public stakeholder, or the LAO to testify. They grill the wrong people for the wrong information during hearings. . . . The Legislature is like

---

[37] Bruce E. Cain and Thad Kousser, *Adapting to Term Limits: Recent Experiences and New Directions* (San Francisco: Public Policy Institute of California, 2004).

the Board of Directors for a company that doesn't know anything about the company.[38]

The May Revise

By May 14, the governor must release the *May Revise* of the budget, which updates revenue and expenditure estimates and contains his final proposals for the budget year. In producing these estimates, DOF staff have the benefit of more recent economic, revenue, and spending data. On the revenue side, corporate taxes are due on March 15 and personal income taxes are due around April 15 so forecasters can incorporate these key trends into their revenue estimates, along with more recent economic indicators, including unemployment and personal income growth. On the expenditure side, departments have a better idea of their caseloads for the current year, which then feed into the adjustments for the budget year.

Since the May Revise is released a month in advance of the legislature's deadline for budget passage, subcommittees have about one to two weeks to review the updated plan and hold hearings on it before they must make their recommendations to the full budget committees. This expedited review period disadvantages the legislature because their staff and the LAO do not have time to adequately review the new and revised proposals. As a result, governors have been accused of deliberately leaving out major proposals from the initial January budget and loading them into the May Revise. For example, with his 2000 May Revision, Governor Davis proposed to exempt certain K-12 teachers from the income tax, which was unprecedented since it would be the first time that an entire class of citizens was exempt.[39] Such "May surprises" are an attractive option for governors since they are subject to less scrutiny in the legislature because of the compressed time schedule for review.

Final Legislative Stretch

After the subcommittee review process concludes, usually in late May, the legislature performs two perfunctory tasks to move the budget bills to the two-house conference committee and then onto the final negotiations between the governor and legislative leaders. First, the subcommittees recommend their actions to the full budget committees in the assembly and senate. With few exceptions, the full committee usually adopts the recommendations of the subcommittees, which signifies the importance of the latter's work. Second, each chamber considers in floor sessions the amended budget bill as reported from the full budget committees. Until 2011, a two-thirds vote in each chamber was required to pass the bill in each house before it could be sent to the conference committee

---

[38] Quoted in Cain and Kousser, *Adapting to Term Limits*, 78–79.

[39] John Decker, *California in the Balance: Why Budgets Matter* (Berkeley: Berkeley Public Policy Press, 2009), 20.

Cartoon 2.1. Solving the Budget Crisis

Source: Tom Meyer.

to reconcile the differences between the Senate and Assembly versions. As discussed earlier, Proposition 25 changed this vote requirement to a simple majority.

The conference committee is composed of three senators and three assembly members. The conferees are usually the budget committee chairs from the majority party and the vice chairs from the minority party in each chamber. Legislative leaders from the majority party appoint the other two members. The committee is tasked with reaching compromises on any differences in line-item amounts and any related budget-bill or trailer-bill language. These hearings are closed to public testimony, but the committee hears testimony from the LAO, DOF, and the Legislative Counsel's office, which acts as the legislature's attorney. Although the majority party seeks input from minority members, their votes are not needed to adopt reconciled items. The committee tends to dispense with the low hanging fruit, or less controversial items, early in the hearing process and skip over the more politically charged issues until later in the process. In certain years, the committee has adjourned without completing its work because agreement could not be reached on more controversial items. This usually kicks the process into the "Big 5" negotiations between the governor and four legislative leaders (Senate Pro Temp, Senate Minority Leader, Assembly Speaker, and

Assembly Minority Leader) and, more recently, just the "Big 3" (the governor and two majority party leaders from the Assembly and Senate).

The Big 5

When the state confronted more frequent stalemates and budget shortfalls, the Big 5 process emerged to become a regular part of the annual "dance" between the governor and legislature. Typically, the five leaders sequester themselves in private meetings in the governor's office to discuss major sticking points between the parties. In the crisis era, talks usually stalemated over two main options: cutting spending or raising revenue. The lack of agreement on these approaches normally led to a prolonged impasse that lasted several months into the fiscal year.

The Big 5 began in 1983 when Governor George Deukmejian sought to reduce the number of legislative leaders involved in negotiations to confront a $2 billion deficit.[40] In 1992, Governor Pete Wilson revived the practice shortly after the release of his May Revise to address what was then the state's largest deficit in history. Subsequent Governors Davis, Schwarzenegger, and Brown all continued the Big 5 meetings to various degrees, but their use of them depended on their strategy for securing Republican budget votes. Although Governor Davis convened Big 5 meetings, he also relied on a "pick-off" strategy that would target the requisite number of Republicans and offer concessions, or even appointed positions, to secure their votes. Governor Schwarzenegger, who publicly criticized the Davis pick-off strategy, frequently used Big 5 meetings early in his administration. However, in 2006 and 2007, he allowed negotiations between Democratic and Republican leaders to run their course before he decided to intervene more closely.

Governors who employ a "hands-off" strategy must maintain a delicate balance between nudging negotiations forward and avoiding the public perception of indifference to the state's often precarious financial condition. At one end of the spectrum is a governor who is intimately involved in talks with legislative leaders early in the budget calendar and at the other end of the spectrum is one who waits until the legislative process has been exhausted. Both ends of the spectrum carry their own political risks. With the hands-on approach (the former), if early ongoing negotiations do not produce an on-time budget and satisfactory outcomes for the public, the governor's leadership abilities can be perceived as weak or ineffective, which may hurt his public standing. If the governor does not engage legislative leaders until late in the fiscal year and the budget situation continues to deteriorate, his leadership skills will also be questioned.

Governor Brown's approach in 2011 exhibited a stark contrast with previous governors. From the outset, he exhorted legislators to adopt a budget in March to allow enough time to place measures on the ballot to extend tax in-

---

[40] Kevin Yamamura, "Governor Forgoes Budget Haggling," *Sacramento Bee*, June 27, 2007.

creases authorized in 2009. As one example of his hands-on approach, he became the first governor in 50 years to testify before a legislative committee, defending his budget plan and an expedited budget calendar. During March and April, normally the time for subcommittee hearings, Brown began discussions with what became known as the "GOP 5," five Republican senators who expressed a willingness to place tax measures on the ballot. Similar to Davis's pick-off strategy, Brown circumvented the Big 5 structure and the minority leadership altogether in the hope of gaining votes for his budget. When this strategy produced no compromise, he cast his net wider and met with Republican leaders, while maintaining talks with the GOP 5. In the end, the governor and Republican leaders did not reach an agreement and Democrats passed a spending plan on their own, made possible by the majority vote requirement of Proposition 25.

It is not clear whether Brown's negotiating strategy in 2011 signaled the demise of the Big 5 structure. Since the budget can be adopted with a majority vote, the negotiation structure is likely to further evolve into the Big 3, particularly in years when revenue increases are not proposed. Recent budget negotiations using only the Big 3 suggest this is likely for the future. Since revenue increases are usually proposed in economic downturns, this means that the Big 5 may surface only during poor economic conditions, while the Big 3 structure will finalize the budget in good economic times. Even then, if governors seek tax increases, they may bypass the minority leadership to target rank-and-file members who are willing to deal or, as Brown did in 2012, circumvent the legislature altogether with a tax initiative.

Legislative Adoption and Gubernatorial Vetoes

Once a budget plan emerges from final interbranch negotiations, the Assembly and Senate must vote to adopt an identical version of the budget bill. From 1963 to 2010, the two-thirds vote threshold meant 54 votes were required in the Assembly and 27 in the Senate. Throughout this time period, the majority party typically needed to attract about 10 minority-party votes to reach the two-thirds threshold. In only three of those years did *one* chamber have enough members of the majority party to meet the two-thirds threshold. Senate Republicans did so in 1953 and Assembly Democrats in 1977 and 1978. Thus, in the pre-Proposition 25 era, the governor and majority party nearly always needed to persuade members of the minority party to support the budget.

Before floor debates take place, the governor and legislative leaders usually have an idea which members are going to support the budget agreement. Nevertheless, this does not stop floor debates from producing highly partisan rhetoric and overly dramatic pleas to alter aspects of the budget. Legislative leaders have also been known to lock members in their chamber to ratchet up pressure on unpredictable legislators and deliver a final budget bill to the governor. In 2007, Senate President Pro Tem Don Perata locked members in the Senate chamber, but it did not lead to an adopted budget.[41] Former Assembly Speaker Willie Brown was known to use similar tactics. When the budget is late, legislative leaders attempt to rush the negotiated budget bill through a floor vote without members having an adequate chance to review it. Only after the final budget is sent to the governor, or perhaps even later, do all the details of the bill emerge in various media reports.

When the budget bill is passed by each house, the governor has 12 days to sign it and issue line-item vetoes. California governors have some of the strongest veto powers of any governor in the 50 states.[42] The governor has line-item veto authority, which allows him to reduce or eliminate an appropriation in the bill. He cannot, however, add an item or increase an appropriation. The veto gives the governor a significant advantage over the legislature since he gets the final input on each line-item.

However, while the governor retains considerable veto powers, past governors have been reluctant to strike much from the budget bill sent to him by the legislature. Figure 2.5 shows the percentage of the Budget Act vetoed each year from 1978 to 2013. The average percent vetoed over this time period is a little less than 1 percent, indicating that the veto is exercised very cautiously. Although we cannot draw any definitive conclusions given the small amount of variance, the percentage vetoed by recent governors has been declining. Governor Deukmejian is particularly notable for his higher level of vetoes. His veto average was more than three times that of the percentage for recent governors.

What accounts for the relatively low percentage of appropriations that are vetoed from the Budget Act? The most likely explanation is that governors do not want to renege on agreements and commitments that were made as part of the negotiations with the legislative branch. These negotiations largely involve discussing the amount of funding that will be allocated to each purpose. Therefore, once a compromise is reached, there is an assumption among negotiators that these appropriation amounts are not subject to further adjustments. If the governor significantly modifies these implicit agreements, his credibility with legislative leaders will decline, which makes negotiations for subsequent budgets more difficult and strained. Figure 2.5 lends credence to this rationale because outgoing Republican governors, in particular, seem to veto a higher percentage than they did in the previous years of their administration. This suggests that governors are cognizant of not having to negotiate another budget. Term limits may mitigate some of this veto reluctance because of higher turnover among legislative leaders, but staff who are likely to remain from one leader to the next can convey the distrust to the next leader.

---

[41] "California Senate Deliberates Budget Impasse," *USA Today*, July 21, 2007, accessed January 23, 2012 at http://www.usatoday.com/news/nation/2007-07-21-calif-budget_N.htm.

[42] Thad Beyle, "Gubernatorial Power," accessed January 23, 2012 at http://www.unc.edu/~beyle/gubnewpwr.html.

Figure 2.5. Percentage of Budget Act Vetoed (General Fund)

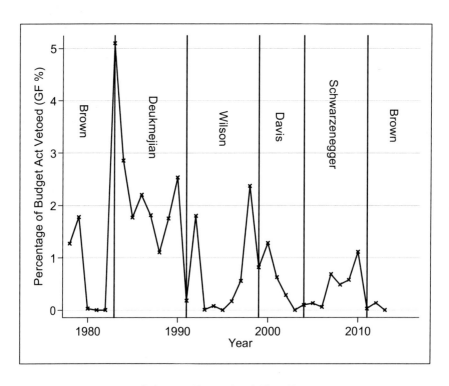

Source: Department of Finance, Chart P-1 and Chart H.

Despite the outcomes of budget vetoes being relatively small, this does not reflect the conflict with the legislature often fomented by the potential and actual use of the veto. It is not uncommon for governors to threaten a veto during nego-tiations in order to leverage concessions from legislators.[43] In 1991, Governor Pete Wilson held on to the budget bill sent to him by the legislature until the last minute of the 12-day period before sending it back to the legislature. That start-ed another 12-day period in which the sides could reach a compromise.[44] When the legislature sent Governor Schwarzenegger a budget in September 2008 that included a weak rainy day fund and a plan to accelerate revenues through in-

---

[43] For an examination of how veto threats shape legislation at the national level, see Charles M. Cameron, *Veto Bargaining* (Cambridge: Cambridge University Press, 2000).

[44] Steve Wiegand, "Governor Will Veto Budget Proposal," *Sacramento Bee*, September 16, 2008.

creased tax withholding, his threatened veto caused legislative leaders to fashion a new bill to his liking. He signed the revised budget bill several days later.

Up until 2011, no California governor had ever vetoed an entire budget bill. Governor Brown had repeatedly claimed that he would veto a budget that did not legitimately balance the books. With a new majority vote requirement, and facing the potential loss of their salary for missing the legislature's constitutional budget deadline, Democrats sent Governor Brown a budget chocked full of spending deferrals and more special fund borrowing on the June 15 deadline. Brown vetoed the entire bill stating that it was not a "balanced solution," which sparked consternation and alarm among his fellow legislative Democrats. Several days later, Democrats passed a new plan that was favored and signed by the governor, which triggered additional spending cuts if projected revenue did not materialize.

Although the governor ordinarily gets the last word on the budget, the constitution still gives the legislature an opportunity to override executive vetoes. The vote requirement to override was the same as that for budget passage for most of the last century—two-thirds. However, with few exceptions, the legislature has not exercised its override powers. The last exception took place in 1979 under the first Jerry Brown administration when the legislature overrode eight vetoed items in the budget bill.[45] Despite having a two-thirds majority to pass the budget, Democrats have not been able to reconstitute that supermajority to override vetoes. If Republicans support an override and thus increase spending, they risk violating party principles that stand for smaller government. When Republican governors are in office, legislative Republicans do not want to undermine the authority of their party leader.

What Happens When the Budget Is Late?

In 1969, for the first time in state history, Governor Ronald Reagan (R) and the legislature did not pass a budget by the start of the fiscal year on July 1. A legal cloud hung over the capitol as it was not clear whether state contractors, employees, and legislators would be paid. Governor Reagan declared that "any time or other service expended by a State employee to be paid from the general fund . . . would have to be treated as a voluntary contribution."[46] This impasse was resolved a few days later, but it signaled a new era of perennially late budgets and the administrative issues that accompany them. Much of the legal uncertainty has been clarified since then because of subsequent court rulings that authorized certain types of state spending in the absence of a budget act.

A large portion of state expenditures still get paid by the state controller when a budget is not adopted by the start of the fiscal year. There is no official estimate of the amount that continues to be paid, but payments made in October

---

[45] *California's Legislature* (Sacramento: Assembly Clerk's Office, 2006).

[46] Quoted in Earl C. Behrens, "Budget Deadlock Is Still Unbroken," *San Francisco Chronicle*, July 2, 1969.

2010 by State Controller John Chiang (D) provide an illustration. Of $21 billion that would normally have been paid in this month, about $19 billion, or 87 percent, was disbursed.[47] The authorization for these payments falls into three categories:

(1) Continuing appropriations are funding amounts set aside for a particular purpose that do not need authorization from one year to the next. The enabling legislation for these programs or services specifies the amount and timing of dispersal. Income tax refunds and welfare payments fall under this category.

(2) Self-executing provisions of the constitution direct the controller to make payments for a specific purpose. For example, debt payments for state bonds are required to be paid, while only a portion of K-12 education payments must continue. [48]

(3) Mandated payments are authorized under federal law and include state employee salaries and certain benefit programs, such as food stamps and child support.[49]

Payment of state employee salaries has been part of an ongoing legal battle between the governor and state controller. The issue arose out of the 1997 and 1998 budget impasses when the Howard Jarvis Taxpayers Association filed a lawsuit claiming the state constitution prohibited the controller from paying employee salaries and other expenses without a state budget. In 2003, the state Supreme Court ruled that the controller must pay state workers the federal minimum wage during a budget impasse because of the Federal Labor Relations Act, but the remainder of their salaries did not have to be paid until a budget was enacted. The salary issue resurfaced again in 2009 when Schwarzenegger ordered Controller John Chiang to pay state workers the federal minimum wage. Chiang refused, arguing that the state's antiquated computer system did not allow adjustments to regular wages in a timely manner. A Superior Court later upheld the earlier 2003 ruling after the state spending plan had been passed.[50]

Although in 1969 state officials feared that the state would come to a screeching halt without a budget in place, the reality over the years has been much different. As noted above, a significant portion of state and local services continues without a budget plan. Political observers believe that budget stalemates last longer when the bulk of state payments are made without a budget enacted. With relatively little disruption in state services and payments, there is less pressure on state leaders to reach a budget compromise. This is not to say that there are not consequences for vendors and others who primarily rely on state government for their business activity or for other state and local agencies that do not get paid. Every time a budget is late, news reports describe how the

---

[47] John Chiang, "What the State Controller Can and Cannot Pay without an Enacted State Budget," (Sacramento: State Controller, October 2010), accessed June 2, 2014 at http://www.sco.ca.gov/october_2010_payments.html.

[48] *Ibid.*; White v. Davis, 2003. S108099. Supreme Court of California.

[49] *White v Davis*, 2003.

[50] Michael Rothfeld, "Governor Schwarzenegger's Minimum Wage Order Upheld," *Los Angeles Times*, March 20, 2009.

budget stalemate pushes smaller nonprofit groups and organizations out of business because of the lack of revenue. What does seem to make an impact, though, is when legislators' own paychecks are on the line as demonstrated by the 2011 budget process, when Chiang refused to pay legislators until they enacted a budget that Chiang regarded as truly balanced.

Budget Gridlock

For much of the past four decades, perhaps no other problem in California politics has received as much attention as budget gridlock, or the state's frequent inability to pass a spending plan by the start of the fiscal year. Budget gridlock has served as the prime example of how the state's political system is broken. Aside from the consequences for those who rely directly on state funding, budget gridlock also negatively affects the state's credit rating, which results in higher borrowing costs for infrastructure and short-term financing. Although the state has avoided gridlock in recent years because of the lower budget vote threshold, it is important to understand the state's history with this problem and its causes. It is premature to say whether gridlock is a thing of the past or whether it will rear its head again.

Nature of Budget Gridlock

California did not always have difficulty passing its annual, and, at one time biennial, budget.[51] For much of the 20th century, the state enacted a budget before the beginning of the fiscal year and, for about a third of the time, adopted a budget well before that deadline. As noted above, it was not until 1969 that the state encountered its first late budget, and even then it passed a few days after July 1. Figure 2.6 provides a graphical display of late budgets from 1901 to 2014. Until the mid-1960s, California usually adopted its budget well before the start of the fiscal year. Gridlock became much more frequent in the 1970s and 1980s. By the 1990s and 2000s, stalemates occurred more than 80 percent of the time and lasted about a month and half on average. The 2010 standoff between Governor Schwarzenegger and the legislature lasted a record 100 days. Gridlock disappeared in 2011 once Proposition 25 was effective.

Causes of Gridlock

There has been much speculation about the reasons for more severe budget gridlock in the last several decades. Many argue that the two-thirds vote requirement to pass the budget was the main factor behind this trend of stalemates,

---

[51] For a detailed analysis of budget gridlock, see Jeff Cummins, "An Empirical Analysis." The data and analysis here are based on that article.

Figure 2.6. History of Late Budgets, 1901–2014

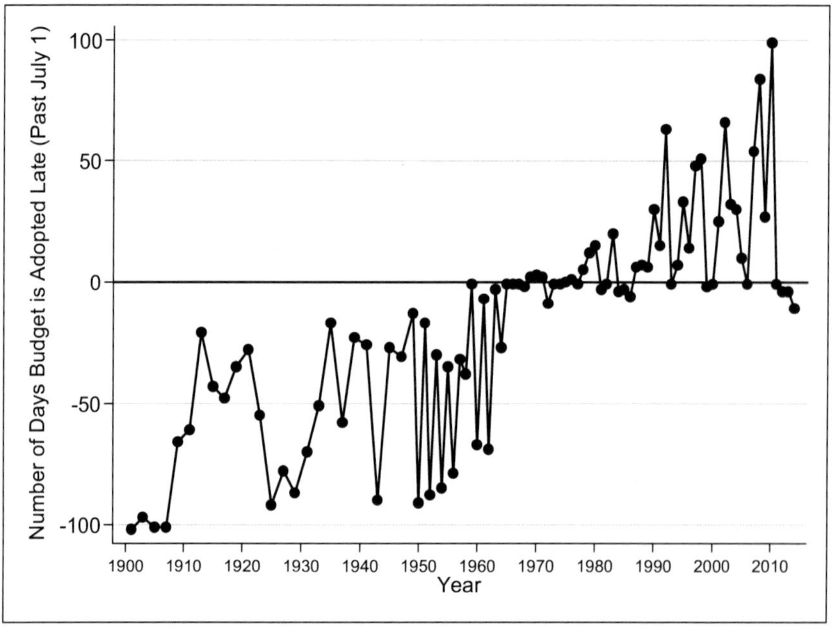

Source: Assembly Clerk's Office and the *California Legislature.*

but that does not address how the state often passed on-time budgets throughout the first half of the 20th century when the two-thirds requirement was present as well.[52] Although the two-thirds vote requirement was an important, if not over-riding factor, other causes played a role as well and perhaps will in the future.

First, political and economic conditions are major contributors to budget impasses. When economic conditions decline in the bust cycle, state revenue follows. High unemployment also places more demand on social welfare pro-grams that support the poor and unemployed. These conditions pull revenue downward and expenditures higher, which then lead to budget deficits. Divided government, or when different parties occupy the governor's office and control the legislature, and party polarization, the ideological distance between the two major parties, make it hard for state leaders to compromise and significantly prolong impasses. Divided government, in particular, could be a pivotal factor in

---

[52] See, for example, George Skelton, "A Simple-Majority Vote Would End the Madness on Passing State Budget," *The Los Angeles Times*, August 20, 2007.

the future occurrence of gridlock if a Republican is able to capture the governor's office.

Another significant contributor to budget stalemates is tax policy and, specifically, the volatility of income tax revenue.[53] Because of a series of policy decisions by the legislature and voters, the share of general fund revenue generated from income taxes has been increasing and now constitutes well over 50 percent of revenues. In California, highly progressive income tax rates generate significant revenue from stock options and capital gains when the stock market grows and lead to precipitous declines when the stock market nosedives. These rapid swings in both positive and negative directions make it difficult for Democrats and Republicans to agree on how to spend money when it flows into state coffers and how to close deficits when the spigot turns off.

California is one of 24 states with the initiative process, and voters have approved several initiatives that substantially affect the budget process each year. Since Proposition 13 limited property tax revenues, the state has backfilled the loss of revenues with general fund support, which has, in turn, limited the amount of money available for other programs. Proposition 98 also contributes to impasses because it mandates a minimum level of spending on education and therefore reduces the discretion of policymakers to balance the budget.

As noted above, term limits drastically changed the environment in Sacramento, which had significant implications for the budget process. Short stints in office encourage a short-term mindset that leads to temporary budget fixes. Legislative leaders are less likely to know the preferences of their colleagues and more ill-equipped to negotiate budget agreements. At the committee level, inexperienced chairs and members do not have the expertise to ferret out poor budget proposals or further refine proposals to make them more efficient.[54] Term-limited legislators are also more likely to rely on lobbyists for information, whose guidance may ultimately hurt the state's fiscal condition.[55] In short, term limits seem to weaken the legislature's capacity to confront fiscal challenges, which destabilizes the budget process and increases the chances for gridlock. Again, time will tell whether the longer tenures allowed in the legislature by the new term limits law will mitigate some of these effects and help legislators more easily forge compromises.

---

[53] For an analysis of the state's revenue volatility, see the Legislative Analyst's Office report on *Revenue Volatility (2005)*. The next chapter also discusses this trend and its importance to the state budget.

[54] Thomas H. Little and Rick Farmer, "Legislative Leadership," in *Institutional Change in American Politics: The Case of Term Limits*, ed. Karl T. Kurtz, Bruce Cain, and Richard G. Niemi (Ann Arbor: University of Michigan Press, 2007).

[55] Christopher Z. Mooney, "Lobbyists and Interest Groups." In *Institutional Change in American Politics: The Case of Term Limits*, eds. Karl T. Kurtz, Bruce Cain, and Richard G. Niemi (Ann Arbor: University of Michigan Press, 2007).; Bruce E. Cain and Thad Kousser, *Adapting to Term Limits: Recent Experiences and New Directions*. (San Francisco: Public Policy Institute of California, 2004).

Evaluating the Structure and Process

During the last crisis budgeting era, there was little disagreement among budget watchers and policymakers that the budget system was broken. Perennially late budgets, a structural deficit, and frequent declarations of fiscal emergency all highlighted the dysfunctional system. With improving fiscal conditions and a key change to the budget process, the crisis nature of budgeting in California has subsided. Still, this does not mean that California's budget structure and process could not be significantly improved. To evaluate the structure and process, it is instructive to outline what an ideal process should look like. Scholars of budgeting have offered a set of criteria, often referred to as budgeting norms, which can guide us in an examination of the process.[56]

It is important to note that these norms do not judge the allocation of funding between different departments and programs because ultimately these are decisions about what values are translated into budget priorities. Rather these norms address the means by which these decisions are made and whether the current process is the best way to channel that decision-making. Although Wildavsky and Caiden conclude that a normative theory of budgeting (what ought to be) is not possible, "Budgeting is supposed to contribute to continuity (for planning), to change (for policy evaluation), to flexibility (for the economy), to rigidity (for limited spending), and to openness (for accountability)."[57]

There are five criteria below that are used to examine the current structure and process. This is not an exhaustive list of criteria, as others have identified more, but they do represent the most common criteria used to address the central issues confronting California.[58]

Periodicity

One of the most common features of any budget is the length of time used to execute the budget and account for the income and outgo. Annual budgets are the most common calendar used in US states (30 states use them) and at the federal level. A two-year, or biennial, cycle is the second most commonly used, but

---

[56] These norms are adapted from Wildavsky and Caiden, *The New Politics*; John W. Ellwood and Mary Sprague, "Options for Reforming the State Budget Process," In *Constitutional Reform in California: Making State Government More Effective and Responsive*, ed. Bruce E. Cain and Roger G. Noll (Berkeley: Institute of Governmental Studies Press, 1995), 329–52.; Juliet Musso, Elizabeth Graddy, and Jennifer Grizard, "State Budgetary Processes and Reforms: The California Story," *Public Budgeting and Finance* 26, no. 4 (2006): 1–21.

[57] Wildavsky and Caiden, *The New Politics,* 184.

[58] Ellwood and Sprague, and Musso, Graddy, and Grizard lay out eight criteria, while Wildavsky and Caiden identify three. With the exception of efficiency, all criteria here are employed by either Wildavsky and Caiden or Musso, Graddy, and Grizard. We added efficiency to address some of the specific aspects of the California process that either duplicate activities or slow the process down.

some states still conduct budgeting activities in the off-year.[59] Since 1949, California has used an annual cycle. However, in practice, the actual decision-making on expenditures has taken on more of a semiannual cycle.

In the "typical" budget calendar outlined above, budget decisions are finalized in late June before the start of the fiscal year. During the crisis budgeting era, late budgets were approved well into the fiscal year sometimes surpassing the first quarter of the fiscal year. Even once the budget was adopted, policymakers frequently had to revisit the spending plan to balance the books. This pattern of semiannual budgeting became more common and is likely to return in future crisis periods.[60]

Some budgeting experts believe that the state should move back to a biennial cycle because it would have several advantages over the current annual process. In biennial states, the development and passage of the budget usually occurs in the first year, while the second year is dedicated to reviewing long-term issues, as well as conducting program review and evaluation. A biennial process could be more conducive to long-term planning that would help the state address its future challenges.

On the whole, however, a large, complex, highly populated state like California is not a good candidate for a biennial cycle. Most states that use a biennial cycle usually have short biennial legislative sessions so the budget cycle often coincides with the regular legislative calendar. With the exception of a few states (Texas and Ohio for example), most biennial states are rural with small populations. Hence, the policy issues that they confront are less complex and time intensive than those dealt with by a country-sized state like California. When comparisons of the political environment between the states and federal government are made, political scientists suggest that California government is most akin to the complexities of the US Congress.

Several other aspects of the budgeting environment in California make it particularly suitable for the annual cycle. One downside to biennial budgeting is that adjustments often must be made in the second off-year when forecasts miss their targets. Given the state's highly volatile revenue system and the forecasting challenges that accompany it, the governor and legislators already have to make adjustments within the span of a one-year period. If adjustments were not made, fiscal imbalances would become even more frequent, further jeopardizing the state's long-term planning and solvency. There is some evidence, though not conclusive, that states with biennial cycles have higher spending levels. It is likely harder to control expenditures when the legislature is not in session much because there is less opportunity to monitor budget activity. Such an environment may only exacerbate the state's inability to align expenditures and revenue. Finally, term limits also populate the legislature with members who lack

---

[59] Ronald Snell, "Annual Versus Biennial Budgeting: The Experience of State Governments," *National Conference of State Legislatures*, April, 2009.

[60] Dan Walters, "California Budget Fix Lasts Just Six Months," *The Sacramento Bee*, September 25, 2011.

knowledge and institutional memory about budget issues. Budget knowledge and expertise for legislators mainly come from budget hearings and involvement in the annual process. A two-year cycle would further reduce legislators' exposure to the process and knowledge of issues because they would no longer have a stake in the outcome in each year.

On balance, the politics and institutions of California seem more suitable for an annual budget. When the state's fiscal situation stabilizes more consistently, it will be more feasible to integrate systematic program review and evaluation, as well as apportion time for long-term planning.

Comprehensiveness

Another traditional budget norm is comprehensiveness. This refers to the extent to which the budget process centralizes decision-making over state revenue and expenditures. Full comprehensiveness would mean that all revenues are placed in a central account, such as the general fund, and that legislators and the governor would have full discretion over the allocation of expenditures. The advantages to this approach include tighter expenditure control through departmental appropriations and clearer lines of accountability. If expenditures exceeded available departmental resources, the department would have to answer to policymakers who would then answer ultimately to voters. Greater discretion over the state's resources also allows policymakers to respond more easily to fiscal issues that arise throughout the year, such as natural disasters or spending deficiencies.

Unfortunately, for a variety of reasons, the state has deviated considerably from this norm. A sizeable portion of the state's total budget—that is both general and special fund spending—is not subject to the annual appropriation process. This includes the continuous appropriations discussed earlier that operate on autopilot each year and are estimated to comprise at least 30 percent of total expenditures. The initiative process also hampers comprehensiveness because voter-passed initiatives have earmarked revenues for certain programs (e.g., Proposition 63 and mental health), mandated a minimum level of spending (e.g., Proposition 98 and K-14 education spending), and placed restrictions on specific funding sources (e.g., vehicle license fees). A prime example of these restrictions occurred in 2009 when legislators and the governor placed measures on the ballot to utilize unspent reserves in mental health and childhood development programs. Since both were authorized through the initiative process, any modifications in spending must be approved by voters. Voters rejected both measures forcing policymakers to look elsewhere for expenditure reductions.

Efficiency

Although not a norm traditionally recognized by researchers, an efficient process can move the main budget through the process quickly without unnecessary redundancies and with an adequate review period that incorporates stakeholder input. There are two components of the current process that do not lend themselves to efficiency. First, the budget bill is introduced in both houses and undergoes the same committee review process in each chamber, which is a common feature of bicameral legislatures. Assembly and Senate budget subcommittees then each hold their own hearings on the same departments. Agency, DOF, and LAO staff, along with lobbyists and members of the public, attend both sets of hearings and offer testimony that is largely the same in each hearing. Often committee members duplicate requests for information from the department, DOF staff, or the LAO, which results in additional workload for these participants and likely detracts from evaluating other programs and services. These redundant processes are particularly magnified after the release of the May Revise when both houses schedule subcommittee hearings to review the revisions before the budget is moved to chamber floors. The expedited review period, usually about two weeks or less, coupled with overlapping hearings hampers the effectiveness of legislative review at this point. Moreover, the two-house conference committee then spends additional time reconciling the budget plans produced by each house. Moving to a process that allowed one chamber to review and pass the budget would go a long way toward improving efficiency.

The second aspect of the process that does not lead to efficiency is the two-thirds vote requirement to make tax changes. Prior to 2010, this efficiency concern also applied to the two-thirds vote requirement to pass the budget, but with the change to a simple majority, an important obstacle has been removed. Two-thirds vote requirements are inefficient because they require a level of consensus that is hard to attain and they reduce accountability for those decisions. Delegates to the nation's Constitutional Convention abandoned supermajoritarian vote thresholds that were stipulated under the Articles of Confederation because they could not pass laws to address the country's problems. James Madison and others believed that supermajoritarian requirements should be reserved for special circumstances, such as altering the structure of a country's constitution, and not for conducting the ordinary business of government. Since appropriating resources (budgeting) and raising revenue are essential to the day-to-day operations of government, they should be considered "ordinary business." Furthermore, since it is rare for either party to gain a two-thirds majority, members of the minority must consent to fiscal decisions. This obscures responsibility for poor budget decisions because both the majority and minority party participate in the decisions so there are no alternatives for voters in a two-party system. Therefore, neither party is punished by voters for the state's ongoing fiscal problems.

Even with the two-thirds requirements, the main stumbling block is essentially political—Republican orthodoxy has drawn a hard line against any tax increases. Republican candidates for office now routinely sign pledges not to raise taxes at the insistence of antitax groups such as Americans for Tax Reform. Republican legislators fear retaliation for supporting tax increases by conservative voters in their next campaign.[61] It is important to remember that at one time governors could find Republican support for tax increases. For instance, Republican Governor Wilson received Republican support for tax increases on sales and income in 1991, while Democratic Governor Pat Brown did on corporate taxes in 1959.[62]

Transparency

The norm of transparency is actually one area where California scores fairly high, with the exception of the latter stages of the process. Transparency entails several components: (1) budget information is available to the public; (2) there is a budget review period that receives public input; and (3) information can be used to hold policymakers accountable. With the internet, budget documents are now readily accessible to the public and interested stakeholders on the Department of Finance website. Press conferences with the governor and DOF director and all budget-related committee hearings are available online through the California Channel. Members of the public who are concerned about particular budget issues can testify at committee hearings. Once the budget is finalized, there are several different publications that can be used to examine how spending was allocated, including the LAO's annual spending plan report.

Where transparency falls short is with Big 5 and Big 3 meetings that take control of the process and the hastily scheduled floor sessions to pass the final budget. As noted earlier, a frequent complaint of the Big 5 meetings is that they are not conducted in public and rank-and-file legislators do not always know the tenor of these discussions. When budget deals do surface, legislative leaders quickly usher them to the floors for passage to avoid missing the legislature's constitutional deadline. Rank-and-file members often grumble that they are not familiar with the contents, but do not want to hold up the budget and jeopardize their pay. Formulation of the budget is at its worst at these times because there is little scrutiny of decisions with far-reaching implications.

Despite these latter unsavory stages of the process, the Big 5 (or Big 3) aspect of them may be unavoidable at certain times, while transparency improvements to floor sessions at final passage are more feasible. The Big 5-style meetings actually represent an efficient means by which to forge compromise rather than hashing out compromises on chamber floors. If the meetings were public, talks may yield to public posturing, which would slow progress. At the Constitutional Convention, delegates recognized that more headway could be made with

---

[61] Interestingly, out of six Republicans who supported tax increases in the 2009 budget package, only one did not win his next election. See Steven Harmon, "One of Six Does Not Constitute 'Most,'" *Political Blogger, Bay Area News Group*, January 13, 2011, accessed January 23, 2012 at http://www.ibabuzz.com/politics/2011/01/13/two-of-six-does-not-constitute-most/.

[62] Greg Lucas, "Pete Wilson: The Negotiator," *The Los Angeles Times*, June 15, 2008.

closed sessions since discussions could be more open and frank. To improve transparency at these latter stages, a requirement for a public review period of the final budget bill before voting might shed light on the contents, but also may lead to more delay from backtracking legislators.

Balance

Balance is the last budgeting norm and plays a central role in the development and evaluation of a budget. Rubin argues that balance is implicit in the term budget: "Budgets have to balance. A plan for expenditures that pays no attention to ensuring that revenues cover expenditures is not a budget."[63] This sentiment is especially true for states, which have to comply with balanced budget requirements, and do not have the ability to run long-term deficits like the federal government. Balance drives the entire budget process from the beginning to end since spending levels are supposed to remain below available resources. The prospect of falling out of balance initiates further legislative action to remain in balance.

California's performance on this norm ranks it among the lowest of any of the states. Few other states have encountered deficits as frequently as California. From 2001 to 2011, the Legislative Analyst's Office projected a deficit in nine out of 11 years, or 82 percent of the time. Even once deficits were no longer projected in 2012, questions remain as to whether the state's budget is really balanced given the enormous amounts of long-term debt.

There are numerous reasons why the state continues to encounter deficits, and they will be addressed more fully in future chapters. For now, it is important to note how the process and procedures in place attempt to prevent deficits, but have been unsuccessful. Many states that avoid deficits have procedural mechanisms to avoid overspending, commonly referred to as balanced budget requirements, but California has one of the weaker rules (see Chapter 7). Voters did approve a stronger rainy day fund in 2014 with a larger target balance level, but it is unlikely to have enough stashed away to prevent budget deficits in the future.

Conclusion

The budget dance ultimately comes down to the ability of policymakers to forge compromises that meet the state's short-term and long-term needs. The structure and process can facilitate the dance and build proper incentives for accountability, but the current budget system in California does not do this. With duplicative committee hearings, an expedited legislative review period post-May Revise, and other shortcomings, the process needs reform to improve its efficiency and effectiveness.

---

[63] Irene Rubin, *The Politics of Public Budgeting: Getting and Spending, Borrowing and Balancing,* 4th ed. (Washington, DC: CQ Press, 2000), 4.

The general public is concerned about the budget situation, but is also a major contributor to the ongoing dysfunction. In an analysis of budget gridlock, election years did not pressure policymakers to adopt a budget any earlier than nonelection years.[64] Without fear of retribution for poor budget performance, it is unlikely that policymakers will have a strong incentive to resolve the state's budget problems. Moreover, the public is unwilling to give policymakers more authority on taxing and spending, which could ultimately lead to stronger accountability. Instead, an overwhelming 79 percent of the public believes that California voters should make some budget decisions, while only 16 percent support the governor and legislature making all of these decisions.[65] While the public values its ability to formulate budget policy through the initiative process, it increasingly places roadblocks in the path of potential compromises between the governor and legislature. With less discretion and authority over budget policy, it will be progressively harder for voters to blame elected officials in institutions that have not made many of those decisions.

Review Questions

1. Describe five significant budget developments and how they have impacted California's budget process.

2. Discuss the pros and cons of the Big 5 and Big 3 meetings. Are there better ways to finalize the budget?

3. Explain the patterns of budget gridlock in California. What factors seem to drive gridlock?

4. What are budgeting norms and how does California meet or not meet these norms?

Additional Resources

Department of Finance

http://www.dof.ca.gov/budgeting/budget_faqs/information/

This is the state's main website for budget information. It has budgets online, historical information, and instructions for state departments on how to prepare their budget.

---

[64] Cummins, "An Empirical Analysis."
[65] Public Policy Institute of California Statewide Survey, *Californians and Their Government*, (San Francisco: Public Policy Institute of California, September, 2012).

Legislative Analyst's Office (LAO)

http://www.lao.ca.gov/laoapp/main.aspx

The site has their analyses of the governor's budget going back decades and other publications and reports in various formats.

Assembly Budget Committee and Senate Committee on Budget and Fiscal Review

http://abgt.assembly.ca.gov/
http://sbud.senate.ca.gov/

These sites have press releases, hearing agendas, budget documents and analysis, links to subcommittees, and lists of committee members.

Chapter 3

The Economy and Taxation in the Golden State

> Upon this subject (adoption of a property tax), your committee (has) the fullest confidence that there never existed a community who will more cheerfully and promptly meet their taxes.
>
> —California Senate Finance Committee Report
> on 1850 property tax bill, 1850.[1]

California is often regarded as a country unto itself. Its size, population, and economy all characterize a political jurisdiction that is larger than most nations in the world. Much of California's history and population has been shaped by its economic growth and development. At the same time that California is renowned for its economic prosperity, this has not always translated into a sound, stable fiscal system that one might expect from a wealthy and resource-rich state. Although California weathered economic downturns relatively well prior to the 1990s, in recent decades, its economy has suffered deeper downturns than the nation as whole and encountered weaker periods of recovery. The state's elastic tax structure, which is highly reactive to economic growth and decline, makes it particularly vulnerable to economic trends and is the root cause of California's boom-and-bust budget cycles. As a result of the transition to a more service-oriented economy, the state's tax structure has failed to keep pace with the changing nature of economic activity.

---

[1] Quoted in David R. Doerr, *California's Tax Machine, A History of Taxing and Spending in the Golden State, 2d ed.* (Sacramento, CA: California Taxpayers' Association, 2008), 10.

61

In this chapter, we provide an overview of the state economy, including its diverse set of industries, review recent economic performance, and analyze the interrelationship between the economy and the state's revenue system. As the foundation for the budget, the economy allows the state to generate revenue to address social problems, invest in education to prepare the current and future workforce, and support the infrastructure network to facilitate further economic growth. After a discussion of the economy, we then turn to an overview of the state's tax structure, criteria for evaluating the structure, and describe its major sources of revenue. California is often criticized for a high tax burden that detracts from economic growth, but the burden varies quite substantially depending on which type of tax one is considering. The next section examines several major issues confronting our revenue system, including the tax burden and business climate, revenue volatility, the outdated sales tax system, and tax expenditure programs. We conclude by evaluating ways to improve the revenue system.

Overview of the Economy

Most discussions about the California economy revolve around its size. As such, we begin by looking at various measures of its size and comparing it to other nations to put it into perspective. The most common measure of the state's economy is the Gross State Product (GSP), which is equivalent to the Gross Domestic Product (GDP) used at the national level. Both measure the total value of goods and services produced within the state or nation. Another way to think of it is the amount of economic activity occurring within the state, which includes the income generated through salaries and wages, products manufactured such as computers and cell phones, and services like haircuts or entertainment, among other components. Figure 3.1 shows California's GSP compared to the other top economies in the world in 2012. The US economy is the largest with $16 trillion in total value, while China is second at $8 trillion. California is essentially tied for eighth place with the Russian Federation and Italy at $2 trillion, followed closely behind by India and Canada. California has fallen in the rankings over the last decade as the economies of Brazil and Italy have strengthened. When compared to other states, California, of course, is the largest in the United States. Texas and New York are second and third, at $1.4 and $1.2 trillion, respectively. No other state in the top 10 surpasses the trillion dollar level.[2]

Aside from the sheer size of the state's economy, another positive characteristic is its rich diversity. California is home to many different types of industries, which is advantageous because the overall economy is not as vulnerable to the decline in one particular sector. When one sector declines, another sector's growth can offset the loss of production and jobs in the declining area. This economic diversity is depicted in Figure 3.2, which shows the breakdown of jobs in

---

[2] Center for the Continuing Study of the California Economy, "California Poised to Move Up in World Economy Rankings in 2013" (Palo Alto, CA: Center for the Continuing Study of the California Economy, July 2013).

Figure 3.1. California Economy Compared to Other Nations, 2012

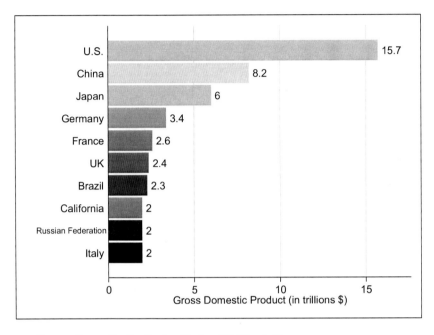

Source: Center for Continuing Study of California Economy.

California by major industry.[3] The largest share of jobs, nearly 20 percent, re-sides in trade, transportation, and utilities, followed closely behind by govern-ment jobs at the national, state, and local level. At the lower end of the employ-ment sectors, financial activities, involving banking, investing, and insurance, represent a little more than 5 percent of employment, while construction falls just below 5 percent.

Economic Performance

California has had a history of strong economic performance, which has cata-pulted it into one of the leading economies in the world. Various events, from the gold rush at the beginning of statehood, to World War II in the 1940s, to the rise of Silicon Valley in the 1980s and 1990s, have helped bring people and sus-tained employment growth to the state. At the same time, California has not

---

[3] The industries are shown according to the North American Industry Classification System (NAICS) developed by the US Department of Commerce. It replaced the older Standard Industrial Classification System (SIC) in 1997.

Figure 3.2. Jobs by Industry, 2013

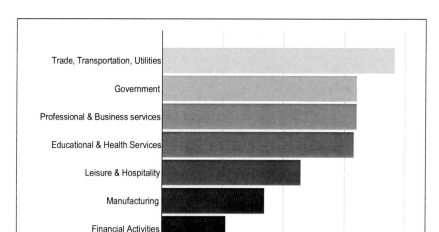

Source: Bureau of Labor Statistics.

managed to avoid the business cycles that other states and the nation as a whole have confronted. Strong and rapid job growth produced by major industries such as defense and technology have significantly contributed to the vitality of the state economy, yet the decline of these same industries at different times has led the state into deep recessions as well.

Figure 3.3 displays the annual change in real gross state product for California from 1980 to 2012 and illustrates the boom and bust cycles that the state economy has encountered. The negative GSP growth indicates the four recessions that the state and nation have encountered over this time period, including the 1980–81, 1990–91, 2001, and 2007–09 recessions, the latter of which is the Great Recession. The figure also shows the solid economic growth that occurred in the middle and late decades of the 1980s and 1990s. Positive economic growth occurred in the early to middle 2000s, but the Great Recession hit in the latter part of the decade to break up the pattern of late decade growth. For the entire time period, the average annual growth was 2.4 percent, while it was near-

Figure 3.3. Real GSP Change Over Time, 1980–2012

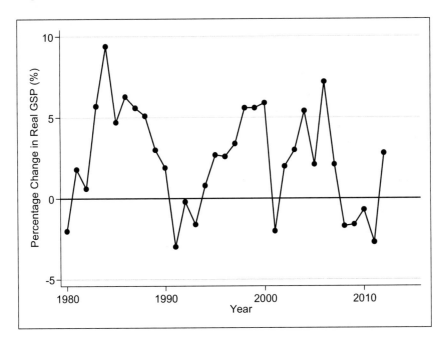

Source: U.S. Bureau of Economic Analysis.

ly a point lower (1.7) in the crisis budgeting era from 2000–12. Usually, an annual average of 3 percent or more is considered strong growth in the United States.

We can further assess economic performance in the state by looking at employment conditions in recent decades. Figure 3.4 shows the annual unemployment rate over the 1980–2013 time period. The trend line follows a pattern similar to what we see with real GSP. Unemployment increases in the early recessionary years of the decades and in 2007, while it improves in the intervening years. While the average unemployment rate over the 30-year period was 7.4 percent, it rose over 12 percent in 2010, indicating the severity of the Great Recession.

The Great Recession

The Great Recession of 2007–09 had severe consequences for the state economy and budget. California was hit hard on both fronts because the real estate market enjoyed a rapid rise in housing prices starting in 2001 that fed into

Figure 3.4. Unemployment Rate, 1980–2013

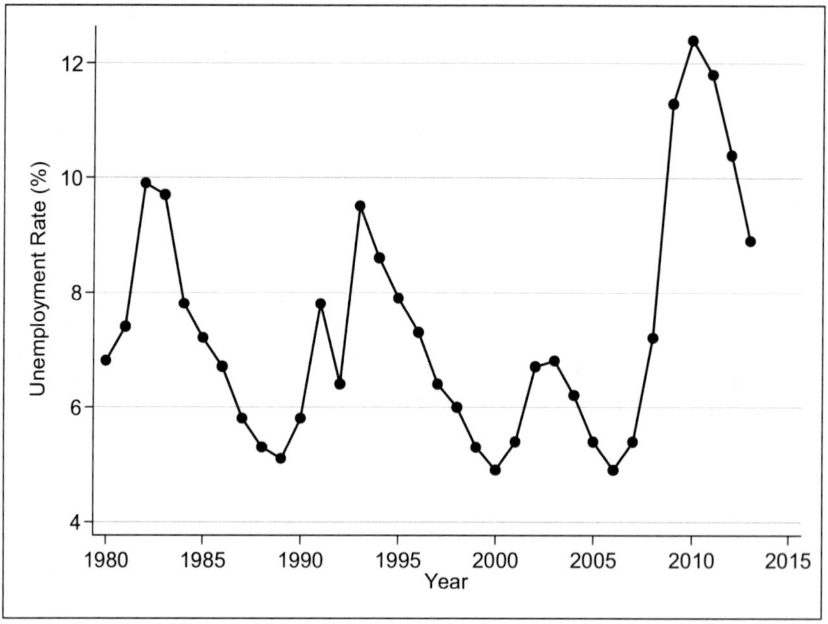

Source: Bureau of Labor Statistics.

a precipitous decline in 2006 when the market collapsed. As such, many of the regions in California faced steeper declines in the housing market than regions in other states that had also enjoyed strong sales in housing. With regard to the budget, the state was already dealing with a structural deficit that was amplified by the drop in revenues and the increased pressure on safety net spending brought on by the Great Recession. To fully understand the implications for California's economy and budget, it is useful to discuss some of the main factors behind the recession.

The Great Recession began with the collapse of the housing market in 2006. There are several reasons why the market collapsed in general and why California was more severely affected than other states. We refrain from a full-blown analysis of the housing and financial crisis here because its origins will be debated for years, if not decades, to come and the details are not necessary to comprehend its effects on the California budget. Nationally, the origins of the housing collapse can be traced to the availability of cheap capital. After the 2001 recession, the Federal Reserve Board, which sets monetary policy, held short-term interest rates unusually low (around 2 percent) for over a three-year period.[4] This federal funds rate is the interest rate that banks charge one another for short-term loans and reverberates throughout the credit and loan markets, affecting everything from credit cards to mortgages. Since low interest rates allow consumers and businesses to borrow money cheaply, it fueled the housing market and the subsequent run-up in housing prices.[5]

Another key factor in the housing collapse was lax lending policies that allowed consumers to obtain mortgages even if they had previously been unable to because of a questionable credit history. These borrowers are known as subprime, since they have weaker credit histories and fall below the "prime" borrowers. Traditionally, buyers were required to provide a down payment of 5 percent or more in order to qualify for a loan, depending on the type of lending program that they qualified for, and demonstrate an income and credit history that established confidence that mortgage payments could be made. Federal lending regulations were loosened in the late 1990s and early 2000s and allowed mortgage lenders to offer no-doc[umentation] or low-doc loans, that required very little evidence that consumers could afford their mortgages. In addition, banks and lending agencies offered various loan packages, such as teaser rates or interest-only loans, that delayed or minimized the actual monthly mortgage payment and resulted in balloon payments after a certain period of time. These generously structured mortgage packages, along with more common adjustable-rate mortgages (ARMs), helped lure more homebuyers into the market and allowed many to afford higher-priced homes than they otherwise could. However, once the initial generous loan terms expired, many homeowners had a difficult time making their mortgage payments. In mid-2005, the Federal Reserve Board decided to douse the flaming housing market by beginning a series of federal funds rate increases that eventually led to a target rate of 5.25 percent in June 2006.[6] Because a sizeable portion of homeowners relied on varying types of adjustable mortgages, their mortgage payments reset at higher and higher interest rates in accordance with the rise of mortgage rates.

One of the most important and complicated contributors to the housing collapse and subsequent financial crisis was the role of the secondary mortgage market and the securitization of mortgages. Through the secondary market, mortgage lenders can sell their mortgages to financial institutions who, in turn,

---

[4] Board of Governors of Federal Reserve, "Open Market Operations," accessed June 5, 2014 at http://www.federalreserve.gov/monetarypolicy/openmarket.htm.

[5] Numerous books have been published that describe and explain the roots of the Great Recession. For a day-by-day chronicle of the events leading up to the housing collapse and credit crisis, see Andrew Ross Sorkin, *Too Big To Fail: The Inside Story of How Wall Street and Washington Fought to Save the Financial System—And Themselves* (London: Penguin Group, 2009). Carmen M. Reinhart and Kenneth S. Rogoff, *This Time is Different: Eight Centuries of Financial Folly* (Princeton: Princeton University Press, 2009) provides a statistical analysis of financial crises throughout the last six centuries, including the Great Recession. Of particular note is their conclusion that it takes, on average, 10 years for nations to recover from financial crises.

[6] Board of Governors, "Open Market Operations."

package the loans into securities to sell to investors seeking a steady rate of return. Mortgage lenders received more capital to lend out to more borrowers and collected fees on top of these transactions. Investment banks, such as Lehman Brothers and Goldman Sachs, along with the government-sponsored agencies, the Federal National Mortgage Association and the Federal Home Loan Mortgage Corporation, more commonly known as Fannie Mae and Freddie Mac, were major financial players who bought the mortgages and packaged them to sell to investors. This structure was highly profitable for mortgage lenders, investment banks, and Fannie Mae and Freddie Mac, and finally for institutional and individual investors who gained steady returns on their securities as long as new borrowers were brought into the housing market and prices continued their rapid ascent. However, this lucrative web began to crumble as borrowers began to default on their mortgage payments once new, higher payments kicked in on their loans. The housing market peaked in late 2006 and rapidly declined thereafter.

In addition to those factors discussed above, California has additional characteristics that made its housing market particularly volatile and sent the state's economy spiraling downward more quickly. First, California is an attractive place to live given its climate and location along the coast. In normal times, demand in the housing market in the state is strong as exemplified by the higher median sales price compared to other states. As prices rose during the housing market expansion, homeowners and investors scurried to buy property whose values were likely to rise quickly and, they thought, remain high for some time. Second, Proposition 13 limits the level of property taxes (1 percent plus local assessments) and limits increases in the assessment value to no more than 2 percent a year. Since property taxes are relatively low on a home, this allows homebuyers to spend more of their money on the purchase price of the home and anticipate a very gradual increase in property taxes. When coupled with low mortgage rates, even more money and income can go towards the purchase price and the subsequent principal payments of the mortgage. Thus, property tax limitations allowed housing prices to rise higher (and perhaps faster) than they otherwise would.

Figure 3.5 shows the median sales price of single-family homes in California from 1985 to 2013. The hot market is obvious from the rapidly rising trend line from 2001 until 2006, while the subsequent drop is obvious as well. The housing market in California peaked in April 2007 with a median sales price of $594,110, almost 9 months after the national peak in July 2006.[7] Two years later, in April 2009, the median price dropped 57 percent to $253,110. The housing collapse had devastating consequences not only for the construction and real estate industry as tens of thousands of jobs were lost, but also for the spillover product markets that are affected by home purchases, such as the durable goods market, which provides appliances for new homeowners.

---

[7] California Association of Realtors, "Market Data," accessed June 5, 2014 at http://www.car.org/marketdata/data/housingdata/.

Figure 3.5. Median Sales Price for Existing Single-Family Houses, 1985–2013

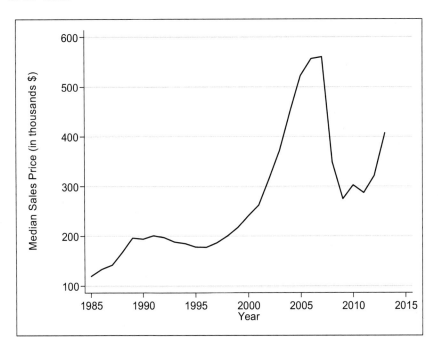

Source: California Association of Realtors.

Although early assessments of the impact of the housing market collapse on the overall economy indicated that it was largely "contained" within the housing sector, the deteriorating housing market eventually led to the financial crisis. Large financial institutions, such as Bear Stearns, JP Morgan, and AIG, had significant vulnerabilities if the housing market collapsed and mortgage default rates rose. Once Lehman Brothers filed for bankruptcy in September 2008, becoming the largest institution in US history to do so, banks became extremely reluctant to lend to one another and businesses and consumers faced considerable difficulty trying to secure ordinary loans that they could normally obtain with ease. The entire US economy slowed nearly to a standstill and California was not immune. Now, mired in a deep recession, the likes of that not seen since the Great Depression in the 1930s, businesses began cutting their expenditures to survive by reducing their labor costs. In California, the unemployment rate went from 5.4 percent in 2007 to over 11 percent by 2009.

Normally, economic recessions have significant consequences for all government budgets, but this is particularly true for state and local governments who are subject to balanced budget requirements. At the national level, policy-makers can run a deficit and attempt to stimulate the economy through various fiscal measures. California, like all states, loses revenue during economic downturns at a time when demand for social programs is on the rise. Both trends push budgets toward imbalances.

By the time the Great Recession unfolded in California in 2007, the state was still trying to pull itself out of a structural deficit that began after the 2001 recession. As workers lost their jobs in significant numbers, this reduced revenue from income and sales taxes and eroded corporate profits and, in turn, corporate tax revenue. As Californians turned to the social safety net, this forced more spending on unemployment insurance, food stamps, welfare, and health insurance programs. The depth and length of the Great Recession exceeded recent previous recessions in 2001 and 1991 and ripped an even larger hole in the state budget. California's precarious budget conditions before the recession positioned the state for potentially disastrous consequences in the wake of such a steep economic downturn, sending the state near the brink of insolvency.

The Impact of the Economy on State Budgeting

The relationship between the economy and budgeting is reciprocal, dynamic, and intricately intertwined. Generally speaking, the economy and state revenue, and subsequently government spending, rise and fall together, though the pattern of revenue and expenditures tends to lag that of the economy. A fast growing economy is likely to flood government coffers with revenue, while economic recessions can quickly drain resources. Unless a state has a healthy rainy-day fund and tight restrictions on access to it, a declining economy will almost always lead to a stressful budget environment. The tax structure and other policies also play a role in how strongly the economy affects state revenue.

Overall, the economy affects budgeting in both the short and long term. First, in the short term, the economy lays the foundation for development of the budget for the upcoming fiscal (budget) year. Since the basic purpose of budgeting is to establish a plan for future spending, budget agencies must determine their expectations for the level of demand for government services. This demand is heavily influenced by the performance of the economy. Thus, to project the level of demand for services, the state must first forecast future economic conditions. The Department of Finance and the Legislative Analyst's Office are the two main state agencies responsible for forecasting the economy.[8] Once this forecast is made, these agencies use these projected economic conditions to determine what the overall revenue level will be and the anticipated level of expenditures. Combining the projected levels of revenues and expenditures then

---

[8] Several academic institutions, banks, and private institutions also generate economic forecasts, including the Anderson School of Management at University of California Los Angeles, the University of the Pacific, and the Center for the Continuing Study of the California Economy.

allows these agencies to determine whether the state will end the budget year in the red (deficit) or black (surplus). Depending on whether there is a projected surplus or deficit, the governor or legislature may propose to cut spending, raise revenue, or distribute tax rebates.

Second, the economy can also influence budgeting in real-time during the budget execution phase. This means that currently changing economic conditions may reduce the amount of revenues coming into state accounts below what was anticipated or produce a level of demand for expenditures higher than what was budgeted. In these instances, budgeting becomes highly reactive and in order to head off a year-end deficit, policymakers consider expenditure adjustments and deferrals and short-term borrowing schemes. Revenue adjustments are difficult to make in the current year budget so policymakers must rely on these other alternatives. As opposed to the role economic forecasts play in the budget development phase, usually through slower and more deliberative decision-making, the impact of the economy on budgets during the execution phase is more immediate, often times forcing policymakers to make urgent budget decisions.

A third way that the economy can impact budgeting is when long-term economic conditions are likely to affect the budgetary needs of the state in the more distant future. This refers to how shifting economic and demographic patterns over the next 10, 20, or 30 years may alter revenue patterns and expenditure demands. For example, in California, as well as nationally, the overall population is expected to become older because of the aging baby boomer generation. This demographic shift is likely to impact a wide variety of consumption patterns from housing purchases to furniture sales and affect the level of demand for different services such as health care. The long-term economic outlook can also shed light on where budget planning is falling short in terms of meeting future economic needs. For instance, projections by the Public Policy Institute of California reveal that there will not be enough college graduates to fill jobs that require a college education by 2025.[9] If these employment needs are not met, it could slow the state's future economic growth. As policymakers consider the allocation of funding between now and 2025, they should incorporate these needs into budgets for higher education. However, while the state should consider these long-term needs in an ideal budgeting environment, the recent crisis budgeting era was not conducive to such considerations.

Aside from the larger implications of the economy for budgeting in California, the economy also affects specific revenue sources because of the structure of these individual taxes. The steeply progressive income tax system makes this source of revenue particularly responsive to economic growth and decline, especially because of high-income taxpayers. High-income taxpayers generate a portion of their income from capital gains and stock options and tend to have surges

---

[9]Public Policy Institute of California. *California's Future Workforce: Will There Be Enough College Graduates?* (San Francisco: Public Policy Institute of California, 2008), http://www.ppic.org/main/publication.asp?i=809.

in their income when the stock market rises. While state coffers benefit from the additional revenue during good times (the boom), they also get hit with a sudden drop in revenue (the bust) when these good times end. In the late 1990s, this is exactly what happened when a surging economy and stock market generated a significant increase in revenue from capital gains and stock options, to the point that the state offered tax rebates, and then resulted in a huge drop in revenues when the stock market plunged and the 2001 recession struck.

The economy also affects sales and property taxes, but in different ways. Both sales and property tax are less responsive to the economy so revenue does not decline as quickly as it does for income taxes.[10] As we discuss below, sales tax revenue has not been growing as fast as it used to because the economy is becoming more service-oriented and few services are taxed in California. For the property tax, there is a longer lag time between changing economic conditions and the impact on revenue collection because of how the property tax is administered. This makes it the most stable major revenue source. Property tax limitations imposed by Proposition 13 have made it even more stable since both assessment values and tax rates are limited. During the steep climb in housing prices from 2001 to 2006, property tax revenue surged, primarily benefiting cities, counties, and other local government entities. Property tax revenue also declined when the housing market crashed and foreclosures rose, albeit more slowly than income tax revenue. Subsequently, many local governments struggled financially to overcome the loss of property tax revenues and the protracted housing recovery. Because the state's share of K-14 funding is offset by property tax revenue, weak growth from property taxes also puts additional pressure on the state's general fund.

The State Tax System

Few areas of government ignite as much political controversy as the tax system. The visceral negative reaction to taxes in general harkens back to the founding of the nation when colonists rebelled against what were believed to be oppressive tax policies imposed by the British Parliament on the colonies (ironically, British citizens paid higher taxes than colonists). Throughout the nation's history, new and higher taxes have been imposed with less fanfare and resistance than more recent times, but these were usually enacted during national crises such as the Great Depression or around World Wars I and II. However, since the genesis of the conservative antitax movement in the late 1970s, spawned by Proposition 13 in California, simply mentioning the word "tax" invites disdain and negative attacks from certain segments of the population, particularly conservatives. California, considered to be the cradle of the antitax movement, has seen its share of fierce political fighting over the prospect of raising taxes or

---

[10] William F. Fox and LeAnn Luna, "State Tax Collections: Eroding Tax Bases," *The Book of the States* (Lexington, KY: The Council of State Governments, 2005), 411–16.

even over reforming various components of the tax system. Republicans and Democrats alike are reluctant to casually banter about the high-stakes issue of taxation without the fear of intense media attention and retribution from antitax groups, such as the Howard Jarvis Taxpayers Association and the California Taxpayers Association. Here we examine California's tax system in more detail, starting with a discussion of the purposes of taxation.

Purposes of Taxation

Although many Americans would probably prefer to pay very little in taxes, if any, taxes actually play a very fundamental role in any governmental system. Simply put, government could not exist if it did not have the authority to raise revenue and support a system of law and order. Our nation's early experiment with a confederation under the Articles of Confederation illustrated how a central government can be impotent without adequate resources necessary to administer a growing republic and enforce its laws. The American Revolution was nearly lost because the Continental Congress lacked authority to levy and collect taxes from its member states.

California's tax system, like any, generally serves several purposes. First, in an abstract sense, the ability for a state to tax its residents fulfills a key component of the social contract between a nation's citizens and their representative government. John Locke and other political theorists wrote of an implicit contract between a state and its inhabitants whereby a mutually beneficial exchange occurs between the two parties. The state provides order and security, punishes crimes, and generally protects its citizens from harm. In exchange for this protection, citizens are required to pay taxes, abide by the laws, and face the possibility of conscription to defend it. Taxation, in general, is thus part of this implicit agreement between a government and its citizens.

On a more practical level, government is concerned about the welfare of its citizens and improving their living conditions. In the US, the government relies on the market economy to distribute goods and services to meet the needs of its residents. As such, another purpose of taxation is to provide government with resources to facilitate economic growth and prosperity. A sufficient level of revenue allows the state to fund K-12 and higher education to prepare individuals for the workforce, support technological advancements, and invest in infrastructure to transport goods and services.

Although we rely on capitalism for the primary means of resource distribution, market failures exist, which inhibit a sufficient level of resources or services for all citizens. A third purpose of taxation is to address market failures that inevitably exist in a capitalist system. Revenue generated through taxation allows the government to address these market failures through income support programs, housing assistance, and health care insurance programs, among other services. Even individuals with decent jobs and income may fall victim to these market failures when market forces do not offer certain goods or services at reasonable prices, such as the case with health insurance. When resources and income are maldistributed on a wide scale, the tax system can help redistribute resources from the well-off to the less well-off. Progressive income tax systems, such as California's, are a common instrument for such redistribution because higher income groups pay a higher marginal rate than lower income groups.

For policymakers, another purpose of the tax system is to encourage or discourage certain types of economic behavior. Tax exemptions, credits, and deductions can be used to promote the purchase of certain items, such as houses, cars, or energy efficient appliances, because they are valuable to policy goals. For example, in the wake of the housing crash in 2006, both the state of California and the federal government offered tax incentives for purchasing a home. This was intended to jumpstart the housing slump and the slow pace of economic recovery since economic growth is an important policy goal of government. On the other hand, taxes, usually excise taxes on certain goods, can be imposed to increase the cost of an item and deter consumers from purchasing that product. In this case, the purpose can be twofold: (1) government may seek to curtail certain types of consumption that may be harmful to the public, such as excessive alcohol use or tobacco use; and (2) government may seek to recover the public costs from such behavior.

Criteria for Evaluating Tax Options

To evaluate the effects and administrative characteristics of various types of taxes, economists and policy analysts use a set of criteria to determine whether a given tax will meet certain goals. Using these criteria, analysts evaluate how well a tax option stands up against each criterion. Tax options that fair well against most of the criteria and that do not have disproportionately large negative effects may be viewed as potential mechanisms for raising revenue. It is important to remember that tax policy is ultimately subject to a political process where politicians attempt to manipulate the estimated effects of tax proposals to suit their desired goals.[11] However, as noted above, the ability for government to raise revenue is an indispensable component of its existence. These criteria provide a framework for examining which tax instruments might best help in this endeavor.

Equity

Aside from the criterion of economic effects (discussed below), no other criterion tends to be as contentious as equity, which evaluates the distribution of the tax burden on taxpayers. Essentially, equity boils down to the "fairness" of a tax, but it is difficult to remove one's ideological predispositions about what is considered to be fair. Two approaches are commonly used to evaluate equity: (1) the *benefits-received principle*; and (2) the *ability-to-pay principle*.[12] The

---

[11] Deborah Stone, *Policy Paradox: The Art of Political Decision Making* (New York: W. W. Norton & Company, 1997).

[12] All of the criteria for this section are largely based on John L. Mikesell, *Fiscal*

principle of benefits received applies to whether the individual taxpayer who pays the tax is the one who also receives the services. Generally, we would say that the tax is fair or equitable if the costs borne by the taxpayer are linked to the services provided to that same taxpayer. This concept closely relates to the idea of a quasi-marketplace where consumers, or taxpayers, are purchasing a product, or benefit.

Not all government-provided services are conducive to such an exchange between the consumer (resident) and seller (government) and the nexus between the cost (tax) and the benefit (service) must be sufficient so that the beneficiaries see a direct or, in some cases, indirect link between the tax paid and the service. One condition that is necessary for the benefits-received principle to apply is that it must be feasible to measure the good or service in quantifiable units where users can be charged based on their higher demand. For instance, California passed a law requiring residential water use to be metered in order to charge based on its demand.

Metered water is also an example of a direct link between the costs and benefits of a service, but the link for other types of services may be more indirect. School districts often receive voter approval for bond measures to build or renovate schools within their jurisdiction, but not all residents who pay property taxes benefit as directly as others. Property owners with children are the ones who most directly benefit if they send their children to public schools, while other property owners may not have children. However, these other residents and businesses may benefit indirectly from lower crime rates that accompany a better school system, increased property values, and a potential supply of educated workers. The intuitive appeal of this principle is evidenced by the relatively high passage rate for school-related tax measures, which pass more than 50 percent of the time.[13]

The ability-to-pay principle refers to how certain groups of taxpayers may have more resources that allow them to absorb the cost of taxes easier than other groups. The level of services received is not considered here; only the capacity to bear the costs. There are two central components to administering such a tax: (1) the measure of ability to pay; and (2) the rate structure.[14] The typical measure used in California is income, generated from salaries, wages, and investment earnings, but other indicators of wealth can also be used, such as luxury purchases (e.g., yachts) or estate values, which are applied in the case of inheritance taxes.

When considering the rate structure, economists analyze the distribution of the tax burden on different taxpayers using the concepts of *horizontal* and *verti-*

---

cal equity.[15] Horizontal equity refers to whether two taxpayers who earn the same level of income are required to pay the same amount of taxes. If there is a discrepancy, then horizontal equity is not maintained. This can occur because the state may grant preferential tax status to households with children or home-owners who are allowed to deduct mortgage interest on their home. In both cases, these would reduce the taxes owed compared to the taxpayer who cannot claim these deductions.

In contrast, vertical equity is employed to evaluate the tax burden for households at different income levels (e.g., $100,000 vs. $40,000). Under this criterion, there is an assumption that a higher income individual has the capacity to pay a larger amount of taxes without infringing on his or her standard of living, but there is no objective way of determining what that additional burden should be. Higher income taxpayers argue that they earned their income like other taxpayers who earn less so they should not be punished for making more income. Three types of tax structure characterize the burden for taxpayers at varying levels of income. All use the relationship between income (or whatever wealth measure is used) and the effective rate of taxation (tax paid divided by income) to determine the structure. A *regressive* tax is one where effective rates are higher for lower income groups while rates are lower for higher income groups. The tax burden thus hits low income groups harder than the high groups, which violates the ability-to-pay principle.

A *proportional*, or flat tax, is one where effective rates are the same for all income levels. Republicans often champion these types of taxes because they argue they are the fairest way to distribute the tax burden; every taxpayer is treated the same. Theoretically, policymakers can then avoid the predicament of attempting to select a rate that should apply to higher income groups. However, while the rate may ultimately be fair, since it is the same for everyone, in practice this structure could place low-income households below the poverty line, which would then make them eligible for welfare programs. Proponents usually counter this argument with a proposal to exempt from the tax households below a certain income level. Because of these concerns, a progressive rate structure has been used for personal income taxes in California and the US.

A *progressive* rate structure is where the effective rates increase as income levels increase. There is an assumption that individuals can pay more taxes when they earn higher levels of income without harming their standard of living. This type of tax best exemplifies the ability-to-pay principle.

Economic Effects

Another important criterion that tax analysts use to gauge the impact of taxes is their influence on economic behavior, and especially economic growth. As John Mikesell notes, "It is important to design tax structures and their administration so that they are not needlessly harmful to the economy."[16] Generally,

---

[15] *Ibid.*, 352–53.
[16] *Ibid.*, 360.

this means that tax rates should be as low as possible to generate adequate revenue to meet the demand for public services and not distort individual or business behavior in the process. Imposing a certain kind of tax can push businesses to locate to other jurisdictions or drive consumers to make purchases in other states or cities. Given California's boundaries, residents are not likely to cross state lines to make many purchases, but they may buy products in neighboring cities if their rates are substantially lower than the buyer's home city.[17]

Public discussion of increasing tax rates usually occurs when the state has projected budget deficits resulting from economic downturns, since this is one way to close the gaps. Opponents argue that increasing taxes during recessions will deter economic growth by reducing consumer demand and business hiring, but the effects are typically small and may even encourage growth depending on how the tax increases are targeted. For example, despite sales and income tax increases adopted in 2012, California's economy grew in 2013 at a faster pace than the national economy. This does not mean that taxes *cause* economic growth, but, instead, it means that economic growth may operate more independently from marginal changes in tax rates than we might assume.

Transparency

History is full of examples where corrupt governments misused public resources or imposed tax systems in an arbitrary or capricious manner. These abuses, in part, contributed to the executive budget movement around the turn of the 20th century discussed in the previous chapter. To allay fears that public resources are misused and to ensure the integrity of an open, democratic process, the state's tax system should be transparent to the public.

There are three main components of transparency.[18] First, there should be transparency at the *adoption* stage so that taxpayers know when, how, and why tax laws have been changed or newly imposed and how the distribution of the burden will fall. The process for these tax law changes should be open to the media and the public for input. Second, the *administration* of the tax should be transparent. Submitting tax payments should be fair and objective, with an opportunity to appeal any penalties or outstanding obligations. It should not be burdensome for taxpayers to seek feedback on their tax status from administering agencies. The third component of transparency is *compliance*. Individuals and businesses should understand how the tax was calculated, what their responsibilities are for paying it, and which level of government is imposing it. Lengthy personal income tax codes at the state and national level are frequently

---

[17] Some California residents cross state lines to buy recreational vehicles or boats in the hopes of avoiding the state's sales tax, but they are still subject to the state's use tax depending on when they return to the state with their new purchase. For background, see Legislative Analyst's Office, *California's Taxation of Vessels, Vehicles, and Aircraft: Out-of-State Purchases* (Sacramento, CA: Legislative Analyst's Office, 2006).

[18] Mikesell outlines four components, but we combine the third and fourth here. *Fiscal Administration*, 369–72.

criticized based on ease of compliance. The difficulty in filing personal income taxes is evidenced by the fact that over half of taxpayers seek the assistance of tax experts to complete their annual taxes.

Collectability

A particular tax loses its revenue generating capacity if it is difficult for tax agencies to collect and for taxpayers to pay. The criterion of collectability addresses the ease with which a particular tax can be administered and paid. If it is costly for government to hire staff to process tax returns or for individuals and businesses to comply with the requirements, then collectability is low. In either case, it can lead to tax avoidance, where taxpayers do not comply with their tax obligations. Generally, larger tax gaps—the difference between taxes owed and taxes paid—indicate that collectability is weaker. In 2005, the Legislative Analyst's Office reported that the tax gap for personal and corporate income taxes was $6.5 billion per year.[19]

Adequacy

One last criterion for use in evaluating tax instruments is adequacy, or the degree to which the tax system or a particular tax generates sufficient revenue to cover authorized expenditures. There are two elements that contribute to adequacy: (1) buoyancy, or tax yield; and (2) stability. Buoyancy refers to whether the tax source generates more revenue as the economy and tax base grow. It should not be necessary to raise rates because the tax is already structured in such a way that it taps into economic growth. Economists typically evaluate buoyancy using tax elasticity measures. Tax elasticity measures how responsive a given tax is to economic growth. A tax with high elasticity, such as the state's personal income tax, is very responsive to the economy, whereas the property tax tends to be less responsive to economic growth and depends more on growth in the housing sector.

While buoyancy is generally viewed as a positive characteristic of a tax, it can also lead to problems of stability. Just as the amount of revenue generated during good economic times may increase rapidly, revenue is also likely to significantly fall during economic downturns producing revenue volatility. Substantial volatility, like what the state has experienced, makes it difficult to plan a budget in the short and long term. Volatility in a particular revenue source can be easier to cope with if other tax sources are more stable or help offset the downswings, but most tax sources rise and fall together, just to varying degrees. Responsive tax policy changes can also mitigate these revenue shortfalls, but policymakers are usually reluctant to increase taxes given the political repercussions.

---

[19] Legislative Analyst's Office, *Tax Gap Handout* (Sacramento, CA: Legislative Analyst's Office, 2005), http://www.lao.ca.gov/handouts/revtax/2005/Californias_Tax_Gap_030105.pdf.

Major Revenue Sources

California's mix of major revenue sources has been altered fundamentally twice since statehood in 1850. Each transition to a new mix of revenue sources was marked by an accumulation of fiscal and administrative problems with the existing structure. These problems eventually led to ballot measures to abolish a major tax or authorize the imposition of entirely new sources. With this in mind, California's tax structure history can be divided into three tax regimes: (1) 1850 to 1910; (2) 1910 to 1935; and (3) 1935 to present.

The first regime lasted from early statehood until 1910. During this time, the property tax served as the state's primary source of revenue, accounting for over 70 percent of total revenue.[20] The state property tax was imposed on top of local government levies; assessment values were locally determined. To avoid paying higher state taxes, underassessment of property values was common among local assessors. These assessment practices and other problems resulted in the abolishment of the state property tax and ushered in the second tax regime.

In 1910, voters adopted Proposition 1, which abolished the state portion of the property tax and left the source exclusively to local government entities, otherwise known as the separation of sources.[21] In its stead, the state general fund relied on several different taxes for its main revenue sources: (1) a gross receipts tax on public utilities; (2) inheritance and gift taxes; (3) the bank and corporate tax; and (4) the insurance gross premiums tax.[22] This tax structure eventually encountered its own problems and resulted in funding shortfalls in the early 1930s. In 1933, voters passed the Riley-Stewart amendment (discussed in Chapter 2), which abolished the gross receipts tax, the state's primary source of revenue at the time, and authorized the legislature to raise additional revenue for school districts.[23] The third tax regime emerged from the wake of the Riley-Stewart plan and serves as the framework for the current system. The state quickly adopted a sales tax to address ongoing budget deficits and later the personal income tax in 1935. Although individual tax rates have been adjusted upward and downward during the existing regime, the broad structure has remained in place. One could argue that Proposition 13 began a new regime in 1978, but it did not abolish an existing tax source or impose a new one. It imposed severe restrictions on an existing one.

Below we provide an overview of the state's revenue system, the major revenue sources, and some minor ones. Even though the property tax is no longer a

---

[20] Marvel Marion Stockwell, *Studies in California State Taxation, 1910–1935* (Berkeley: University of California Press, 1939), 1.

[21] *Ibid.*, 2.

[22] James E., Hartley, Steven M. Sheffrin, and J. David Vasche, "Reform During Crisis: The Transformation of California's Fiscal System During the Great Depression," *The Journal of Economic History* 56, no. 3 (2003): 659.

[23] *Ibid.*, 660.

state revenue source, we discuss its characteristics because it has a substantial impact on state and local budgeting. We also discuss recent issues with some of the sources.

Overview of the Revenue System

California's revenue system is divided into two major categories. The general fund (GF) is the state's main bank account and acts as the primary source of revenue for the bulk of state programs and services. It is by far the largest of the state's accounts and is the one the state struggles to balance most often. The second category, special funds, refers to a group of state accounts whose revenue is legally required to be used for specific purposes outlined in authorizing legislation. In 2012–13, these two funding categories generated $137 billion in revenue, of which $98 billion was general fund and $39 billion was special funds.

Figure 3.6 shows the breakdown of sources of revenue for the general fund. Personal income taxes, corporate taxes, and retail sales and use taxes constitute the "Big 3" revenue sources since they account for over 96 percent of the general fund. At 67 percent of the total, personal income taxes is the largest source, followed by the sales tax at 21 percent, and corporate taxes at 8 percent. Insurance taxes, motor vehicle fees, liquor taxes, and other miscellaneous sources comprise the remainder of GF sources.

Personal Income Taxes (PIT)

The personal income tax was adopted in California in 1935 in response to the Great Depression and consistent state budget deficits. Along with the sales tax, it was considered a source of revenue that would help the state eliminate its perennial deficits. The PIT applies to all sources of income, including salaries and wages, business-related income, and investment income from interest, dividends, and capital gains. The structure is a progressive system where marginal rates increase as the taxpayer's income rises. These rates were set at 1–15 percent when the PIT was originally adopted, but the top marginal rate has been adjusted several times in response to revenue shortages and surges and gubernatorial initiatives. Table 3.1 shows the current marginal tax rates as of 2013. The top marginal rate is 12.3 percent.

Since the early 1980s when it eclipsed the sales tax, the PIT has been the state's main source of revenue. While the amount of revenue generated from the PIT has grown over time, its yield has often been subject to great volatility, which contributed to budget gridlock and structural deficits. Figure 3.7 shows the level of PIT volatility from 1970 to 2012. The percentages reflect the difference between the *average* percentage increase in PIT revenue and the *annual*

Figure 3.6. General Fund Revenue by Source, 2012–13

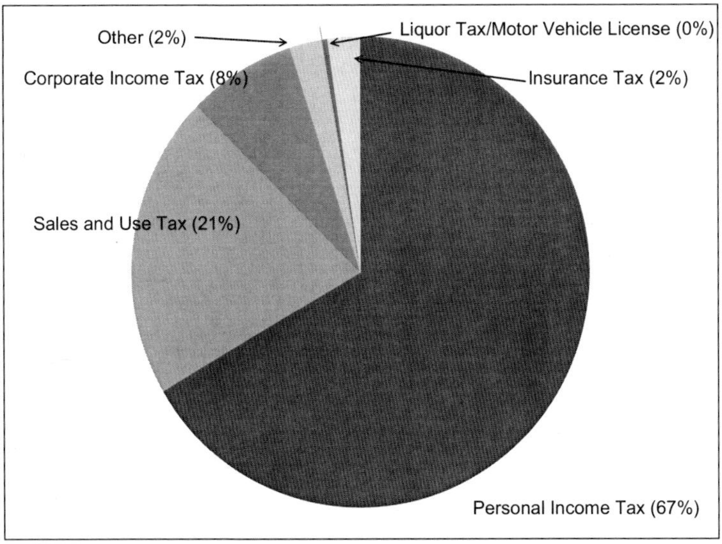

Source: Governor's Budget, Schedule 8.

Table 3.1. Personal Income Tax Rates

If taxable income is:		Tax is:		
Over	But not over		Plus	of amount over
-	15,164	-	1.0%	-
15,164	35,952	151.64	2.0%	15,164
35,952	56,742	567.40	4.0%	35,952
56,742	78,768	1,399.00	6.0%	56,742
78,768	99,548	2,720.56	8.0%	78,768
99,548	508,500	4,382.96	9.3%	99,548
508,500	610,200	42,415.50	10.3%	508,500
610,200	1,017,000	52,890.60	11.3%	610,200
1,017,000	and over	98,859.00	12.3%	1,017,000

Source: Franchise Tax Board. As of January 1, 2013 for married household filing jointly.

Figure 3.7. Personal Income Tax Revenue Volatility, 1970–2012

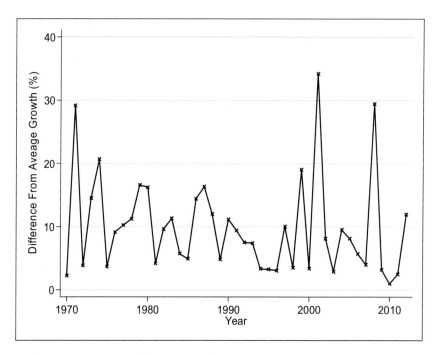

Source: Department of Finance, Schedule 3. Higher percentages represent more volatility.

percentage increase.[24] Higher percentages thus represent more volatility. The early 2000s show how the state enjoyed an enormous surge in revenue followed by several years of lower volatility. This volatility is primarily because PIT revenue depends on a small percentage of taxpayers whose income is heavily influenced by capital gains and stock options.[25] As one example, PIT revenue from capital gains and stock options was $2 billion in 1995–96 and then surged to $17 billion by 2000–01, just five years later. Two years later it fell precipitously to $5 billion.[26] This high volatility makes it difficult to budget for expenditures from one year to the next, especially when the bulk of state expenditures are ongoing in nature.

---

[24] The average percentage growth from 1970 to 2012 is 6 percent.
[25] Legislative Analyst's Office, *Revenue Volatility in California* (Sacramento: Legislative Analyst's Office, 2005).
[26] *Ibid.*, 8.

Sales and Use Tax (SUT)

The second major source of revenue for the state is the sales and use tax. Similar to the PIT, the sales tax was adopted in 1933 and the use tax in 1935 to address ongoing budget shortfalls. In 1955, the SUT for local government was established. The sales tax applies to the retail purchase of most tangible goods, such as clothing, furniture, and automobiles, and is collected by the seller. It is not imposed on intermediate sales transactions, such as from a wholesaler to a retailer. Certain items are specifically exempted from the tax, including prescription drugs, food items, and public utilities. The use tax is imposed on users of a product that is purchased out of state, but whose use is primarily in California. In 2012–13, the SUT generated $20 billion. It is not as volatile as the PIT, but faces a shrinking tax base that significantly reduces it revenue earning capacity (this is discussed further below).

The rate structure is a combination of state and local levies and varies by local jurisdiction. Table 3.2 provides an overview of the SUT components. The largest portion of it, 6.5 percent, goes to the state, but a small portion of that directly supports local services for criminal justice and health and social services. Local governments can also adopt optional add-on taxes that, on average, add another .86 percent to the total statewide rate. These local sales tax options are discussed further in Chapter 8.

Corporation Tax (CT)

Adopted in 1910, the corporate tax applies to income earned from, or attributable to, business conducted in the state. The sources of these taxes include corporations, Subchapter S of corporations, financial institutions, and other business entities.[27] Nonprofit organizations, such as churches, are exempt from liability for this tax. In 2012–13, corporate taxes generated $7.5 billion. There are three components of the CT: the corporate franchise tax, the corporate income tax, and the bank tax. The corporate franchise tax is paid by entities that conduct transactions in the state for the purpose of financial profit and represent the bulk of businesses that pay this tax. The corporate income tax is paid by businesses that generate income from state sources, but do not conduct transactions within the state. Apple, Wells Fargo, and the Chevron Corp. are examples of major businesses that pay corporate income taxes. The initial corporate tax rate was 1 percent, but it has been gradually increased over the last century. Corporations pay a basic tax rate of 8.84 percent on profits and a minimum tax of $800, the latter of which is paid if the business does not earn a profit. Banks and financial institutions pay a higher rate of 10.84 percent, but are exempt from certain local taxes.

---

[27] Legislative Analyst's Office, *Tax Primer* (Sacramento: Legislative Analyst's Office, 2007).

Table 3.2. Sales Tax Structure

Rate	Recipient	Purpose
3.6875%	State	General Fund
0.25%	State	General Fund
0.25%	State	Pay off Economic Recovery Bonds
0.50%	State	Local criminal justice activities
0.25%	State	K-14 Education
0.50%	State	Local health and social services
1.0625%	State	Local revenue fund
1.00%	Local	.25 goes to county transportation; .75 goes to city or county
7.50%	Total	
0.86%		Average Optional Local Add-on
8.36%		**Average Total State/Local**

Source: Board of Equalization; *CalFacts*, Legislative Analyst's Office.

One controversial aspect of corporate taxation has been the tax treatment of multistate and multinational businesses. The central issue in the taxation of such entities is apportionment, or the percentage of a company's profits that can be taxed by the state. Because company profits are only reportable at the national level, each state determines its method for calculating how much of a company's profits are attributed to that state. Depending on how a state constructs its formula, the state can either generate higher revenue from corporations or provide incentives for the corporation to locate its business activities in the state, which often can bring economic benefits. In 1966, California adopted the Uniform Division of Income for Tax Purposes Act (UDITPA), which authorized a three-factor apportionment formula based on the percentage of a corporation's property, payroll, and sales in the state. Each factor was weighted equally in the calculation of profits, but California, and other states, began to realize that weighting sales more heavily could incentivize businesses to locate their firms in the state and potentially increase job growth.[28] In 1993, California modified its apportionment formula so that sales were double weighted, which effectively reduced the tax liability for having more property and employees in the state. This for-

---

[28] Legislative Analyst's Office, *Reconsidering the Optional Single Sales Factor* (Sacramento: Legislative Analyst's Office, 2010), 8.

mula was further adjusted as a result of the 2009 budget agreement. Under this new framework, multistate corporations could choose between the three-factor formula and a single sales factor and could opt for the one that most reduces their tax liability. The method was changed once again in 2012, when voters passed Proposition 39, which required multistate businesses to use the single sales factor. The new requirement is expected to annually generate an additional $1 billion in revenue, about half of which is dedicated to energy efficiency projects in the first five years.

Property Tax

Prior to 1910, the property tax served as the main source of revenue for state and local government. Today, it principally serves as a major source of revenue for cities, counties, special districts, school districts, and community colleges. The state's role in the administration of the property tax is overseen by the Board of Equalization and is now limited to performing assessments of certain types or property, such as public utilities and privately owned railcars. However, revenue from the property tax has substantial implications for the state budget process each year, and the state-local fiscal relationship in general, so it is important to have an understanding of its background and relationship to the state revenue structure.

The property tax is the oldest tax in California since it was adopted at the time of statehood in 1850. In 2012–13, property taxes generated $49.9 billion in revenue. With few exceptions, the tax applies to all types of property including residential, commercial, industrial, agricultural, open space, and certain personal property.[29] Real property is assessed based on the value of land, buildings, fixtures, and other elements attached to the land. Personal property is a smaller component of total property and includes equipment, jewelry, machinery, and aircraft.

The value of most property is determined by local county assessors, while a small share of it, including railroads and utilities, is assessed by the Board of Equalization. Prior to the passage of Proposition 13 in 1978, the value of property was based on the market value and the tax rate was set by each local jurisdiction the property was located in. Thus, county and city government (and special districts) each imposed their own rate. Just prior to the passage of Proposition 13, the average statewide rate was 2.67 percent of assessed value. Since Proposition 13, the assessed value of most property is based on the purchase price. A uniform rate of 1 percent is applied and any locally approved levies are added to this base rate. In 2012–13, the statewide average tax rate was 1.14 percent.

Proposition 13 did not stipulate how the revenue from the base tax rate should be allocated, which left it to the legislature to decide. Assembly Bill 8, passed in 1979, established the formula in each county for how revenue would be distributed to each entity within the county. These formulas were based on

---

[29] Legislative Analyst's Office, *Tax Primer*.

the percentage allocation of property tax revenue that existed prior to Proposition 13. To address state budget deficits over the last several decades, the governor and legislature have modified these formulas to shift funding between education agencies and the other local jurisdictions.

The property tax has remained a central point of contention in state tax debates since its inception. The administration of the property tax has a history of questionable assessment practices at the local level. At times, these assessment practices favored homeowners and businesses by intentionally undervaluing property and decreasing tax liabilities. These practices were driven by the fact that the state offset lower property tax revenue with state revenue to support the school system. In the 1960s and '70s, assessment values increased sharply as a result of reforms to standardize assessment procedures and what some believed were overly aggressive county assessors.[30] Population and economic growth in California played a role as well as it fueled demand for housing. The run-up in property values led to increasing calls for property tax relief that were never satisfactorily addressed by the legislature and governor and culminated in the adoption of Proposition 13.

As discussed in the previous chapter, the level of property tax revenue plays an instrumental role in the state budget process because funding support for school districts and community colleges is a combination of property tax revenue and state general fund revenue. Because Proposition 98 sets a minimum level of funding support for K-14 education, a higher estimated level of property tax revenue means that the state can reduce its contribution to the Proposition 98 mandate. The implications of the property tax for local government are more fully discussed in Chapter 8.

Other Revenue Sources

While the Big 3 taxes generate the largest portion of revenue for the state, there are a number of other revenue sources that make smaller contributions to the general fund or are deposited in special funds with restricted purposes.

Insurance Tax
The state's fourth largest source of general fund revenue is the insurance tax. Adopted in 1911, the tax is imposed on insurance companies that charge premiums to customers for property, assets, injury, and death. In 2012–13, the state collected $2.2 billion from insurance companies who sold coverage.

Vehicle License Fee (VLF)
The vehicle license fee, otherwise known as the "car tax," is a major source of revenue for counties and cities, but is administered through the state Department of Motor Vehicles (DMV). The annual fee, which is based on the depreciated purchase price, is charged to registered owners of vehicles in California and

---

[30] Doerr, *California's Tax Machine*, 93–107.

is imposed in lieu of a property tax on vehicles. When adopted in 1935, the rate was set at 1.75 percent of the car's market value and later increased to 2 percent in 1948 until an unusual series of adjustments began in 1998.

With state coffers overflowing, Governor Pete Wilson (R) and the legislature approved several incremental decreases to the 2 percent VLF rate, which were contingent upon the condition of the general fund. Legislation adopted in 1999 further accelerated these downward rate adjustments. Since this revenue stream supports city and county services, the state "backfilled" the lost revenue with general fund money. When the state faced large deficits in 2002, Governor Gray Davis (D) unilaterally increased the rate back to the previous level of 2 percent because of the poor condition of the general fund. In October of 2003, Davis was recalled and replaced with Arnold Schwarzenegger, who had campaigned on repealing the car tax increase. Before Schwarzenegger was inaugurated, VLF bills had already been sent to car owners with the higher 2 percent rate. Governor Schwarzenegger's first action in office was to reduce the car tax rate down to the .65 percent level that had been in effect prior to Davis's administrative action. This unusual set of circumstances led state officials to instruct vehicle owners to calculate their own car tax liabilities using the new (old) reduced rate of .65 percent. This reduced rate remained in effect until 2009 when Governor Schwarzenegger and legislative leaders agreed to temporarily raise the rate to 1.15 percent to combat another large projected deficit. This higher rate expired in 2011.

Alcohol

Like other states, California levies an excise, or "sin," tax on the production of alcohol on a per-gallon basis. The basic idea behind such excise taxes is to discourage certain types of undesirable excessive behavior by raising the cost of such activities. California rates vary from a low of 20 cents per gallon on beer, wine, and hard cider to a high of $3.30 per gallon for distilled spirits. In 2012–13, the alcohol tax yielded $357 million in general fund revenue.

Tobacco

Another so-called sin tax is levied on tobacco products, the most common of which is cigarettes. The total tax per pack (20 cigarettes) is 87 cents, and the revenue is apportioned between the general fund and special fund accounts. A portion of the tax is a result of two initiatives, Proposition 10 (50 cents) passed in 1998, and Proposition 99 (25 cents) passed in 1988. Revenue from these propositions is earmarked for tobacco prevention, childhood development, and other health-related programs. Tobacco taxes are generally thought to have a deterrent effect on sales, particularly among youth, and lead to the sale of cigarettes on the black market. Tobacco taxes generated close to $900 million in 2012–13.

Lottery

California voters authorized a state-run lottery system in 1984 with the passage of Proposition 37. The initiative determined the allocation of the proceeds: one-half is distributed to ticket purchasers, up to 16 percent is distributed for administration, and at least 34 percent is used to support K-12 and higher education. Advertised as a way to boost education spending, the lottery actually provides a very small percentage, less than 2 percent annually (or about $1 billion), of the state's overall education funding.

Fuel Tax

The state imposes a number of specific taxes and fees that support special fund-related activities, such as hunting and fishing, but the largest amount of special fund revenue comes from motor vehicle fuel taxes. About $5.5 billion was generated in 2012–13 from excise taxes on gas, also known as the gas tax, and diesel fuel. As a result of the fuel tax swap in 2010 the state levies a 36-cent per gallon tax on gas and an 8-cent per gallon tax on diesel fuel, both of which are adjusted annually to replace lost revenue from the elimination of the sales tax on fuel. The imposition and allocation of revenue from this source has frequently been the subject of budget negotiations in recent years with a portion of this revenue being redirected to bond payments (See Box 3.1 on Creative Financing).

Major Tax Issues

Tax Burden in Perspective

Discussions about California government and taxes often turn to the subject of the tax burden. Conservative critics of the state's tax system are quick to point out that California is a high tax state when comparing its burden to other states or the national average. Liberals offer a more nuanced view of the tax burden and emphasize that burdens are higher for certain types of taxes, but also lower for others. To assess the magnitude of the burden in California, it is instructive to look at the overall tax burden compared to other states, as well as the burden by major individual taxes. We will look at the most common way that economists typically measure the tax burden: the amount of taxes paid as a share of personal income. Another common measure used is taxes paid per capita, but adjustments are not typically made for the cost of living in states so it does not give us a standardized measure.

Table 3.3 shows the state's tax burden using overall measures for state and local government, the state by itself, and indicators for major and some minor tax sources. The total state and local tax burden (combines state and local revenue sources) is shown because state and local finances are often intertwined with one another and not just in California. Using this total state and local measure, California ranks twelfth among states, with a burden slightly more than the na-

---

Box 3.1. Creative Financing

Over the last several decades, budget agreements have led to creative ways of funding existing state and local services, modifying programmatic responsibilities between the state and local government, and capturing funding streams to plug budget deficits. The complicated schemes that emerge often are designated with terms or labels that become commonly used in subsequent legislative and public discussions. Since these schemes are designed by executive and legislative staff, who are fiscal experts, few people outside the capital normally understand the mechanics of these schemes. Here are explanations of some of the common terms.

Realignment. This term is used to describe the shift in programmatic responsibilities and associated funding from the state to the county level that occurred in the beginning of each of the last three decades (1990s, 2000s, 2010s). The main purpose was to better match the delivery of the program services with the level of government, mainly counties, that is responsible for the outcomes in the hope that more efficient and effective services could be provided. Examples of some of the programs shifted to the county level include mental health, social services, and health programs in 1991 and adult corrections, substance abuse, and child welfare in 2011. The state authorized dedicated funding streams to support the shift in responsibilities, but local governments have complained that the funding sources have never been adequate.

ERAF Shift. In response to budget deficits the state faced in 1992-93 and 1993-94, state leaders permanently shifted over $3 billion in property tax revenue from cities, counties, and special districts to school districts and community colleges. This transfer reduced the state's share of the Proposition 98 obligation. The acronym ERAF stands for the Education Revenue Augmentation Funds that were established in each county for local government entities to deposit their property tax dollars. The amount of ERAF contributions is determined by property tax growth rates. To offset the loss of revenue to local governments, voters approved Proposition 172 in 1993 to provide counties and cities with a share of revenue from a half-cent increase in the sales tax.

Triple Flip. Authorized by Proposition 57, the local sales tax rate was reduced by .25 percent and the state portion of the sales tax increased by the same percentage. Revenue from the "new" state portion was dedicated to pay off the budget deficit bond of $15 billion. The lost revenue from the tax rate decrease for local government was offset with additional property tax revenue. This arrangement will last until the deficit bond is paid off.

Fuel Tax Swap. In 2010, the governor and legislature eliminated the sales tax on the purchase of gasoline and increased the excise tax on a gallon of gasoline by 17.3 cents per gallon. The swap was made in a revenue neutral manner, but allowed excise tax revenue to offset general fund obligations for debt service on transportation bonds. The Board of Equalization adjusts the tax amounts annually on gas and diesel fuel in order to replace the lost sales tax revenue.

Sources: Legislative Analyst's Office – *ERAF and the 1997-1998 State Budget* (1997); Transportation Funding Overview 2011-12 (2011); and 2011 Realignment: Addressing Issues to Promote Its Long-Term Success (2011). California Local Government Finance Almanac – *A Primer on California City Finance* (2005).

Table 3.3. Tax Burden Rankings (Revenue as a Percentage of Income)

Type	% Personal Income	CA Rank	Average State %
State and Local Taxes 2011	17.1	12	16.0
State Taxes Only 2013	7.5	9	6.2
Personal Income Tax 2010–11	3.1	6	2.1
Sales and Use Tax 2010–11	1.9	23	1.9
Corporate Tax 2010–11	.60	4	.32
Property Tax 2009–10	3.5	24	3.7
Tobacco Tax 2010–11	.06	46	.14
Alcohol Sales Tax 2010–11	.02	42	.05
Motor Fuels Tax 2010–11	.35	22	.32

Source: State and Local Taxes and State Taxes: Federation of Tax Administrators; All others: California Budget Project. *Principles and Policy: A Guide to California's Tax System* (April, 2013).

tional average of 15.7 percent. Judging by this statistic alone, California would not be considered a high-tax state, but it also does not tell the whole story. The state tax burden by itself puts California in the ninth-ranked spot. When we look at individual types of taxes, California is in the top 10 states for personal (6) and corporate (4) income taxes, while it falls out of the top 20 states for the remaining tax sources.

Overall, the best way to probably measure the tax burden in the state is with the total state and local measure since it captures the total burden for residing in the state. Using this measure, it would put California above the national average, but just outside the top 10 states. However, one reason California has been tagged with its high-tax reputation, and deservedly so, is that its tax *rates* on major sources are all very high (the property tax rate is the exception). California has both the highest PIT rate (top rate) and sales tax rate among all states, while its corporate income rate is eighth.[31] Using tax rates alone, it is safe to say that California is a high-tax state.

What explains the difference between California's tax burden and its rates? One major factor in this discrepancy is the shrinking tax bases for each of the state's major taxes. Each type of tax has its own characteristics that contribute to the shrinking tax base, but one factor common to all is the growing amount of tax expenditures. These tax loopholes, as they are commonly known, will be discussed in more detail below, but for now it is important to note that the forgone revenue lost from the loopholes reduces the overall burden for taxpayers in the state. Thus, to ensure growing revenue, it becomes necessary to increase tax rates that apply to a decreasing amount of income and activity subject to taxation. The shrinking base and high tax rates violate one of the core principles of a sound tax system; that is, the base should be broadly construed and subject to low rates. However, the political nature of the budget process often compels elected leaders to grant special tax treatment to favored constituencies.

Another component of the tax burden that often surfaces in legislative debates is the distribution of the tax burden among different income classes of taxpayers. This raises concerns about vertical equity because high-income taxpayers shoulder a disproportionate share of tax liabilities, while it also leads to adequacy problems, particularly with stability. The stability problem arises because the income of high-income taxpayers is particularly volatile, especially when they represent a very small percentage of personal income taxpayers. The disproportionate share of the tax burden for personal income taxes is illustrated in Figure 3.8. Figure 3.8 shows the share of tax returns by income group and the share of tax liabilities associated with those income levels. Those households earning $100,000 or less comprise 73 percent of total tax returns, but account for less than 20 percent of the liabilities. Households making $200,000 and over represent about 8 percent of tax returns, but are 62 percent of the tax liabilities.

---

[31] Federation of Tax Administrators, 2014 Tax Rate Tables, accessed June 9, 2014 at http://www.taxadmin.org/fta/rate/tax_stru.html.

Figure 3.8. Tax Returns and Liabilities by Income Group, 2012

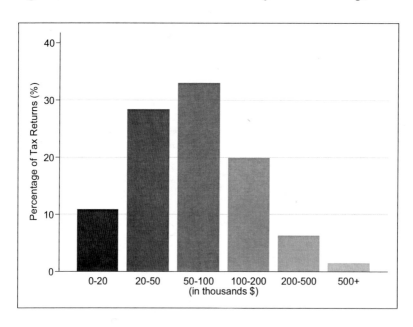

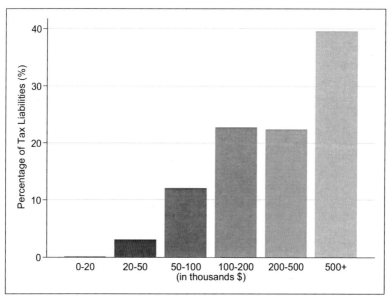

Source: Franchise Tax Board.

The highest income group alone, those earning over $500,000, make up just 1.5 percent of returns. They earn nearly 20 percent of total gross income and account for nearly 40 percent of liabilities. This means that California relies on an extremely small segment of taxpayers for a rather large chunk of its revenue whose income also tends to be very volatile. This distribution of the tax burden is one of the reasons why some observers have recommended spreading tax liabilities among income groups more proportionately.

Business Climate

Related to concerns about the tax burden is the state's business climate. The business climate entails the extent to which the state is business-friendly. It addresses the question of whether regulations and the tax burden deter new businesses from locating their operations in the state and whether it is desirable for existing businesses to expand their operations. Republican and Democratic representatives alike have both recognized that the burdensome regulatory scheme and high tax rates in California may repel certain types of business from locating to the state. Republicans and conservative observers like to cite the latest publications that rank states' business climate. For instance, according to the 2014 Tax Foundation's Business Tax Climate Index study, California ranked 48th out of all states based on an index of major tax sources. In its rankings of the best states for business, *Forbes Magazine* ranked the state 39th based on the labor supply, quality of life, business costs, regulatory environment, and other indicators. While these publications may provide a rough indicator of whether California is an attractive option for business decisions, there are likely many other reasons why firms may choose to expand operations or conduct business in the state. These reasons may include access to ports and shipping and proximity to certain specialized industries, such as high technology, and a large consumer market.

Ultimately, business climate indicators are seeking to gauge whether businesses will start or expand operations in a given state, and the extent to which this will lead to job growth, but a better way to gauge the impact of the business climate on the economy and job growth is to examine data more systematically. When observers claim that businesses are fleeing the state, they often cite anecdotes of a business moving to another state, but that anecdote and others do not reflect overall trends. Unfortunately, there are few actual studies that investigate business movement in and out of the state and the jobs that follow.

In 2007, the Public Policy Institute of California published the first comprehensive study of business and job migration in California and updated the analysis in 2010.[32] These studies found that a very small percentage of job losses in

---

[32] Jed Kolko and David Neumark, *Business Location Decisions and Employment Dynamics in California* (San Francisco: Public Policy Institute of California, 2007), http://www.ppic.org/main/publication.asp?i=710. Jed Kolko, *Business Relocation and Homegrown Jobs, 1992–2006* (San Francisco: Public Policy Institute of California,

any given year can be attributed to businesses leaving the state. "Between 1992 and 2006, jobs leaving the state never accounted for more than 2.3 percent of job losses in any given year."[33] In terms of cumulative jobs lost to other states during this period, California ranked below the national average as the 21st state. The report concluded that while California may rank high in the number of businesses leaving the state in absolute terms that is mainly attributed to the size of its population compared to other states. When examined as a share of total jobs lost, "job displacement resulting from establishments leaving the state is less common in California than in most other states."[34]

In another economic analysis, the Center for Continuing Study of the California Economy addressed several other claims often publicized about the impact of the business environment on the economy. One aspect about the job market the study analyzed was the loss of jobs in manufacturing. The loss of these types of jobs is often highlighted because they tend to be higher paying and represent one of the nation's and state's stronger sectors historically. The study notes that during three different periods from 1997 to 2009 California's job losses in manufacturing were no worse than the national average. In addition, the state's share of all US jobs in manufacturing has remained the same when the aerospace industry is excluded (due to defense downsizing in the early 1990s) in the period from 1990 to 2008.[35]

Overall, the business climate in California does not appear to be as bad as some would claim. Certainly, there are businesses and families that leave California for other states because it is costly to do business or raise a family, but there are also many reasons why most stay—the climate, beaches, state university systems, access to labor markets, and so on. If business investment is any indication of the state's competitive position, then California is in a better position than many other states. Its share of US venture capital—that is, investment in startup businesses—has been consistently growing over the past few decades and represents more than 50 percent of the US total.[36] This demonstrates that the state is likely to remain an attractive place to set up business in the future.

Erosion of the Sales Tax Base

One trend that is impacting the sales tax system in California and other states is an eroding tax base. This is primarily caused by two factors: (1) the transition from traditional in-store purchases to more online sales transactions;

2010), http://www.ppic.org/content/pubs/report/R_910JKR.pdf.

[33] Kolko, *Business Relocation and Homegrown*, 3.

[34] *Ibid.*, 5.

[35] Center for Continuing Study of the California Economy, *Numbers in the News: Are Businesses and High-Income Residents Fleeing California?* (Palo Alto: Center for Continuing Study of California Economy, 2009), http://www.ccsce.com/PDF/Numbers-July09-Fleeing-Calif.pdf.

[36] Marc Lifsher, "California is By Far the Leading State in Luring Venture Capital," *Los Angeles Times,* April 5, 2012.

and (2) the movement away from a goods-based economy to a more service-oriented economy. The erosion has occurred because the state is limited in its ability to collect sales tax from online purchases, and services are largely exempt from the sales tax in California. In effect, the sales tax system is disconnected from the new economy. In terms of evaluative criteria, the SUT suffers from shortcomings in buoyancy (adequacy) and collectability. Revenue generated from the SUT is not keeping pace with economic growth, while online purchases make it difficult to collect liabilities.

One way to illustrate the lack of buoyancy is to examine the amount of economic activity that is subject to the SUT. Essentially, this is a measure of the tax base. Figure 3.9 shows taxable sales as a percentage of personal income. In 1980, taxable sales represented close to 50 percent of personal income and have slowly declined ever since. In 2009, the taxable sales base declined to less than 30 percent of personal income.

As noted above, one contributor to the deterioration of the sales tax base is the fact that economic activity is primarily growing in the service sector, where consumers increasingly purchase services, such as auto repairs, accounting services, or movie tickets, rather than tangible goods, but most services are not subject to the sales tax. In 1933, the service sector represented 48 percent of economic activity, whereas in 2010 it represented 67 percent of the economy.[37] A 2007 survey by the Federation of Tax Administrators found that California taxed only 21 out of 168 services, which placed it among the states that tax the fewest number of services.[38] A report by the state Board of Equalization estimated that the state lost up to $8.7 billion by exempting most services from taxation.[39]

The second contributor to the declining tax base is that consumers are increasingly purchasing goods online, which, for the most part, are not subject to direct taxation. Researchers estimated that nationally electronic commerce (e-commerce) sales rose from $3 trillion in 2010 to $4 trillion in 2012, a 33 percent increase over two years.[40] Online retailers are not required to include sales tax in their transactions unless they have a physical presence, such as a distribution center, in the state. In cases where the seller does not impose a sales tax, the state's use tax is supposed to apply, however the Board of Equalization estimated that less than 1 percent of consumers who owe use tax actually pay it.[41]

---

[37] California Budget Project, *Extending Sales Tax to Services* (Sacramento: California Budget Project, 2011), 1.

[38] Federation of Tax Administrators, *2007 Survey of Services Taxation*, accessed June 9, 2014 at http://www.taxadmin.org/fta/pub/services/services.html.

[39] California Budget Project, *Extending Sales Tax*, 5.

[40] Donald Bruce, William F. Fox, and LeAnn Luna, "State and Local Government Sales Tax Revenue Losses from Electronic Commerce," *State Tax Notes* 52, no. 7 (2009): 537–58.

[41] Board of Equalization, *Economic Perspective* (Sacramento: Board of Equalization, 2011), http://www.boe.ca.gov/news/pdf/EP2-11.pdf.

Figure 3.9. Taxable Sales as a Percentage of Personal Income

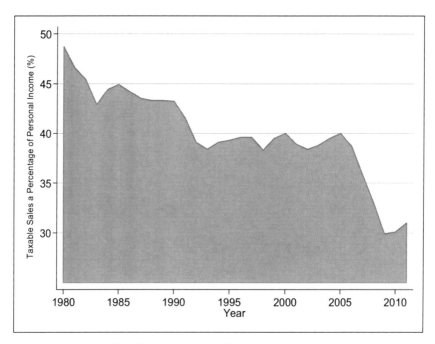

Source: Board of Equalization; Bureau of Economic Analysis.

According to the e-commerce study, state and local government in California lost an estimated $1.9 billion in sales tax revenue from e-commerce.

The key obstacle for California and other states is a pivotal Supreme Court ruling from 1992. In *Quill Corporation v. North Dakota*, the Court ruled that a seller must have a substantial nexus, or physical presence, in the state before a taxing entity could force the seller to collect taxes on their transactions with residents.[42] The ruling left open the possibility that Congress, under its Commerce Clause powers, could authorize states to collect taxes from online transactions, but lobbying efforts by the National Governors Association and other organizations representing states have so far fallen short.

Debates about e-commerce taxes raise issues of equity and administrative feasibility. In terms of equity, traditional brick-and-mortar retailers, such as Wal-Mart, argue that e-retailers have a competitive advantage over them because customers can pay lower prices for their online purchases. Depending on

---

[42] California Budget Project, *Narrowing the Gap: Options for Boosting California's Sales Tax Collections from Online Retailers* (Sacramento: California Budget Project, 2011), http://www.cbp.org/pdfs/2011/110427_Use_Tax_BB.pdf.

the jurisdiction in California and its sales tax rate, this could be close to a 10 percent discount on online goods. Executives at Amazon.com have indicated that the main component of their business plan has been to avoid sales taxes.[43] With regard to the administration of internet taxes, e-retailers point out that calculating the sales tax rate for thousands of local jurisdictions across the country is too complicated and burdensome. This ignores the fact that most online retailers, particularly larger ones such as Amazon.com or Overstock.com, employ hundreds of employees who develop software to efficiently promote their products.

After a pitched public battle with Amazon.com, Governor Jerry Brown (D) signed legislation to tax major e-retailers in 2011. When the "Amazon tax" bill was initially considered, Amazon executives threatened to gather signatures for a referendum, but later capitulated when state policymakers agreed to delay tax collection for a year. In exchange, Amazon agreed to construct distribution centers in California and create 10,000 jobs in the process. The state began collections in late 2012, but businesses with less than $1 million in sales are exempt.

Tax Expenditures

One of the major contributors to slow revenue growth is tax expenditure programs or TEPs. As defined in the Government Code, a "tax expenditure is a credit, deduction, exclusion, exemption, or any other tax benefit provided for by the state" (Section 13305). Although this is the legal definition, it does not technically include other types of favorable tax treatment that are typically considered tax expenditures under a broader working definition.[44] Commonly referred to as tax loopholes, tax expenditures can be more broadly thought of as provisions of state law that reduce the amount of revenue that the state would otherwise collect. All of the Big 3 taxes (personal income, corporate income, and sales and use tax) are subject to these expenditures, although the bulk of forgone revenue occurs in personal income taxes. For 2013–14, the Department of Finance estimated that tax expenditures cost the state $51 billion in lost revenue. That amount has doubled since 2002–03 when forgone revenue totaled $24.3 billion. The biggest chunk was from personal income tax revenue at $34 billion, followed by SUT loopholes at $11 billion. The corporate income tax accounted for $6 billion of the total lost.

Tax expenditures are authorized by the legislature for a variety of reasons. Many provisions, such as one for the home mortgage interest deduction, the state's largest TEP, are enacted to conform the state tax code to the federal system because it makes it easier for taxpayers to determine their federal and state liability, particularly for personal income taxes. Any major restructuring of the

---

[43] *Ibid.*

[44] Department of Finance, *Tax Expenditure Report, 2013–14* (Sacramento: Department of Finance, 2013), http://www.dof.ca.gov/research/economic-financial/documents/Tax_ExpenditureRpt_13-14.pdf.

federal tax code is typically followed by a revamping of the state tax system. State elected leaders may also adopt a tax deduction or exclusion to grant tax relief to certain groups of taxpayers or to encourage certain types of consumer spending.

In the case of SUT tax expenditures, California has exempted most food items, prescription drugs, and utility services, to make the tax burden less regressive for low-income households and senior citizens who may live on fixed incomes. These types of expenditures are considered necessities for everyone and could significantly burden those with meager forms of income.

Some tax expenditures have emerged as a result of budget negotiations when Republicans sought tax concessions from Democrats. Enterprise zones, which allow businesses to deduct certain types of expenditures (i.e., hiring) from their taxes if they base their operations in depressed economic areas, were expanded in the 2009 budget package as a concession to Republicans for supporting tax increases. Although studies indicate that such tax loopholes produce marginal positive economic effects at best, they are symbolically important to the tax-cutting philosophy of Republican legislators.

Tax expenditures contribute to the erosion of tax bases by creating holes in the tax structure. Both the creation of new expenditures and the expansion of existing provisions reduce the liability for taxpayers. The biggest tax expenditure program, home mortgage interest, accounted for $3.3 billion in lost revenue in 2002–03 and $4.4 billion in 2013–14, a 33 percent increase. The estimate for another popular TEP for charitable contributions grew from $1.2 billion in 2002–03 to $1.9 billion in 2013–14, a 58 percent increase. Elected policymakers remain reluctant to reduce or eliminate any TEPs because of the sizeable public opposition to the more popular ones and the intense lobbying efforts from those businesses that financially benefit from industry-specific ones, such as the film production tax credit or the software exemption. If the trend in tax expenditures continues, the state's revenue system will likewise continue to fall short of supporting service levels for a growing and aging population.

Tax Reform—Evaluating What Needs To Be Done

It is widely recognized that California's tax system is a major contributor to the state's recurring budget woes. Referring to a commission that Governor Schwarzenegger established in 2008 to address this problem, columnist Dan Walters described the purpose this way: "It's to straighten out countless taxing irrationalities and to generate more revenue stability to flatten out a roller-coaster budget that flies upward one year and plunges the next."[45] Although these goals are generally shared by many observers, the specific tax changes to reach these goals are what invite more controversy and partisan rancor. To outline these goals, it is useful to return to the tax criteria discussed earlier to assess

---

[45] Dan Walters, "State's Crazy Tax System Needs an Overhaul," *Sacramento Bee*, October 6, 2008.

what reforms should look like (we discuss pathways of reform in Chapter 9). Since particular problems with the tax system have been well-documented, such as volatility and buoyancy, the most relevant criteria for the formulation of a tax overhaul are adequacy (both stability and buoyancy), equity, and economic effects. As noted earlier, overreliance on the personal income tax has led to considerable year-to-year volatility for the general fund, and the erosion of the sales tax base has reduced the buoyancy of this source. The disproportionate share of PIT liabilities is inequitable for high-income groups, while the regressive nature of the sales tax and exemptions for most services, which favor higher-income households, raise further equity concerns as well. Any tax reform should also consider the economic effects so it minimally distorts economic behavior and encourages economic growth and an attractive business climate.

There are two main ways to address revenue volatility.[46] One is to change the mix of taxes so that a larger share of revenue is generated from more stable sources. Since the sales and corporate income tax are less volatile than the PIT, this would entail increasing the share from the first two sources. Suggestions to raise the share of sales tax revenue typically elicit claims that it is regressive and would unfairly burden lower-income groups, but this could be avoided if the tax base was expanded to services, primarily consumed by upper-income groups, and the overall rate was reduced. In addition, some states like Hawaii provide a tax refund to low-income groups to further reduce the regressive nature of the sales tax. To avoid opposition from raising the share of corporate income tax revenue, the tax rate could be reduced to bring it in line with neighboring states or the national average. However, to generate more revenue, tax loopholes for corporations would need to be reduced. (See Table 3.4 for a summary of tax reform options and main criteria addressed).

To further counter the volatility of the PIT, the state could consider alternative methods of reporting capital gains and stock options, which are the most volatile components of income. For instance, income generated from capital gains and stock options could be averaged over several years so that a surge does not occur in one particular year.[47] Another way to decrease PIT volatility is to reduce the progressiveness of the tax brackets, but this suggestion by the last tax reform commission in 2009, the Commission for the 21st Century Economy, ran into stiff opposition from Democrats and labor groups.

The second way to address volatility is to maintain a strong rainy-day fund. With adequate funding stashed away during the boom years, the state can fill in spending holes when revenues take a nosedive. Rainy-day funds deal with the symptoms of revenue volatility rather than the root cause. They are discussed in more detail in Chapter 7.

Although the alternatives above would help increase revenue stability, it might come at the expense of horizontal or vertical equity. Eliminating some tax expenditure programs and broadening the sales tax base to services, however,

---

[46] Legislative Analyst's Office, *Revenue Volatility*, 14.
[47] *Ibid.*, 15.

Table 3.4. Tax Reform Options

Options	Main Tax Criteria Addressed
Sales Tax	
• Extend to services and:	Equity; Adequacy (buoyancy)
o Lower rate	Economic effects
o Offer refund to lower income groups	Equity
• Extend further to e-commerce	Equity; Adequacy (buoyancy)
Personal Income Tax	
• Reduce and eliminate tax expenditure programs	Equity; Adequacy (stability)
• Flatten marginal rates	Equity; Adequacy (stability)
• Average income from stock options/capital gains	Adequacy (stability)
Corporate Tax	
• Reduce and eliminate tax expenditure programs and:	Equity
o Lower rate	Economic effects
Property Tax	
• Increase rate slightly	Adequacy (stability)
Other	
• Adjust major tax rates countercyclically	Adequacy (stability)
• Strengthen rainy day fund	Adequacy (stability)

might increase equity in some ways. For example, those industries that benefit from enterprise zones or film production credits already receive favorable tax preferences that raise equity concerns for those industries that do not. Businesses that provide services are already favored over those that primarily sell goods. In this regard, adopting some of these changes would level the playing field for some businesses and taxpayers. At the same time, extending the sales tax to services and e-commerce would produce more buoyancy by generating growing revenue from these expanding economic sectors.

The positive side of many of these suggested changes is that they do not have deleterious economic effects. When changes to the tax system are suggested at various times, the common goals are to lower tax rates and broaden tax bases, which most agree is good for economic growth. The above reforms would move the state's tax system more in this direction. What sometimes gets lost in tax discussions is that the generation of additional revenue allows the state to pay for infrastructure projects, colleges and universities, and health care services that all have positive impacts on the economy. Inadequate funding for a dilapidated transportation system slows down the transportation of products and services, while decreasing university support reduces the supply of trained workers for new or expanding businesses. Although tax reform might result in a higher level of revenue, which some may view simply as higher taxes, a modernized tax system would do it more efficiently, produce fewer economic distortions, and permit the state to make more long-term investments to spur further economic growth.

Aside from those reforms mentioned above, the state could also look at other ways of smoothing over the boom-and-bust budget cycles and perhaps soften the blow of economic recessions. Instead of using spending cuts to balance the budget during economic downturns, David Gamage suggests adjusting tax rates for the three major revenue sources.[48] Gamage points out that California's response to economic downturns, and the ensuing budget shortfalls, much like other states, is ineffective because policy responses adopted are countercyclical. That is, to stave off larger deficits, the state reduces spending on social safety net programs such as welfare and job training at a time when support for these programs should be increased. Not only would the spending assist more households hit by job losses, but it would help stabilize the declining consumer demand. On the tax side, he argues that broad-based tax rates should adjust automatically depending on economic conditions. When the economy declines, tax rates should be increased to generate an amount of revenue similar to pre-recession levels and decreased when the economy is growing strongly again. Stabilizing the level of revenue during the economic downturns would allow the state to support increased demand for safety net programs and allow the largest consumer, the state, to plug the hole in economic activity created by the loss of private sector demand. Gamage also notes that these adjusted tax rates should target higher-income households because they are less vulnerable to economic conditions and have more resources at their disposal (i.e., savings, borrowing, etc.) to continue their spending activity.

Another way to address the state's budget problems through tax changes is to revisit Proposition 13. While Proposition 13 dramatically cut property taxes and imposed constraints on future revenue growth, it also severely restricted the state's most stable revenue source. This induced volatility in local government and K-12 finances because both became more dependent on state revenue sources. Adjusting the tax rate upward somewhat and offsetting that tax increase somewhere else (i.e., income taxes) could provide more stability. Another proposal that frequently surfaces is to create a split roll where residential property taxes would continue to be assessed based on the acquisition value, but commercial property would be based on market value. This would address an equity

---

[48] David Gamage, "Preventing State Budget Crises: Managing the Fiscal Volatility Problem," *California Law Review* 98 (2010), 749–811.

concern because commercial property changes ownership much less frequently than residential property. Unlike residential purchases, a transfer of ownership for a business can be structured in a way to avoid triggering a reassessment of the property value. Even though revenue from property taxes primarily supports local government, additional property tax revenue from these proposals would reduce the financial commitments and obligations of state government to support counties, cities, and K-14 education, freeing up state funds for other service areas.

From a policy perspective, adjusting tax rates automatically and more frequently and revisiting Proposition 13 would seem like effective tools for alleviating the state's main revenue problems. However, those most affected by either of these proposals—high-income taxpayers, homeowners, and businesses—are likely to vehemently resist any such changes to their tax burden. Since these groups make up the bulk of voters or, in the case of businesses, have considerable resources to influence policy outcomes, these tax policy options are not likely to gain much traction.

Conclusion

With one of the largest and most dynamic economies in the world, the state has a unique capacity to generate revenue from a variety of sources and support a large and growing population. The state continues to be an attractive location for doing business and a hotbed for technological development. Throughout the state's history, it has encountered periods of rapid economic change that preceded a restructuring of the tax system. The accumulation of problems with the existing tax structure eventually catalyzed enough political pressure to make fundamental changes to the system. In the previous transition in the 1930s, precipitated by the Great Depression, a series of state budget deficits highlighted the inadequacy of the tax system. The current environment is not much unlike this earlier period. Although budget conditions stabilized in 2012, there is still an underlying need to update the tax system to strengthen the state's long-term financial outlook.

One factor that is present today that was not in the first budgeting crisis era is the antitax (and government) movement and mentality that has effectively handcuffed any efforts at significant reform. Not only is there significant opposition to any revenue increases, but there is also opposition to any tax reforms, even revenue neutral ones. The uncertainty behind potential changes instills fear in the average person that their tax status may be worse than the status quo. Another obstacle to fundamental change is that any tax reforms, even revenue neutral ones, are subject to a two-thirds vote in the legislature, which, in the past, has meant that some Republicans must agree with the changes. Often tied to signed commitments to not raise taxes, Republican legislators avoid any proposal other than a tax cut like the plague.

Instead, fundamental tax changes might have to come as they have in the past—at the ballot box. The abolishment of the *state* property tax, the adoption of the sales and income tax (Riley-Stewart amendment) and property tax reductions all came about, either directly or indirectly, as a result of voter propositions.[49] In 2012, California voters again showed their willingness to raise revenue by adopting Propositions 30, which increased sales and income tax rates, and 39, which modified corporate tax calculations for out-of-state businesses. These propositions, along with the "Amazon tax," help the state align revenues with expenditures in the short term. However, Proposition 30, the largest source of this additional revenue, fully expires in 2018, and this will further test the adequacy of California's tax system.

Review Questions

1. Explain how the Great Recession affected the California economy.

2. How does the tax structure contribute to California's boom-and-bust budget cycles?

3. Discuss the state's major revenue sources and the major issues affecting them.

4. Which tax reform options will best address revenue volatility? Would the general public support these options?

Additional Resources

Center for the Continuing Study of the California Economy

http://www.ccsce.com/

The site has reports on California's major economic indicators and provides recent data on economic issues in the news.

Commission on the 21st Century Economy

http://www.cotce.ca.gov/

The commission website has the final report and recommendations, meeting agendas, and the mission.

Economic Research Unit, Department of Finance

http://www.dof.ca.gov/research/economic_research_unit/index.php

---

[49] Stockwell, *Studies in California.*

This site has updated information on the state economy, a brief history of the California economy, and forecasts of the state and national economies.

Chapter 4

The Spending Plan

I intend to resist the siren song of permanent spending, whether it comes from the left or the right. I will stand up to anyone who tries to convince the Legislature that they should spend most or all of this money on ongoing expenses.

—Governor Gray Davis in May 2000 after the
Department of Finance announced $12.3 billion in new revenue.[1]

Budgeting, in essence, is a plan to spend money. It outlines the total amount to be spent and how and where that money will be spent in a given year. Budgets implicitly acknowledge limitations since a budget assumes a certain level of revenue that can be spent and that departments and agencies should not spend more than their allocation. Throughout California's history, the state has been reminded time and again about these spending limits as it encountered periodic episodes of overspending. As Governor Davis (D) warned in 2000, it is difficult, if not impossible, for elected officials to resist the "siren song of permanent spending" that arises when California experiences a revenue upswing. Governor Davis and legislators ultimately succumbed to the call and plunged the state into its second crisis budgeting era.

During episodes of budget deficits, casual observers and Republicans often point to spending as the driving factor behind these imbalances. In a 2003 gubernatorial recall debate, Republican candidate Arnold Schwarzenegger famously quipped that the state had "an addiction problem," referring to its proclivity to overspend. Throughout much of his administration, Schwarzenegger repeatedly

---

[1] Quoted in David Doerr, *California's Tax Machine, A History of Taxing and Spending in the Golden State*, 2d ed. (Sacramento: California Taxpayers' Association, 2008), 384.

claimed the state had a spending problem. Although he vowed to tame the problem, when Schwarzenegger left office in 2011, the state's fiscal condition was no better off than when he entered office, and probably worse.[2] Even as a Republican, Schwarzenegger was not alone in his inability to control state spending. Before him, Republican Governor Ronald Reagan, the standard-bearer for fiscal conservatism, oversaw large increases in government spending. Although at times California has indulged itself with profligate spending, its subsequent cutbacks often restrain its spending trajectory.

In this chapter, we discuss overall state spending levels and how this spending is allocated among the major service areas. Since critics often claim that California has a spending problem, we provide some perspective on this problem by analyzing historical spending patterns and comparing California's expenditure levels with other states. We also examine the primary factors that contribute to spending growth, including population trends and inflation, and contributors that affect specific policy areas. Since solutions to budget shortfalls often involve attempts to curtail spending, we discuss several of the more commonly used tactics and their potential to align spending and revenue. We conclude by exploring two of the state's long-term spending obligations—state pensions and retiree health care—and potential solutions to address them.

Spending Overview

To operate state government and provide a significant portion of funding for local government, California's level of spending, like its economy, rivals that of many large developed nations. In 2012–13, the state spent a total of $134.3 billion from its general fund and special funds. Of that total, $97 billion came from the general fund and $38 billion was supported by various special funds. California received another $70 billion from the federal government. All told, more than $200 billion flows through the budget process each year.

It is important to remember that government spending reflects the state's values and priorities since larger amounts of money are allocated to priority areas. The governor or legislative leaders may espouse the importance of particular programs or pet projects in their speeches or campaign rhetoric, but where the money is actually spent is what matters. In California, public opinion polls have consistently shown that K-12 education is the top priority and public comments by policymakers routinely echo this sentiment. Figure 4.1 is a breakdown of how general fund spending was allocated among major policy areas in the 2012–13 fiscal year and demonstrates that elementary and secondary education is the

---

[2] It is difficult to pinpoint the exact size of the state's general fund deficit at these two times since we are not comparing apples to apples. The Legislative Analyst's Office (LAO) projected a deficit of $10.2 billion in November 2003 when Schwarzenegger entered office and a deficit of $25.4 billion in their November 2010 report before he left office.

Figure 4.1. Where the Money Goes, 2012–13

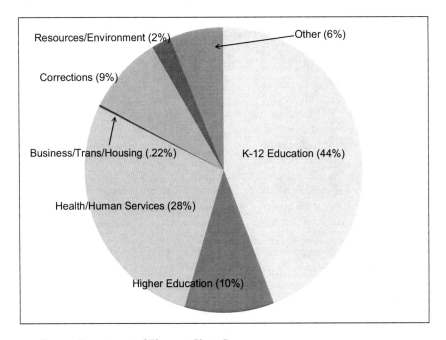

Source: Department of Finance, Chart C.

state's top priority. Approximately $43 billion, or 44 percent, was spent on K-12 education, followed by health and human services at $27 billion, or 28 percent. Higher education, including the community colleges, and the California State University and University of California systems, received the third largest amount at $10 billion, representing about 10 percent of general fund spending. Although corrections spending has been gaining ground on higher education, it still ranks fourth at $8.6 billion, or 9 percent of the budget. The remaining $8 billion (8 percent) was spent on environmental programs, transportation, housing, and other areas.

Is Spending Out of Control?

As alluded to at the beginning of this chapter, one of the frequent complaints about the California budget is that spending is out of control and that this leads to the recurrent budget imbalances. However, analysis of spending trends does not paint a clear picture of the state's free-spending ways. If we look at particular types of spending or certain policy areas, a conclusion that spending is abnormally high is fairly reasonable. In contrast, if we examine some of the traditional standards of government spending, California's spending levels and rates are somewhat average, and, in some cases, below average.

Two of the traditional standards for measuring spending growth are presented in Figure 4.2, along with spending rates for the state's two major types of spending (general fund and special funds) and their combined total. One of the traditional standards presented is the sum of annual inflation rates and population growth. The inflation component addresses how the cost of providing the same level of services for the state may rise from one year to the next. Population accounts for the fact that a larger number of people may place more demands on government services. In reality, this demand depends on the composition of that population increase, such as whether there are more school-aged children, but for now we just consider overall population changes (this is discussed further below). The second standard measure in Figure 4.2 is the average general fund spending rate for all states. This indicates the extent to which California's spending is an outlier compared with other states. All rates represent annual averages from 1979 to 2012. This time span includes several recessions when state spending dipped and periods of substantial economic growth when states ramped up spending in response to growing revenues.

California's general fund spending rate of 5.4 percent is about the same as the national average and slightly less than the population/inflation measure of 5.5 percent. By these numbers, the "spending problem" label does not seem appropriate since California is not different than the average state. However, if we focus on the state's special fund spending rate, then this type of spending appears excessively high at 9 percent compared to the standard measures. A more telling sign of the state's spending behavior is the total rate for general fund and special fund spending. It exhibits a rate of 5.9 percent, which is slightly more than the standard measures, but again does not signal an unusually high rate. Overall, we can conclude that the rate of at least one type of spending, special funds, is rather high, but the spending rate for the state's main account, the general fund, which is often the focus of media and public attention, and for the state's overall spending is roughly equal to standard measures of government spending.

We should note two caveats about these measures. First, despite its frequent use in state tax and expenditure limits (TELs), the population/inflation benchmark represents a fairly conservative standard by which to measure government growth. It assumes that a government does not adopt new programs that would increase spending beyond those already in effect (unless the state is replacing programs or increasing efficiency). It implies we should not expect government to adopt new programs to address ongoing or newly emerging social problems or market failures. The second caveat concerns the fiscal sustainability of peer groups. Just because California is right around the average state spending rate does not mean that California and its peers are not heading off a fiscal cliff. In other words, an "average" spending rate could still mean future trouble.

Another way to gauge whether the state has a spending problem is to examine the size of state government. One concern that arises from excessive gov-

Figure 4.2. Spending Rates in Perspective, 1979–2012

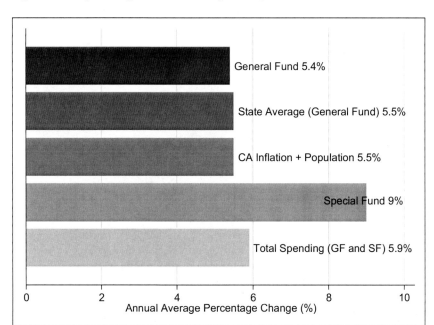

Source: Department of Finance, Chart G; *Fiscal Survey of the States,* National Association of Budget Officers (NASBO).

ernment spending is that the public sector will grow too large and inhibit the market economy. This slowdown in economic activity might occur from a high tax burden that is necessary to support a large government sector and from the cumbersome regulatory structure that we associate with a robust bureaucratic state. A common measure of government size is the level of state spending relative to the gross state product (GSP). This is a measure similar to that used to assess tax burdens in the previous chapter, but substitutes spending for revenue. Figure 4.3 provides this measure of government size for California, three highly populated states that California is often compared to, and the national average in 2012. California's spending as a share of the economy (GSP) approaches 6 percent and is higher than both Florida and Texas. However, it is well below New York at 7 percent and the national average at 8.2 percent. The national average is high compared to these large states because some of the smaller states, like Alaska and Wyoming, have state government sectors that are much larger compared to their economies. The larger states have more economies of scale from their population sizes and more diverse economies. Nevertheless, by this measure too California's size does not appear to be an outlier.

Figure 4.3. State Spending Relative to Gross State Product (GSP), 2012

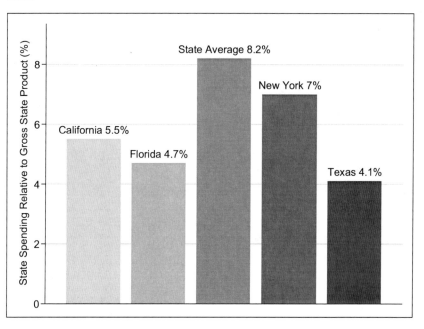

Source: Bureau of Economic Analysis; *2013 State Expenditure Report*, National Association of State Budget Officers. State spending is general fund and special funds.

The total size of government can also be reflected in the number of employees on the state's payroll. In Figure 4.4, it shows that California is the 4th lowest state in terms of the size of its workforce relative to population. California has 104 full-time equivalent positions for every 10,000 residents in the state. This is slightly lower than Arizona at 105.9 full-time equivalent positions for every 10,000 residents. Florida has the lowest ratio of any state at 93.8 full-time equivalent positions. California's ratio is much lower than the national average of 171.7 full-time equivalent positions for every 10,000 state residents. As with other measures of government size, the national average ratio is bolstered by smaller states (i.e., Alaska, Montana) who do not maintain the economies of scale that larger states do. Alaska, for example has a ratio of 373.1 full-time equivalent positions per 10,000 population.

Figure 4.4. State Employees per Population, State Comparisons, 2012

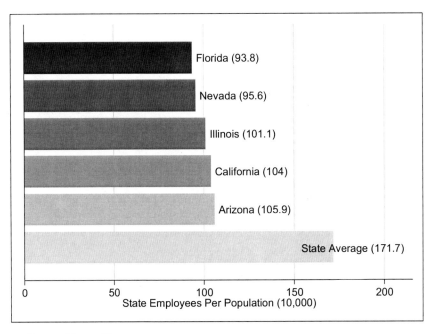

Source: Census Bureau.

Where is California's Spending Growth Occurring?

A secondary topic in discussions about California's spending behavior is the rate of spending in specific policy areas. A common misperception is that spending on prisons is the fastest growing segment of the budget, but debt-service on bonds far outpaces spending on prisons when we review spending over the last two decades. Spending trends in major policy areas from 1990 to 2012 are presented in Figure 4.5. Debt-service on bonds has grown the fastest over this time period, followed by corrections. Spending on environmental programs and K-12 education are virtually tied, while health and human services and higher education grew the slowest.

One point to remember about the fastest growing areas is that their base year amount in 1990–91 is much lower than some of the other areas that have slower growth (i.e., K-12 education). It does not take very large increases in their budget allocation to boost their growth rates beyond the other larger policy

Figure 4.5. Fastest Growing General Fund Areas, 1990-2012

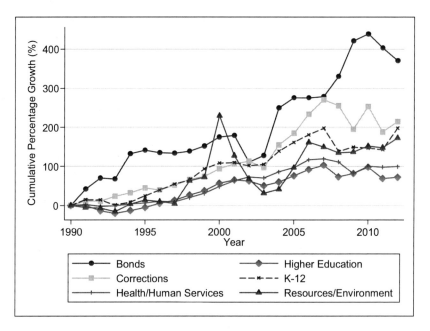

Source: Department of Finance, Chart C.

areas. For K-12 education and health and human services, which have been the two largest areas of the budget, it takes significantly more funding in these areas to increase their spending rates commensurate with bonds or corrections. Still, even with this caveat in mind, bond debt-service and corrections spending have grown extremely fast.

Some critics of the state's spending behavior also frequently point to legislators as the primary culprits behind spending growth. But it is important to note that authority for spending in the two fastest growing areas does not fully rest with the legislature and governor. Bonds, and the debt-service to pay them off, have to be approved by voters and a portion of corrections spending in recent years has been driven by federal court mandates. The state prison system was placed in federal receivership in 2005 because the prison population was over-capacity and the court required the state to spend significant sums of money to reduce the population. At least part of the blame here can be placed on voters since they also approved the three-strikes sentencing law in 1994 and generally support stiff prison sentences for criminals, which both increase prison costs.

Factors behind the Spending Growth

There are several factors that drive spending growth for any state. In some cases, the state retains some discretion over these factors. For instance, a state's tax policies may make it more attractive for elderly people to take up residence in the state, which may drive down support for education spending and increase it for health care. Generally speaking, though, many of these factors are beyond the control of the state, but still have a substantial impact on the direction of state spending.

Inflation

Budgeting processes usually have built-in mechanisms to account for the costs of inflation. For certain programs, these cost-of-living adjustments, or COLAs as they are known, are determined by state statute or constitutional law. If a department or agency does not have a statutorily determined COLA, then the Department of Finance usually provides these agencies with a COLA adjustment that can be used to formulate their budgets. During the crisis budgeting era, state agencies frequently went without COLAs, which erodes the level of services that an agency can provide over time.

Population

As discussed earlier, population changes are commonly considered to be legitimate reasons for spending growth, which is why they are incorporated into tax and expenditure limitation laws. As the population grows, demand for services generally grows in all policy areas, including K-12 education, higher education, health care, corrections, and transportation. The budgets of many state programs, such as CalWORKs (welfare) and Medi-Cal (health care), are determined by the caseload, or number of individuals enrolled in these programs. Some departments have very complicated formulas and statistical models for projecting their caseload from year-to-year and for estimating the level of spending necessary to meet the service demand. Population and migration trends within and without the states can alter the demand for services in certain parts of the state and for certain programs. For example, the aging of the baby boom generation is expected to increase spending on Medi-Cal, since a portion of their enrollees are eligible for Medi-Cal and federal Medicare, and on supplementary social security, which provides income support to low-income seniors.

Market Failures

One of the rationales for government intervention, and the spending that typically accompanies it, is the development of market failures. In these sectors of the economy, the private marketplace has failed to provide a necessary good or service at a reasonable price that consumers can afford or failed to provide the service at all. For instance, the affordability of health insurance has often been cited as a reason why six million Californians did not have insurance coverage. In response to this need, the federal government has partnered with states to provide low-income households with health insurance coverage. The cost of these programs, such as Medi-Cal in California, has been borne by the state and federal government. With the passage of the Affordable Care Act in 2010 at the federal level, California's share of costs will rise substantially when the law is fully implemented.[3] To the extent that the state (and/or federal government) attempts to address other market failures, this places additional demands on state spending.

Economic Conditions

Economic conditions also impact the level of spending in the state. When the economy encounters a recession, individuals lose their jobs and are eligible for social safety net programs like unemployment insurance, welfare, and food assistance. Revenue normally declines during economic recessions so the state usually attempts to balance the budget by reducing spending for these programs, which is counterintuitive. When economic conditions are improving, this presents a good time to make infrastructure investments in transportation or utilities and increase support for colleges and universities because a growing economy requires more educated workers. In sum, spending demands do not subside during positive or negative economic times, but the demand for different types of spending does.

Infrastructure Needs

Yet another pressure on spending growth is support for infrastructure such as highways, roads, public transportation, government buildings, prisons, and water supply facilities. As shown in Figure 4.5, debt-service on bonds has been the fastest growing segment of the budget because a number of bond measures for infrastructure have been approved by voters in the last two decades. As the population has grown and existing infrastructure required maintenance and renovation, more spending has been necessary to build new transportation networks and repair existing ones. Because infrastructure projects are funded by bond proceeds, the state has had to pay higher interest rates on those as a result of the state's low credit rating. In addition, when the legislature passes bond measures and sends them to voters, the bills are usually loaded up with pork projects that set aside funding amounts for specific projects in legislators' districts. This pork adds to the overall cost of the bond, but is viewed as a necessary evil of the political process to pass them.

Political Aggrandizement

One last factor that deserves mention involves the nature of politics and legislator ambition. Individual legislators usually seek to move to higher office and, in order to pad their resume, pursue the expansion or creation of programs. Politicians on the campaign trail want to tell voters that they are responsible for pro-

---

[3] George Skelton, "California Could Take Big Hit from Healthcare Overhaul," *Los Angeles Times*, March 24, 2010.

grams that have addressed a social problem or assisted those in need and "claim credit" for it. Few politicians want to run on the platform that they cut spending for K-12 education or for higher education when these tend to be popular programs. Thus, there tends to be an inherent incentive in the political environment to spend money so that politicians can claim credit for the programs created under their tenure.[4]

Major Program Areas

K-12 Education

K-12 education receives the largest amount of total funding of any state-supported program. This reflects education's priority level among the public and policymakers. In 2012–13, K-12 education received about $68.4 billion in funding from all sources.[5] Of that total, $37.9 billion came from the general fund, another $15 billion was from local property taxes, and the remaining $15.5 billion came from federal funds, the state lottery, and other miscellaneous sources. Like many state programs, state support for education has declined as a result of revenues that have not returned to prerecession levels. At its peak funding level in 2007–08, K-12 education received $42.5 billion from the general fund. The 2012–13 level is thus a 10 percent decline from that previous high.

The financial statistic that garners the most attention in discussions about school finance is the per-pupil spending level. The figure typically includes the amount spent on teacher and staff salaries and benefits, books and supplies, and other operating costs. The measure is used as a gauge of how supportive a given state is of its education system. Common benchmarks that are used for comparison purposes are the national average and spending amounts for similar-sized states. These benchmark spending levels are presented in Figure 4.6 for 2009–10, alongside California's per-pupil spending level. At $10,762 per student, California spent slightly more than Florida and Texas, but lagged far behind the national leader New York ($19,704). California spent $1,374 below the national average of $12,136. Among all states, California ranked 34th.[6] The per-pupil spending level is commonly substituted as a proxy for the education performance or quality of a state's education system. It is assumed that higher levels of per-pupil spending will produce higher test scores, but studies have not found

---

[4] David Mayhew coined the term "credit claiming" in his classic book, *Congress: The Electoral Connection* (New Haven, CT: Yale University Press, 1974). He argued that reelection is the primary motive of elected representatives and credit claiming is a key ingredient in persuading voters to support candidates.

[5] California Department of Education, "2012–13 Budget Tables," http://www.cde.ca.gov/fg/fr/eb/budgettablemain2012.asp.

[6] National Center for Education Statistics, *Digest of Education Statistics*, http://nces.ed.gov/programs/digest/d12/tables/dt12_215.asp.

Figure 4.6. Per-Pupil Spending Comparisons, 2009–10

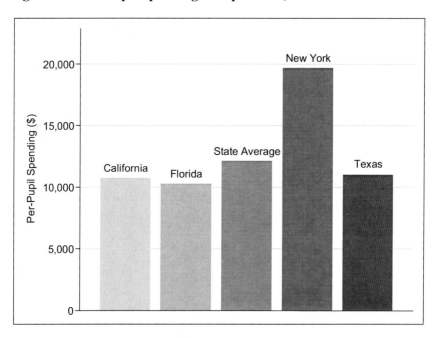

Source: *Digest of Education Statistics*. Amounts are total expenditures (with capital outlay) and include local, state, and federal funding.

this to be true.[7] School performance more likely depends on teacher quality and parental income and education levels.

Proposition 98

It is often said that there are few people in Sacramento who fully understand the state's education funding formulas because of Proposition 98. Passed in 1988, Proposition 98 lays out complicated formulas for determining the level of funding each year for K-12 education and community colleges. Pushed by the education community, it was intended to set a floor on the funding level for education because school districts and interest groups feared that Proposition 13, which limited property taxes, would constrain school spending since property taxes were previously their main source of revenue. The proposition sets the

---

[7] Susanna Loeb, Anthony Bryk, and Eric Hanushek, "Getting Down to Facts: School Finance and Governance in California," *Education Finance and Policy* 3, no. 1 (2008): 1–19. Available at cepa.stanford.edu/content/getting-down-facts-school-finance-and-governance-california.

funding level through the application of three tests that are based on school enrollment and growth in the economy and general fund (see Box 4.1). Although it was intended to help depoliticize education spending, annual scuffles over the level of spending have not subsided after Proposition 98 and may have intensified. As noted in Chapter 2, while Proposition 98 set a floor for K-14 funding, policymakers still consider whether to suspend the minimum guarantee in tight budget times (it has been done twice) and argue over what the level of funding should be. In recent years, the governor and lawmakers have also found ways to circumvent its requirement, which has angered education groups. In 2011–12, Governor Brown and Democrats shifted $5 billion out of the general fund to pay local governments for prison realignment costs.[8] This reduced the Proposition 98 obligation because the education share had to be based on a smaller general fund budget. As state policymakers continue to deal with spending mandates imposed by Proposition 98, these types of tactics are likely to become more common.

Education Outcomes

Ultimately, education funding is spent to facilitate student learning and prepare students for college and the workforce. As such, strong emphasis in California and across the nation has been placed on standardized test scores. Since the passage of Proposition 13, California has seen a long downward trend in its performance on these tests and ranks near the bottom of states nationally. In 2011, California fourth grade students ranked 46th nationally in reading and math on the National Assessment of Educational Progress (NAEP), a standardized test used to compare performance across states.[9] Education advocates usually point to the low per-pupil spending levels, but, as mentioned above, California ranks in the middle when compared to other states. California's low test score ranking is likely attributed to many other factors besides just funding levels. While the K-12 student population in California has remained relatively steady in recent years at around 6 million, the ethnic and income composition is extremely diverse. As a destination for immigrants from countries all over the world, elementary and secondary-age students arrive in California with low levels of proficiency in the English language. In some large, urban districts there may be numerous languages other than English spoken in students' homes. For example, in the Los Angeles Unified School District, there are over 100 languages other than English spoken by students.[10] Providing instruction to English

---

[8] Kevin Yamamura, "California's School Funding Measure under Seige in Tough Times," *Sacramento Bee*, February, 4, 2012.

[9] Comparisons for eighth grade students were worse. Reading scores were tied for 49th and math scores were 47th. The results are discussed by John Fensterwald, "Not Much Good News from NAEP," *Thoughts on Public Education* (November 1, 2011). Available at http://toped.svefoundation.org/2011/11/01/not-much-good-news-from-naep/. Full NAEP results are available at http://nationsreportcard.gov/.

[10] See the District Language Census Report here: http://www.lausd.k12.ca.us/lausd/offices/bulletins/r30r2008.pdf.

Box 4.1. Key Provisions of Proposition 98

Test 1—Percentage of General Fund Revenue: At least 39 percent of general fund revenues must be spent on K-14 education.

Test 2—Adjustment by Personal Income: Prior-year funding is increased by growth in statewide K-12 attendance and per capita personal income. This test normally applies in moderate to strong general fund revenue growth years.

Test 3—Adjustment by General Fund Growth: Prior-year funding is increased by growth in statewide K-12 attendance and per capita general fund revenues. This test usually applies when the general fund declines or grows slowly.

Suspension: The legislature can suspend the minimum guarantee with a 2/3 vote and set the level of funding at whatever it wants. This occurred in 2004-05 and 2010-11.

Maintenance Factor: For suspension and Test 3 years, the state records the level of funding that would have been necessary to meet the Test 2 requirement. In subsequent years, the state must accelerate growth in funding to catch up to that Test 2 level. The gap between actual funding levels and the Test 2 baseline is known as the maintenance factor. In years when a maintenance factor exists, the state generates savings since it does not have to fund education at the higher Test 2 level. Restoration to the Test 2 level begins in a year in which growth in per capita general fund revenue exceeds growth in per capita income.

Source: Legislative Analyst's Office, *Proposition 98 Primer*.

Language Learners (ELL) can be complicated, especially with a wide variety of languages. Many studies also show that parental income levels and education are also strong predictors of student achievement. Students from low-income households, who have parents with low education levels, tend to perform poorly on standardized exams. Although additional resources (i.e., higher per-pupil spending) may help compensate for some of these factors, a major study by Stanford researchers from 2008 suggested that significant reforms were also necessary to improve education outcomes even if funding support was increased.[11]

Recognizing that resource allocation could improve student performance for certain targeted populations, the legislature approved Governor Brown's Local Control Funding Formula in 2013.[12] The formula allocates funding based on a

---

[11] Loeb, Bryk, and Hanushek, "Getting Down to Facts."

[12] Legislative Analyst's Office, *An Overview of the Local Control Funding Formula*, (Sacramento: Legislative Analyst's Office, 2013), http://www.lao.ca.gov/reports/2013/

district's average daily attendance (ADA) as it did under the old system with adjustments for cost-of-living and other factors, but districts receive additional funding for students who are ELL or receive free or reduced-price meals (FRPM). School districts determine whether students are ELL based on their home language and their performance on the California English Language Development Test. FRPM students qualify for meals if their family's household income is below 185 percent of the federal poverty line (about $44,000). Districts receive additional funding for each ELL or FRPM student enrolled and more "concentration" funding on top of that if the percentage of these students enrolled in the district exceeds 55 percent. The new funding formula acknowledges that certain student groups may need additional school resources to close achievement gaps with their peers. The impact of the formula on student performance will not be known for at least several years.

Health and Welfare

The second largest program area is health and welfare, which includes Medi-Cal, the state's health insurance program for low-income households, and CalWORKs, which provides cash assistance to low-income adults and children. In 2012–13, the state spent $27 billion from the general fund on all of these programs.

Many, but not all, health and welfare programs are means-tested, where eligibility is determined by household income. The income levels used to determine eligibility are based on the ratio of household income to the poverty level for a given size of family. Typically, an individual is eligible for these programs if their income is 100 percent of the federal poverty level or below, but some programs, such as the Healthy Families program (phased out), had higher income thresholds (up to 200 percent of FPL). In 2014, the federal poverty level was $23,850 for a family of four.[13]

Since program eligibility is based on poverty thresholds, the statewide poverty level is a major factor in the caseload for these programs, and in their spending levels. Not surprisingly, poverty levels rise and fall with economic conditions. Poverty levels rose sharply during the Great Recession and subsided in its wake. By the end of 2012, 16 percent of Californians were below the poverty line. When poverty levels rise, these are precisely the time when demand for poverty-related programs grows, but also the time when state revenue is declining.

There has been increasing attention given to the inadequacy of the federal poverty measure because it is not viewed as an accurate gauge of poverty across the United States. The federal measure was originally developed in the 1960s by the Social Security Administration. Analysts estimated that one-third of a

edu/lcff/lcff-072913.aspx.
[13] The federal poverty thresholds are available here at https://www.census.gov/hhes/www/poverty/data/threshld/.

household budget was spent on food at the time and used that number as the threshold for poverty. It was subsequently adjusted for inflation annually. The current measure is outdated because household budgets have changed considerably and now must consider child care expenses, health care, and transportation costs, among other factors. In a state like California with a high cost of living, the measure is particularly problematic because it does not consider that some states, and areas within states, have substantial variation in living expenses. A study by researchers at UCLA and the California Budget Project estimated that a more accurate poverty level in the state might be twice the FPL based on the average cost of household expenses (e.g., rent, food, transportation, etc.).[14] In 2010, the Obama administration acknowledged the inaccuracy of the measure by issuing the traditional measure and a newly revised one, the supplemental poverty measure, although eligibility for programs will still be based on the traditional measure. For budgeting purposes in California, the traditional measure is used to determine eligibility.

Medi-Cal

California's version of the federal Medicaid program is called Medi-Cal. This insurance program for low-income individuals is supported by a combination of roughly equal proportions of federal and state funding. The state spent $15 billion from the general fund in 2012–13 for support of the program.[15] Prior to the passage of the Affordable Care Act (ACA), individuals were eligible to receive Medi-Cal coverage if their income levels were at or below 100 percent of the poverty level. Since California policymakers opted for the Medicaid expansion under the ACA, those with incomes below 138 percent of the FPL qualify for Medi-Cal. The federal government establishes a minimum level of benefits that must be covered, including hospital inpatient and outpatient care and doctor visits. The state also offers additional optional services, including prescription drugs and dental visits, although these optional benefits were scaled back considerably during the crisis budgeting era. Medi-Cal also partially supports other major programs such as In-Home Supportive Services and mental health services, which are administered by separate state departments. In 2012–13, Medi-Cal had about 8 million enrollees. This number is expected to climb over 10 million with the full implementation of the ACA.

Supplemental Security Income/State Supplementary Program (SSI/SSP)

The state provided $2.8 billion in 2012–13 for support of the SSI/SSP program. The program provides cash assistance to low-income aged, blind, or disabled individuals. The SSI component is paid with federal funds, while the SSP

---

14 UCLA Center for Health Policy Research, *What Does it Take for a Family to Afford to Pay for Health Care* (Los Angeles: University of California, Los Angeles, 2007). The study is available at http://escholarship.org/uc/item/61p8n2s5.

[15] Legislative Analyst's Office, *The Spending Plan* (Sacramento: Legislative Analyst's Office, 2013).

component is supported by state funds. Individuals qualify for cash assistance if their monthly income is below the maximum grant level (around $900), and other sources of income do not exceed $2,000. The caseload was 1.3 million in 2012–13. With the baby boomer generation getting older, the caseload is expected to grow for this program.

California Work Opportunity and Responsibility to Kids (CalWORKs)
The CalWORKs program is the state's primary welfare program that provides cash assistance to low-income children and adults. CalWORKs is the state's version of the federal Temporary Assistance for Needy Families (TANF) program. For its share, the state provided over $1.5 billion in 2012–13. To be eligible for benefits, family income must be at or below 100 percent of FPL and certain work requirements apply for adults. Specifically, to remain eligible they must work 20 to 30 hours a week or participate in educational or job-training programs. Until 2013, adults could time out, or become ineligible for benefits, after a period of four years of assistance. This time period was shortened to two years in 2013 if stricter work requirements were not met. Time limits do not apply to child recipients. California is one of only four states that allow children to receive assistance even though their parents have timed out.[16] In January of 2011, the average grant for a family of three in a high-cost county was $694, while it was $661 in low-cost counties. As shown in Figure 4.7, enrollment ebbs and flows with economic conditions.

Waste, Fraud, and Abuse
A frequent complaint about government programs, especially those involving the social safety net, is that there is rampant waste, fraud, and abuse in these programs. The average person on the street may make such claims based on someone they know or have observed who appears to be claiming benefits they do not deserve or qualify for. In 2009, in an effort to galvanize support for its antifraud proposals, the Schwarzenegger administration claimed that 25 percent of the spending on the state's In-Home Supportive Services program was fraudulent. When reporters dug deeper into the origin of the 25 percent figure, it could not be verified in any state studies. The number appears to have originated from a San Diego district attorney program in 1997 that investigated welfare applicants and found that 25 percent were not eligible for benefits. Despite referring to the wrong program and inaccurately referring to fraud (eligibility denials are not fraud), the high rate of fraud was cited repeatedly.[17]

It is true that fraud and abuse exist in these programs, but evidence does not support the high level commonly assumed. For example, news stories have doc-

---

[16] Public Policy Institute of California, *Just the Facts: California's Welfare Caseload* (San Francisco: Public Policy Institute of California, 2012).
[17] Malcolm Maclachlan, "How Much IHSS Fraud Is There?" *Capitol Weekly*, September 30, 2010.

The Spending Plan

Figure 4.7. CalWORKs Welfare Caseload, 1997–2013

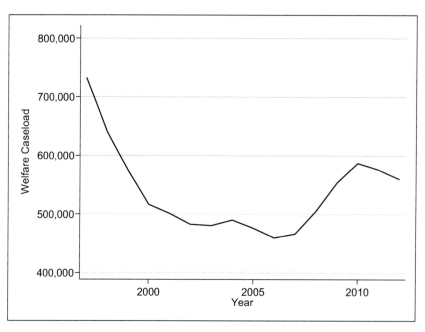

Source: Department of Social Services, CalWORKs Data Trends.

umented schemes to defraud Medi-Cal by stealing Social Security numbers and using those of the deceased to claim payment for medical devices or services. Other reports have shown that caretakers (of usually elderly relatives) in the In-Home Supportive Services program have claimed excessive hours to increase their take-home pay. But even with numerous anecdotes about alleged and actual fraud and abuse, the level is still much lower than some believe. Why is this the case?

First, most major departments have internal auditors that provide oversight and conduct audits of department programs.[18] State and local government also have several independent entities—that is, outside of the departments themselves—at each level that oversee and conduct audits of these social programs. The state controller and Department of Finance at the state level both have audit units that regularly audit state programs, and all programs that receive federal funding are audited by the California State Auditor according to a federally established schedule. In addition, through the Joint Legislative Audit Committee,

---

[18] For a list of these internal auditors, see the Directory of State Internal Audit Organizations at http://www.dof.ca.gov/osae/.

legislators can request performance audits of any state or local program if they have suspicions or evidence of fraud or abuse. County auditors also perform similar oversight of individual county programs, and county district attorneys have established programs to investigate reports and allegations of fraud.

Investigations of fraud by these various agencies do uncover instances of fraud, but it usually is at a much lower rate. For instance, the Sacramento County D.A.'s office reported in 2010 that less than one percent of their IHSS cases revealed fraud in their investigations.[19] Although potential fraud and abuse contribute to the public's resentment over social welfare programs, the resentment also may be based on the question of deservedness. Who deserves what is a central question in any political system and at the heart of public budgeting.

Higher Education

Once considered the top state university system in the United States, if not the world, the funding cuts to the higher education system in the crisis budgeting era significantly affected the affordability and access to California's system, which has led to questions about its position among the top state systems. California's system is comprised of three segments—the community college system, the California State University (CSU) system, and the University of California (UC) system. Each segment targets students who have varying educational goals, ranging from the awarding of associate's degrees to doctoral degrees. The state spent $9.9 billion (GF) on higher education in 2012–13. The biggest portion of this funding supported community colleges at $3.8 billion, followed by the portion for the University of California at $2.4 billion, and the $2.3 billion for the CSU system.

Unlike other major program areas, the higher education segments also receive revenue from tuition and fees. With general fund reductions, the UC and CSU systems have raised tuition significantly to compensate for the revenue loss. In 2013–14, CSU systemwide tuition and fees were $5,472, which more than doubled from the $2,520 amount in 2006–07, just six years earlier.[20] For the UC system, tuition and fees doubled from $6,141 in 2006–07 to $13,200 in 2013–14. The community college system does not set its own fees; the legislature does. The fees there doubled as well from $20 per unit in 2006–07 to $46 in 2012.[21]

The higher education segments have been targeted with funding reductions and will probably continue to for several reasons. First, as mentioned above and unlike other major service areas, they have an alternative revenue source—

---

[19] Maclachlin, "How Much IHSS Fraud is There?"

[20] California State University system, Fee Rates, at http://www.calstate.edu/budget/student-fees/fee-rates/.

[21] California Community Colleges Chancellor's Office, "Key Facts About Community Colleges," at http://californiacommunitycolleges.cccco.edu/PolicyInAction/Key Facts.aspx.

tuition and fees—which can be adjusted to mitigate their general fund reductions. Unlike ordinary tax increases that require a two-thirds vote in the legislature, the governing boards for the UC and CSU systems can raise tuition and fees without jeopardizing their political careers since they are appointed. Second, while community college funding is constitutionally protected under the Proposition 98 umbrella, UC and CSU funding is not. There is no requirement that they be funded at a minimum level. Yet another reason the segments are targeted for cuts is that other major areas either have to comply with court-mandated spending, such as corrections, or federal cost-sharing requirements for programs like Medi-Cal or CalWORKs. In addition, federal loan programs are readily available and allow students to keep paying for rising tuition without feeling the full financial impact.

This disinvestment in higher education will have at least two consequences, both of which ultimately negatively impact the state and national economy. First, affordability and low completion rates reduce the projected number of college graduates in the future. As the number of college graduates does not keep pace with demand for jobs requiring bachelor's degrees, businesses will not be able to meet their employment needs and may find other locations more attractive.[22] Second, rapidly rising tuition and fees have increased students' share of the cost, which has driven up average student-debt levels. As students pay back their larger student debts, they will have less money for consumer purchases, such as houses and cars, which will contribute to slower economic growth.

Criminal Justice and Corrections

The area of criminal justice and corrections includes the judicial branch, Department of Justice, headed by the attorney general, and other criminal justice-related programs, but, by far the largest component of this area is the state prison system, which is overseen by the Department of Corrections and Rehabilitation. Total general fund spending for this area in 2012–13 was $9.7 billion, of which $8.7 billion was spent on corrections. As shown in Figure 4.5, corrections is the second fastest growing area of the general fund budget, behind bond debt-service, and is often mistaken as the largest area of the budget because of its rapid growth in recent years.

Corrections spending is driven largely by its inmate population. Trends in the prison population are shown in Figure 4.8. The population rose substantially in the 1980s and 1990s in response to higher crime rates, harsher sentencing laws, such as "three-strikes and you're out," and extremely high recidivism rates. Because of federal court orders to reduce the inmate population and the state's pri-

---

[22] Public Policy Institute of California, *Closing the Gap: Meeting California's Need for College Graduates* (San Francisco: Public Policy Institute of California, 2009), http://www.ppic.org/content/pubs/report/R_409HJR.pdf.

Figure 4.8. Prison Inmate Population, 1980–2013

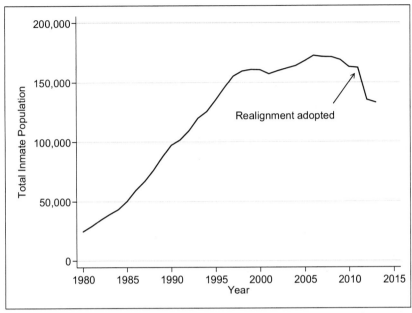

Source: Department of Corrections and Rehabilitation, *Population Reports.*

son realignment program (discussed further below), the population began to decline in 2012.

The corrections budget has been a difficult issue for the state to grapple with for several decades. Since the 1980s, when crime rates were higher, policymakers have been pressured by public opinion and voters to use incarceration as the primary means for dealing with crime. The political repercussions of being "soft on crime" were highlighted in the 1988 presidential race between Vice President George Bush (R) and Massachusetts Governor Michael Dukakis (D). Bush ran television ads that reported how Dukakis, as governor, had released inmates prior to the end of their sentence who later committed violent crimes. Many believe those ads were fatal for Dukakis and vaulted Bush into the White House. Political candidates, both Democrats and Republicans, fearing the "soft on crime" label, have taken stronger and stronger positions on crime that have contributed to a "lock 'em up" mentality.

With high crime rates and a projected increase in the number of inmates, California embarked on an ambitious prison building plan to accommodate the growing prison population (The total number of prison facilities now stands at 33). During this time, California, and other states, adopted stiffer sentencing laws, including "three-strikes and you're out" laws. Indicating the momentum behind this mentality, California's law was adopted in 1994, both as a bill in the legislative process and as an initiative (Proposition 184), and imposed an automatic 25-years-to-life sentence upon conviction of a third felony. The so-called second-strike provisions of the law and other sentencing mandates, along with the three-strikers, significantly increased the length of stay for prison inmates, especially for violent offenders.[23]

Another contributing factor to the rising corrections budgets has been the prison workforce. Prison guards are members of the powerful California Correctional Peace Officers Association (CCPOA), which is considered to be the one of the most influential unions in Sacramento. Through contract negotiations with the governor, CCPOA secured relatively high salaries and generous benefits, which further drove up the costs of housing inmates. Some prison guards make over $100,000 annually by boosting their base salary with overtime and holiday pay.

Prison Lawsuit and Realignment

In 2001, the Prison Law Office in San Francisco filed a federal lawsuit alleging that health care conditions in the prison system violated the Constitution. Poor health conditions were cited in numerous investigations and reports and were rooted in prison overcrowding. Despite the prison building spree in the 1990s, the system did not have the capacity to properly house the number of offenders receiving prison sentences and the population already there. In 2001, at the time the lawsuit was filed, the system operated at *160 percent* of capacity. Newspaper articles reported that inmates were triple bunking in their cells and any useable space within the institutions, such as gymnasiums, was converted to bed space. In 2011, after several lower court rulings, the U.S. Supreme Court ordered the Department of Corrections and Rehabilitation to reduce the population to 137.5 percent of capacity by 2013, which would mean about 30,000 fewer inmates.[24]

To meet the population reduction target, Governor Brown signed legislation in 2011 that shifted some state responsibilities and funding to the county level in a "realignment" of services. The proposal initially provided about $6 billion in revenue from vehicle license fees and the state portion of the sales tax. Policymakers expected this amount to grow over time to support expanding services.[25] The largest component of the 2011 realignment was the transfer of responsibility for lower-level criminal offenders and state parolees. These lower-level offenders would have normally been sent to state prison to carry out their sentence, but

---

[23] For a report on the three-strikes law and its impact on the prison population, see Legislative Analyst's Office, *Three Strikes: A Primer* (Sacramento: Legislative Analyst's Office, 2005).

[24] Public Policy Institute of California, *California's Future: Corrections* (San Francisco: Public Policy Institute of California, 2014).

[25] Legislative Analyst's Office, *The 2011 Realignment of Adult Offenders—An Update* (Sacramento: Legislative Analyst's Office, 2012), at http://www.lao.ca.gov /analysis /2012/crim_justice/2011-realignment-of-adult-offenders-022212.aspx.

counties assumed responsibility for them for certain types of crimes. Counties also began to manage and supervise parolees released from state prison and parole violators. The intention of realignment was to provide incentives for counties to offer more effective rehabilitation programs that would make prisoner reentry into communities more seamless. Since parolees usually return to their home communities upon release from prison, a smoother transition is more likely to occur because offenders are still connected to their community and support services are available locally throughout their entire supervision period. Although realignment helped reduce the prison population by tens of thousands, it was not enough to meet the 137.5 percent target. The three-judge panel overseeing the overcrowding case subsequently extended the deadline to 2016 and required intermediate targets prior to then.

Common Budget Cut Tactics

To meet budget targets or balance the books, policymakers and budget staff often employ common tactics that look good on paper because they reduce expenditures, but result in phantom savings, push expenditures into another fiscal year, or simply delay the fiscal reckoning. These budget "solutions" are simpler substitutes for other alternatives that may ignite political opposition or inflame key political supporters. In some cases, they may increase the costs of providing state programs and services in future years. Of course, it is usually the politically charged alternatives that are the most effective ways for balancing a budget over the long term. Below are some of the options that the state has used in the past and that are frequently present in budget discussions.

Across-the-Board Cuts

One method for reducing departmental expenditures is to adopt across-the-board cuts, which direct most or all departments to reduce their total budget by a certain percentage—say 5 percent. This tool represents a decision by default because it usually comes after the governor or state leaders bypass more controversial cuts. A close cousin of across-the-board cuts is unallocated reductions, where one or a few departments are given a certain budget reduction target. In both cases, policymakers put the burden of making painful decisions on department administrators. On the one hand, these administrators are the ones that know where the department "fat" is so that the least consequential reductions can be made. On the other hand, the governor and legislators are abdicating their responsibility of making tough policy decisions, which is what they are elected to do. If straight across-the-board cuts are adopted for all departments, it also avoids the fact that certain departments and their programs may deserve more priority than others. In addition, departments and agencies with smaller budgets may have a harder time absorbing a 5-percent reduction compared to larger departments who can trim their budgets more easily without significant harm.

The Scalpel and the Hatchet—Furloughs and Layoffs

State worker salaries and benefits can constitute up to 80 percent of departmental budgets. The staff workload depends on how labor intensive the programs and services the department provides are and whether the work is mainly handled by state-level workers or through subventions to local government. The Schwarzenegger administration used furloughs as a temporary measure to reduce employee compensation costs in the late 2000s. A typical furlough looks like this: a worker receives two unpaid days off during the month and, in exchange, their salary is reduced by 10 percent. This option is temporary because a worker could return to their normal work schedule and salary after a year or two of the savings. This avoids the complicated and protracted process for laying off civil service workers and the costs of rehiring new workers once revenue sources strengthen again. Schwarzenegger's furlough proposals ran into a number of legal challenges that ran over into the Brown administration ranging from whether the governor could issue furloughs through executive order and for which employees (agencies supported by federal funds versus state funds) to whether fellow constitutional officers had to comply with the directives.[26] After campaigning on the position that furloughs are a temporary solution for an ongoing problem, Governor Brown pitched his own version of furloughs with the label "personal leave programs" (PLPs) in 2012.

As a budgetary tool, the savings from furloughs and related programs are questionable at best, and may even increase expenditures in the near term. When employees receive frequent days off, they can substitute those for vacation or personal leave days they would normally take anyway. When these employees separate from state service with sizeable leave balances saved up, the state must pay for that leave at the employee's most recent salary. In 24-hour care institutions such as prisons, it can lead to higher costs because workers filling in for those on furloughs may be making overtime pay, which is higher than regular pay.

Although furloughs have been used more frequently and have affected more state workers in recent years, the state conducted layoffs as well to reduce the workforce and payroll costs. Policymakers are reluctant to impose massive layoffs because they have several drawbacks. The layoff process is lengthy and can take up to six months or longer before employees are let go so the budget savings are not immediate. Because of civil service protections, layoffs are seniority-based so no priority is given to better performing employees. Layoffs can also reduce the level of services provided by departments, which can be consequential for certain types of departments. Finally, if the decline in revenue conditions is more temporary, then layoffs are a permanent solution to a temporary

---

[26] The *Sacramento Bee* reported that Schwarzenegger dealt with over 40 furlough lawsuits at the end of his administration. Jon Ortiz, "Gov. Jerry Brown Orders Furloughs for Holdout Unions," *Sacramento Bee*, July 12, 2012.

problem and it may be hard for departments to rehire those skilled and knowledgeable workers.

Kick the Can Down the Road—Spending Deferrals

Balanced budget requirements stipulate that the governor must sign a balanced budget—at least on paper. To meet this requirement, the governor and legislators have often moved an expenditure item from one fiscal year to the next. This has the politically expedient effect of reducing expenditures in the current year, but minimizing the programmatic impact since the funding may be appropriated and available for expenditure just a few days after the close of the fiscal year. A frequently used maneuver is to delay payments for K-14 education, particularly because they are the largest chunk of the annual budget. In 2011–12, state policymakers moved about $2.2 billion in payments to the 2012–13 fiscal year.[27]

Risky Assumptions

Another tried and true tactic is to overestimate the amount of savings from policy or program changes. This may include enacting cuts to specific programs that are contingent upon federal approval, planning on a higher level of reimbursements from the local or federal level, or anticipating that alternative funding sources will offset general fund liabilities. The Brown administration attempted to impose co-payments on services for Medi-Cal recipients in 2011 even though it required federal approval from the Centers for Medicare and Medicaid Services (CMS). Between fiscal years 2011–12 and 2012–13, the new charges were expected to save the state over $1 billion, but federal officials rejected the policy change.[28] For a number of years, the governor's budget anticipated that the federal government would provide a higher level of reimbursement for illegal immigrants incarcerated in state prisons, but the actual reimbursement was frequently much lower. The lower actual reimbursement did not stop the Department of Finance each year from inserting a higher figure in the governor's January budget proposal. In general, these types of tactics provide state leaders with the perception that the budget is balanced at the time of passage when, in reality, it will soon unravel.

Future Fiscal Obligations

California has several long-term spending obligations that could potentially wreak havoc on the state's financial well-being unless prudent measures are

---

[27] Legislative Analyst's Office, *The Spending Plan* (Sacramento: Legislative Analyst's Office, 2012), 19.

[28] Kevin Yamumura, "Obama Administration Rejects California's Medi-Cal Co-pays," *Sacramento Bee*, February 6, 2012.

taken to lighten their burden. In this section, we analyze two of the largest obligations, one of which has received considerable media attention, public pensions, and the other, state retiree health care, which has remained largely below the public's radar. The fiscal decisions that led to these problems are endemic to any budgetary process where policymakers seek to take credit for generous programs and avoid the political costs for raising revenue to support them. These decisions included overpromising on the benefit side and underestimating the cost on the funding side. Thus, viable solutions will have to address both sides.

Public Pensions

It is commonly said that government jobs pay lower than the private sector, but that the public sector offers generous benefit packages, including health care and retirement, to offset these lower salaries. The generous retirement benefits for California workers come in the form of defined-benefit plans. These plans provide an amount of retirement income that is based on the worker's years of service, salary at or near retirement, and type of employment (public safety versus miscellaneous). "In total, about 4 million Californians—11 percent of the population—are members of one or more of the state's 85 defined benefit. . ." plans.[29] The two agencies managing state and local pension plans with the largest membership are the California Public Employees' Retirement System (CalPERS) and the California State Teachers' Retirement System (CalSTRS). Together, these systems have 3.1 million members, including around 750,000 who currently receive payments.[30] Here, we focus our discussion on these two pension plans.

How State Pensions Work
    CalPERS and CalSTRS operate similarly, but the former is more generous in its offerings to members. Table 4.1 provides an overview of the basic components of each pension plan. The calculation of the benefit amounts is generally the same. Here is a hypothetical example for a state worker in CalPERS who is subject to the 2 percent at 60 years-of-age benefit formula. The final salary is $60,000 and the worker has 25 years of service.

- 2% X 25 years of service = 50%
- 50% of $60,000 = $30,000
  Annual retirement benefit = $30,000

Although this is a simple example, a retiree's benefit level could vary based on the formula, age at retirement, and salary factor. For instance, public safety

---

[29] Legislative Analyst's Office, *Public Pension and Retiree Health Benefits: An Initial Response to the Governor's Proposal* (Sacramento: Legislative Analyst's Office, 2011), 5.
    [30] *Ibid.*

Table 4.1. CalPERS/CalSTRS Overview

Category	CalPERS	CalSTRS
Benefit formula	1.25% at 65 to 3% at 50	2% at 60
Employee contribution rate (percent)	0–11	8.15–10.25
Full retirement age	50–65	60
COLA (percent)	2–5	2 automatic
Final salary basis	62% of agencies utilize final year	Final 3-years average
Average benefit, all retirees	$25,386	$39,346
Average benefit, recent career retirees	$66,828	$67,980

Source: Pension Math.

workers might be entitled to a 3 percent at 50 formula, in which case their salary factor would be multiplied by 3 percent instead of 2 percent. In addition, if a worker retires after the age stated in the formula (i.e., at age 63 instead of age 60) the percentage factor increases slightly (i.e., 2.15 percent instead of just 2 percent). Moreover, certain workers in CalPERS, but generally not CalSTRS, also participate in the federal social security program so they receive social security benefits on top of their pension payments.

In recent years, the benefit levels paid to public pension recipients have come under scrutiny as the state struggled to fund its bills and critics argued that the state could not afford such excessive benefits. Much of the attention focused on an extremely small segment of retirees who received more than $100,000 in annual payments, and, even more rarely, more than $200,000. Table 4.1 displays the annual average benefit levels for different cohorts of retirees in the two major pension plans. The average benefit for all retirees in CalPERS and CalSTRS was $25,386 and $39,346, respectively. The CalPERs average is lower because it includes recipients whose jobs may not have required a college education or who had shorter careers and thus did not qualify for a higher benefit level. For recent retirees with longer careers (30 years or more), the benefit amounts are higher overall at $66,828 for CalPERS retirees and $67,980 for CalSTRS retirees.

How They Are Funded

The state's pension plans are funded by a combination of three factors: (1) employee contributions, (2) employer contributions, and (3) investment earnings. The employee and employer contributions are based on a percentage of pay known as the contribution rate. For employees under CalPERS, these rates vary from 0 to 11 percent of pay depending on the specific bargaining unit and job classification, with an average of 7.4 percent.[31] The employer contribution rate in CalPERS is different than that for employees. These rates are based on the normal cost of retirement, which is the "annual cost that current employees are expected to earn," and the cost of unfunded liabilities from the program, amortized up to 30 years.[32] In 2009, the average systemwide contribution rate was 15.7 percent of payroll, with a normal cost average rate of 10.7 percent and 5 percent for the unfunded liability portion. For CalSTRS, the contribution rates are set in statute for employees at 8 percent and for employers at 8.25 percent. The state picks up the unfunded liability component.

The third major funding contributor to state pension plans is earnings on investments. Both CalSTRS and CalPERS have governing boards that oversee asset portfolios in a wide range of investments, including stocks, bonds, mutual funds, real estate, and other ventures. Each system plans to meet its future pension obligations with an assumed rate of return on these investments that is approved by the governing boards. If the actual rate of return falls below the assumed rate over several years, this generates concern that the pension system will not be able to fund its obligations. Because of the economic collapse in 2008 and the related stock market plunge, actual annual rates of return for CalPERS and CalSTRS fell to worrisome levels that triggered their respective boards to lower their expected rate of return to 7.5 percent. Although the historical rate of return over the 20-year time period from 1990 to 2010 for CalPERS, 7.8 percent, and CalSTRS, 8.1 percent, exceeded this expected rate, many analysts still believe that the lower 7.5 rate is too optimistic.[33] Some analysts believe the assumed rate should actually be much lower at 4.5 percent. Employers, including the state itself, affiliated with the pension plans, usually resist changes to the expected rate of return because they are required to pay a higher contribution rate to compensate for the anticipated lower earnings.

The Pension Problem

When the stock market dropped during the Great Recession, the funding outlook for the state's major pension plans declined significantly. Pension plans are required by law to provide actuarial estimates of their funded status, which is

---

[31] Joe Nation, *Pension Math: How California's Retirement Spending Is Squeezing the State Budget* (Palo Alto, CA: Stanford Institute for Economic Policy Research, 2011), 5, at http://siepr.stanford.edu/system/files/shared/Nation%20Statewide%20Report%20v081.pdf.

[32] *Ibid.*, 4.

[33] *Ibid.*, 11–12.

a measure of their ability to meet future pension obligations. If projections show a shortfall between the plan's assets and its liabilities (future payments), then an unfunded actuarial accrued liability (UAAL) has occurred. A UAAL refers to the lump sum amount that would need to be invested at the current time, and added to funds already deposited in the plan and the assumed future investment earnings, to support benefit payments earned to date for current public employees upon their retirement. According to federal accounting standards, this UAAL must be amortized over a period not exceeding 30 years. Pension plans report the unfunded liability amount annually, along with the funded ratio, which is the percentage of future liabilities that projections show are covered by future assets.

The unfunded liabilities of the state's major pension plans have come under intense scrutiny in recent years. First, the methods for conducting actuarial estimates for the pension funds' assets have been called into question, particularly the assumed rate of return on future investment earnings. Since a fund's projected assets are a key component of the funded ratio (numerator), the determination of this amount can swing the ratio dramatically. If a pension plan has a funded ratio of 80 percent, it is generally considered to be healthy, even though it is not 100 percent funded. Funded ratios reported below this 80 percent target raise alarm bells. The funded ratio reported by CalPERS hit 61 percent as of June 30, 2008, which was a low for the previous decade (See Figure 4.9). CalSTRS' ratio was much healthier at 78 percent. The June 2012 ratios have CalPERS at 66 percent and CalSTRS at 67 percent, both worrisome levels, particularly since the nation is out of the Great Recession. A report by a Stanford University economist (and former state legislator) using more conservative assumptions projected ratios in this same range for each pension plan.[34]

One of the main factors in the declining funded ratios is the assumed rate of return. Until 2012, CalSTRS and CalPERS both estimated their funded ratios using a rate of return of 7.75 percent or higher. Only after intense public pressure did they lower it to 7.5 percent to reflect more pessimistic views about the stock market and future earnings. Using the lower rate of return lowers the funded ratio and triggers larger employer contribution amounts for CalPERS (from both state and local governments) and higher contribution amounts from the state for CalSTRS. Some believe even the lower adjusted 7.5 rate is too optimistic. Thus, the risk in future years will be whether each pension plan is funded at a level that will be able to support its future pension commitments.

A related consequence of lower funded ratios for the state is the annual state contribution to each plan's fund. As mentioned above, lower ratios require larger state contributions. These contributions have been rising sharply over the last

---

[34] Nation, *Pension Math*, 17. The report estimates funding ratios assuming a range of rates of return from 4.5 percent to 9.5 percent. It also provides the probabilities of meeting different ratio targets. There is a 51 percent chance that each plan will have slightly less than 70 percent.

Figure 4.9. Funded Status of CalPERS and CalSTRS, 1991–2012

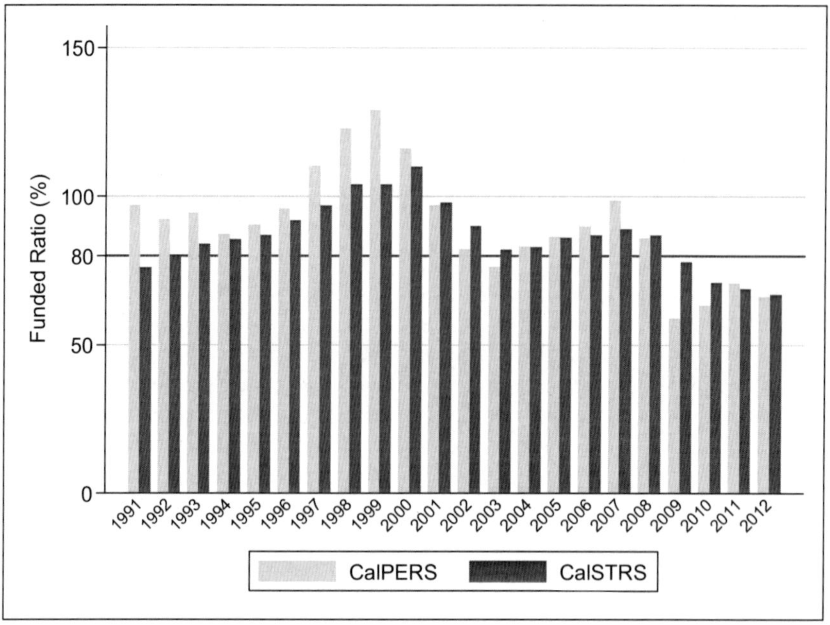

Source: CalPERS and CalSTRS Comprehensive Annual Financial Reports. Funded ratios are as of June 30 of each year. The CalPERS ratios represent market-value based methods. Horizontal line at 80 percent reflects low threshold for a healthy fund.

decades. These larger contributions have spillover effects that leave a smaller share of the budget remaining for other state programs and services. It is anticipated that retirement contributions will continue to rise for a variety of reasons and squeeze out funding for other services.

What Led to the Pension Problem?

The pension problem confronted by the state and local government can be traced to several factors, most of which have been self-inflicted by state and local policymakers. In this regard, the pension problem is symbolic of the state's larger budget problems. Like the state overall, policymakers have approved more generous benefits, which have raised spending levels (liabilities), while they have also reduced contributions, which bring revenue levels (assets) down.

More specifically, though, the seeds of the pension crisis were sown in 1984 with the passage of Proposition 21. The measure "allowed public pension funds to shift most of their investments from predictable bonds to stocks and other investments, with higher yields but also higher risks."[35] In the process, this policy change also shifted the main source of pension funding from more reliable employee and state/employer contributions to riskier and more volatile investment gains. This made pension funds particularly vulnerable to downturns in the stock market as evidenced during the Great Recession. "Public pension funds now commonly expect to get two-thirds to three-quarters of their revenue from investment earnings to cover normal costs."[36]

When funding ratios increased in the mid to late 1990s, legislators introduced and approved a number of bills that reduced employee and employer contribution rates for CalPERS and CalSTRS and provided more generous benefit packages. For example, on the contribution side, AB 1509, adopted in 2000, diverted 2 percent of teachers' pay away from the main CalSTRS fund to a supplemental benefit program.[37] With regard to benefit expansions, several bills authorized longevity bonuses that added amounts to monthly benefit payments based on 30 or more years of service, reduced the full retirement age from 60 to 55, and allowed unused sick leave to count towards years of service. Among these benefit enhancing bills, the most consequential was SB 400 in 1999, which put in place a number of different benefit increases for CalPERS members. Perhaps the most notable provision granted California Highway Patrol (CHP) officers a 3 percent at 50 benefit formula. This allowed some CHP officers to collect up to 90 percent of their salary in retirement at a relatively early age and set a negotiating target for other public safety bargaining units at the state and local level.

What Can Be Done?

In response to growing pension burdens, there have been efforts by policymakers and advocacy groups to rein in pension costs. Near the end of his administration, Schwarzenegger successfully negotiated some minor pension reform changes in collective bargaining agreements with several state employee groups. These changes included larger employee contribution rates and modifying the base salary so that it relied on the highest three years of pay instead of the highest single year. Advocacy groups also emerged to promote pension reform and temporarily floated a ballot initiative to authorize a hybrid pension system that included both a traditional pension plan and a 401(k)-style component.[38] The initiative failed to qualify for the ballot, but in 2012, Governor Brown and legislators negotiated a package of reforms to reduce the state's long-term liability.

---

[35] Ed Mendel, "State Pension Funds: What Went Wrong," *Calpensions.com*, January 11, 2010.

[36] *Ibid.*

[37] *Ibid.*, 2.

[38] Two examples of these groups are California Pension Reform (accessible at http://www.californiapensionreform.com/) founded by late former state legislator Keith Richman and the California Foundation for Fiscal Responsibility (accessible at http://www.fixpensionsfirst.com/).

One major obstacle that has hamstrung pension reform efforts is the limitations on changing benefits for current workers and retirees. Both are protected by contract law under the state and federal constitutions and by case law. This means that when an individual is employed by a government entity the pension benefits are considered a contractual obligation on the part of the employer that generally cannot be modified without the consent of the employee, which usually occurs through the bargaining process.[39] When such modifications have been made, the state Supreme Court has ruled that "comparable new advantages," such as salary increases, must be offered to compensate for the change.[40] Case law has applied these restrictions to employee contribution rates, benefit formulas, and future accrued years of service, among other factors. When state and local policymakers have considered pension reforms, they have primarily targeted new employees because more substantial modifications to their pension plans can be made. However, since future unfunded liabilities are mainly the product of current workers and retirees, the downside to this approach is that it does little to reduce the liabilities.

In 2012, the governor and legislature settled on a package of reforms that was signed into law several months prior to the November election. Democrats intended to use the reform package as a demonstration of how Sacramento could cut state spending so that voters would be more receptive to a measure to increase sales and income taxes (Proposition 30). The major provisions included the following:

- Increase the full retirement age to 62 for nonpublic safety members and teachers
- Increase the full retirement age to 57 for public safety members
- Cap the annual benefit payout ($132,000 in 2012) based on participation in federal social security
- Require employee contributions to be at least 50 percent of the normal cost of retirement

Although all of the changes apply to future employees, some provisions impact current plan members, including a prohibition against pension holidays and air-time purchases. Pension holidays allow employees or employers to skip pension contributions, while air time purchases allow employees to purchase service credit to pad their benefit payout. The combined package of reforms were the most significant changes to state pension plans since the late 1990s when benefits were substantially increased, yet the preliminary estimates of savings did not put much of a dent in pensions' unfunded liabilities. CalPERS, with an unfunded liability over $100 billion, estimated that the changes would generate up to $4 billion in savings (2012 dollars). CalSTRS, with a liability of $65 billion, projected that the reforms would save about $12 billion.[41]

---

[39] Legislative Analyst's Office, *Public Pension*. This report also has a summary of the relevant case law.

[40] Allen v. Long Beach, 45 Cal. 2d 128 (Cal. 1955).

[41] CalPERS, "Actuarial Cost Analysis: California Public Employees' Pension Re-

As part of the 2014 budget package, policymakers took a significant step to shore up CalSTRS finances by authorizing higher contribution rates from the state, school districts, and teachers. The plan will be phased in over seven years and much of the burden will fall on school districts. The state's share is expected to increase to more than $2 billion.

While state policymakers managed to cobble enough political will together to enact major pension reforms and increase CalSTRS contribution rates, the question remains whether they go far enough. Significant unfunded liabilities remain and could get worse if investment earnings fall below projections in coming decades as some analysts believe they will. As they have on previous efforts, public employee unions will continue to resist benefit changes and use their considerable resources to do so.

State Retiree Health Care

Pension obligations are not the only long-term fiscal concern confronting the state. Currently, the state provides health and dental benefits to state worker retirees and their eligible family members. Under a weighted formula, the state pays a portion of the retiree's health care premium that is based on the number of years of state service. A state worker qualifies for a 50 percent contribution after 10 years of service and up to a 100 percent contribution after 20 or more years of service. As opposed to pension programs, which are prefunded (contributions earn interest over time), retiree health care is pay-as-you-go, where the state pays the cost of premiums for all retirees each year. In 2012–13, the state spent $1.3 billion on premiums for health and dental care.

Although the current annual cost for retiree health care is an extremely small share of the general fund budget, the amount has been growing quickly in recent years and is expected to continue to increase as health care premiums outpace inflation. In 2007, in response to new federal accounting standards, the legislature required the state controller to provide an actuarial estimate of the state's unfunded liability for retiree health care. Similar to the unfunded liability for pension plans, the liability represents the shortfall between the future costs of providing health care and the projected funding of the program for current and future retirees. As of June 30, 2013, the state controller reported that the unfunded liability is $65 billion over the next 30 years.[42]

Some observers believe that the situation for retiree health care is even more dire than the condition of the state's pension funds because of the lack of pre-

form Act of 2013," August 31, 2012, at http://www.calpers.ca.gov/eip-docs/about/pubs/cost-analysis.pdf; CalSTRS, "Recent Pension Legislation and Its Impact on CalSTRS Benefit Programs," September 28, 2012, at http://edsource.org/wp-content/uploads/CalSTRS-AB430-reformanalysis0922121.pdf.

[42] "Chiang Unveils Plan to Reduce State's $64.6 Billion Retiree Health Care Liability," State Controller's Office, March 6, 2014, at http://www.sco.ca.gov/eo_pressrel_14701.html.

funding. Without prefunding, earnings on investments cannot help offset the costs of providing the benefits. The state could choose to support retiree health care using the prefunding structure, but its annual contribution is not enough to build up assets that could be invested in bonds and stocks. The report from the controller's office also estimates the unfunded liability if the state were to transition to a prefunded model. This would reduce the unfunded liability by $22 billion, but would also require an annual contribution that is double what the state currently pays. Given the state's struggle to pay its bills for the immediate costs of programs in recent years, policymakers have chosen not to set aside funding for these future obligations.

Aside from changing the funding structure, one policy option available is to decrease the state's share of contribution for retirees' health care premiums. This would, of course, increase the costs for state retirees and likely meet strong resistance from public employee unions. Because retiree health care lacks legal protections, it is a more feasible alternative to cutting pension benefits. "Unlike pensions, there is no widely held view that promised retiree health is a 'vested right,' protected by contract law, under a long series of court decisions. Some think promised retiree health care can be cut, depending on circumstances."[43] Unless the state's fiscal condition improves considerably over the next decade, squeezing retiree health care could become a reality.

Conclusion

With a state as large and diverse as California, the state spends a significant amount to provide essential services to its residents. The state provides the bulk of its resources for the K-12 and higher education systems, health and social welfare programs, and the state prison system. When federal funding is factored in, the state oversees the spending of more than $200 billion. It is not surprising then that there are intense, perennial battles over the allocation of these resources. These vast sums of spending raise inevitable questions about whether it has been spent appropriately (i.e., government waste) and whether the level of spending is the best way to move the state's economy forward and advance the quality of life.

Since the advent of the antitax movement in the late 1970s, the prospect of government overspending has been a primary concern of the public and voters. This concern subsided during the crisis budgeting era as policymakers enacted cutbacks in most program areas, state prisons being the main exception. Overspending is likely to be a concern once again as revenue conditions improve and pent-up spending demands grow for infrastructure, the restoration of program cuts, and long-term pension and retiree health care programs.

---

[43] Ed Mendel, "City Bankruptcies Target Retiree Health Care Costs," *Calpensions.com*, August 6, 2012.

Discussion Questions

1. Based on the breakdown of state spending, what are California's main policy priorities? What do trends in spending growth tell us about these priorities?

2. Discuss the evidence that the state has a spending problem and conversely why it may not.

3. What are some of the factors that drive growth in government spending?

4. Explain California's pension problem and its causes. Has it been fixed? What other solutions may be necessary to address it?

Additional Resources

The Next 10 Budget Challenge

http://www.budgetchallenge.org/pages/home

This website allows users to simulate the budget decisions that California legislators must make each year.

The California Budget Project

http://cbp.org/

This nonpartisan organization conducts research and issues reports on state budgetary matters mainly as they relate to low- and moderate-income residents.

CalPERS and CalSTRS websites

http://www.calpers.ca.gov/ and http://www.calstrs.com/

The websites publish their annual actuarial reports, investment portfolios, and other material for members and the public.

Chapter 5

Ballot-Box Budgeting

> Proposition No. 2 . . . would reduce still further the Legislature's ability to en-
> act an economical and effective budget. It would also increase the incentive of
> other groups to assure themselves of a fixed state appropriation by writing their
> demands into the Constitution.
>
> —1952 ballot argument against Proposition 2
> (Public School Funds), an Initiative Constitutional Amendment
> that required the state to spend $180 per pupil

In 1936, a charismatic and popular radio show host in southern California, Robert Noble (the Rush Limbaugh of his day), began pitching to his largely older
audience a pension scheme to distribute weekly $30 warrants to retirees over age
50.[1] The "Ham and Eggs" movement, as it was later called, was eventually taken
over by "two brothers of, to say the least, dubious character," Willis and Lawrence Allen, who managed to remove Noble from the California Pension Plan's
headquarters, where dues and donations to the movement were sent.[2] In 1938,
the brothers Allen, now heading the incorporated "Retirement Life Payments
Association," turned in 789,104 signatures to qualify the "Retirement Life Payments" initiative, or Proposition 25, for the 1938 General Election ballot.

The measure's purpose echoed the intent of social security legislation at the
federal level, passed just three years earlier, to provide income security to an
elderly population mired in poverty. The rather complicated proposal authorized
the issuance of weekly scrip payments valued at $30 to eligible retirees in an

---

[1] Daniel Hanne, "'Ham and Eggs Left and Right: The California Scrip Pension Initiatives of 1938 and 1939," *Southern California Quarterly* 80, no. 2 (1998): 183.

[2] *Ibid.*, 190.

attempt to free up jobs for younger workers and boost inflationary pressures on the depressed economy.[3] The initiative also required the governor to appoint a well-paid administrator for the new pension program, with extraordinary powers, from a list of three names specified by the Allen brothers. Despite the hefty sum of $300,000 ($5 million in 2014 dollars) behind the proposition, it failed to pass with 45 percent of the vote.

The near taste of victory only emboldened the Allen brothers and their allies to promote a revised proposal again the very next year in 1939. When the new measure qualified for the ballot, under pressure from supporters, Governor Culbert Olson (D), himself only a supporter for political reasons, called a special election solely for the purpose of the measure. That measure, Proposition 1, had a much stronger economic and political impact, as it sent shockwaves through the California municipal bond market and led to two unsuccessful gubernatorial recall efforts.[4] After Proposition 1 was overwhelmingly defeated, supporters launched another effort in 1940. Although the third initiative did not qualify for the ballot, new leaders took up the cause and pushed similar pension measures throughout the 1940s, until their last defeat in 1954.[5] Although the Ham and Eggs movement and its offspring ultimately ended in defeat, it serves as a classic example of the ballot-box budgeting phenomenon and one whose implications reverberate to the present day. Not only do modern-day initiative sponsors place their proposals on multiple ballots until they are successful or, as in the case of Ham and Eggs, defeated, policy entrepreneurs and interest groups also frequently attempt to earmark state resources for a particular service or segment of the population.

Current observers of state politics normally trace the phenomenon of ballot-box budgeting in California to Proposition 98, which carved out the largest chunk of the state budget for K-12 education in 1988. "The use of citizen's initiatives to guarantee, rather than restrict, funding began with the passage of Proposition 98 in November 1988," two scholars wrote in 2008.[6] Others might point to the infamous property tax limitations imposed by Proposition 13, although that measure primarily blunted the main source of revenue for local governments and not the state. If we only look as far back as 1988, or even further to 1978 in the case of Proposition 13, we would overlook decades of numerous ballot measures to alter the state's revenue scheme, allocate funding for specific services, and modify, if not overhaul, the budgetary process. Many earlier measures, some passing and some not, laid the foundation and provided the inspiration for these later propositions.

---

[3] John M. Allswang, *The Initiative and Referendum in California, 1898–1998* (Stanford: Stanford University Press, 2000), 54.

[4] Hanne, "'Ham and Eggs,'" 223, 225.

[5] Allswang, *The Initiative and Referendum*, 57.

[6] Mark Baldassare and Cheryl Katz, *The Coming Age of Direct Democracy* (Lanham, Maryland: Rowan and Littlefield, 2008), 15.

In this chapter, we explore the roots and development of ballot-box budgeting in California and examine the significant impact it has on the state's budgetary process. We start first with an overview of budgeting through direct democracy and how both the "common people" and legislature place measures on the ballot for a popular vote.[7] In the second section, we analyze different types of fiscal propositions and the trends that have emerged in recent decades. We then turn our attention to major issues raised by budgeting through direct democracy, such as earmarking, piecemeal budgeting, and the loss of budget accountability. We conclude by considering some of the proposals to curb the negative effects of ballot-box budgeting.

Understanding Ballot-Box Budgeting

While both academic studies and government reports have summarized and analyzed the initiative process, none has explicitly looked at ballot-box budgeting.[8] Usually, these studies concentrate only on citizen-generated initiatives, although some researchers do expand their inquiries to ballot propositions originating from the legislature. These distinctions in terms are important for understanding budgeting through direct democracy so we will lay the groundwork by defining the scope of ballot-box budgeting, outlining different types of propositions, and describing how these various measures reach the ballot.

Ballot-box budgeting occurs when measures are placed before voters, either by the legislature or through the initiative process, that would modify the tax system, the allocation of spending, or the budgetary process. We should note that this is a more expansive definition of ballot-box budgeting than if we just considered measures emerging from the initiative process. Using a more narrow definition would ignore the voluminous number of times that the governor and legislature have referred measures to the electorate that pertained to the fiscal system or the budget process. Therefore, we can use the term *ballot propositions* to encompass all measures that are placed before voters either through the initiative or legislative process.

Under the umbrella of ballot propositions, *initiative measures* are those that arise from citizen petitions, while *legislative measures*, or *referrals*, are those that are "referred" to voters by the legislature. Ballot propositions also include *referendums*, which allow the electorate to reject or approve an act passed by the legislature, but the referendum power does not apply to certain types of legislative acts, including the budget and tax levies. Thus, referendums pertaining to

---

[7] We use "direct democracy" to refer to voting on both initiatives *and* legislative measures. Typically, it is only used in the context of voting on citizen initiatives.

[8] Allswang, *The Initiative and Referendum*; California Secretary of State, *A Study of California Ballot Measures 1884 to 1993* (Sacramento: Secretary of State, 1994). Matsusaka is the exception. See John Matsusaka, "A Case Study of Direct Democracy: Have Voter Initiatives Paralyzed the California Budget?" in *Book of the States* (Lexington: The Council of State Governments, 2010).

budgetary matters have rarely been used. Each subcategory of measures can further be broken down into proposals to change statute or the state constitution. The legislature is required to place constitutional amendments before voters and, in the decades both before and after the adoption of the initiative in 1911, these constituted the great bulk of measures on the ballot. In the late 1940s, the legislature also began to approve statute measures in order to revise previous voter-passed initiatives. To place constitutional amendments and bond proposals on the ballot, the state constitution requires a two-thirds vote by the legislature.

For initiatives, the process starts with the drafting stage, where sponsors submit a petition to the secretary of state with the proposed statute or constitutional amendment and a $200 filing fee. After the attorney general prepares a title and summary of the measure's main provisions and the Legislative Analyst's Office provides a fiscal analysis, the initiative is cleared for the signature qualification stage, where sponsors circulate the measure to meet signature thresholds to qualify it for the ballot. For initiative statutes, the threshold is 5 percent of the votes cast in the last gubernatorial election (currently about 500,000 signatures), while the threshold is a bit higher at 8 percent (currently about 800,000 signatures) for initiative constitutional amendments. These thresholds are low when compared to other states. Simmons reports that the median signature threshold for initiative statutes for all initiative states is 8 percent, while it is 10 percent for initiative constitutional amendments.[9] These lower thresholds are one of the reasons for the frequent use of initiatives in California since the inception of the process (see Table 5.1 for a list of select fiscal propositions).[10]

Historical Perspective

When the scope of ballot-box budgeting includes legislative measures, the roots of ballot-box budgeting can be traced back to the years just after the adoption of the state's second constitution in 1879. Since the only way the legislature could amend the constitution was to approve a measure and submit it for a popular vote, the California electorate, like that of nearly all other states, was not unfamiliar with weighing in on state law, even before the adoption of the initiative.[11] With increasing frequency, the legislature referred constitutional amendments

---

[9] Charlene Wear Simmons, *California's Statewide Initiative Process* (Sacramento: California State Library, 1997), 9.

[10] Frederick J. Boehmke, "Sources of Variation in the Frequency of Statewide Initiatives: The Role of Interest Group Populations," *Political Research Quarterly* 58, no. 4 (2005): 565–75.

[11] Referendums on constitutional amendments were common by the late 1900s except in southern states. Currently, only Delaware does not have a requirement that constitutional amendments be approved by voters. See Initiative and Referendum Institute, *Constitutional Amendments* (Los Angeles: Initiative and Referendum Institute, 2006), accessed June 7, 2013, at http://www.iandrinstitute.org/REPORT%202006-3%20 Amendments.pdf.

Table 5.1. Select Significant Fiscal Propositions, 1911–2012

Year	Prop	Description	Source	Type
1922	12	Authorized executive budget process and timelines for budget enactment	I	BP
1933	1	Overhauled tax system and established 2/3 budget vote under certain conditions	LM	TEL, Tax, BP
1946	6	Adopted annual budget process	LM	BP
1962	16	Strengthened 2/3 vote requirement for budget	LM	BP
1978	13	Capped property tax rate and restricted assessments; imposed 2/3 vote on legislature for tax increases	I	TEL, BP
1979	4	Limits growth in certain appropriations to population and inflation (Gann initiative)	I	TEL
1988	98	Earmarked at least 40 percent of general fund for K-12 education and community colleges; established formulas for determining allocation	I	Ear
1988	99	Imposed 25 cent tax on cigarette packs; earmarked funding for health services and anti-tobacco education and research	I	Ear
1990	111	Relaxed spending limits under Gann; tweaked Prop 98 school funding formula	LM	TEL, Ear
1993	172	Imposed half-cent sales tax increase and earmarked funding for public safety	LM	Ear
1998	10	Raises tax on cigarette packs by 50 cents and similar amount for other tobacco products; directs revenue to early childhood development programs	I	Ear

2002	42	Permanently earmarks sales taxes from gasoline for transportation purposes instead of general fund	LM	Ear
2002	49	Dedicates about $500 million to afterschool programs	I	Ear
2004	57	Authorizes $15 billion bond to cover state budget deficit	LM	Ear
2004	58	Requires governor to sign balanced budget, establishes formula for reserve fund, and restricts borrowing	LM	BP
2004	1A	Restricts state's ability to reduce local government revenue sources (property, sales, and vehicle license fees)	LM	BP, Ear
2004	63	Establishes additional 1 percent tax on incomes over $1m and dedicates revenue to mental health programs	I	Ear
2010	22	Limits state's authority to redirect fuel tax and property tax revenue	I	BP, Ear
2010	25	Changes 2/3 vote requirement to pass budget to a simple majority	I	BP
2010	26	Broadens types of fees subject to 2/3 vote requirement at state and local level; imposes 2/3 vote requirement on any tax changes	I	BP
2012	30	Temporarily raises sales tax by quarter cent and income tax on higher-income groups and dedicates most to education; guarantees local governments receive revenue for realignment responsibilities	I	Ear
2012	39	Modifies tax formula for out-of-state businesses; dedicates revenue to general fund and energy efficiency programs	I	Ear

Note: For source, LM=Legislative measure; I=Initiative. For type, BP=Budget process; Ear=Earmark; Tax=Tax measure; TEL=Tax and expenditure limitation. Includes measures affecting mainly the state budget process. See Chapter 8 for statewide measures affecting local government.

and bond measures to the ballot from 1884 until 1910. In fact, in 1910, one year before the adoption of the initiative and referendum, there were 12 measures on the ballot, four of which were bond measures. The other eight were constitutional amendments, three of which dealt with fiscal matters. The appearance of fiscal issues on the ballot was common by this point, as one-third of the 107 measures on the ballot between 1884 and 1910 dealt with such budget issues.

Many of the pre-initiative fiscal propositions dealt with a property tax exemption of some kind or another. These included exemptions for "free public libraries, free museums, and young fruit and nut-bearing trees and grape vines."[12] Less frequently, bond measures appeared on the ballot that authorized borrowing for projects in specific regions, such as the San Francisco Depot Act, or Proposition 2 in 1892. It is not entirely clear why the legislature so often referred measures to the ballot prior to the initiative (and after, for that matter), but one contemporary observer attributed it to the overly prescribed nature of the constitution. "[T]he plan of taxing everything, adopted in 1879, has been found to be too burdensome, and is now in course of relaxation."[13] Over time, the legislature realized the constraints the constitution imposed and sought to remedy them by the only means available. Nevertheless, by the time the initiative and referendum process was approved in 1911, California voters were veteran legislators, weighing in frequently on important matters of the day, including taxes and spending. "Hence there is gradually growing up in California a body of law which is 'understood by the people,' which is comprised in manageable bulk and which is grounded on popular approval."[14]

A Role for "the Good People of the State"[15]

There is no indication that initiative advocates were driven by their desire to expand the electorate's role in state budgeting per se. By most accounts, the push for direct democracy in California and its tools of the initiative, referendum, and recall (IR&R) were motivated by the corruption in the state legislature at the hands of the Southern Pacific Railroad (SPP). Progressives, who led the direct democracy movement in California and other states, were primarily concerned with loosening the grip of machine politics and the tyrannical control of the railroad. "The California movement that unfurled the Progressive banner originated with a small group of business and professional men who were determinedly opposed to machine control of the political and economic institutions of the state by the Southern Pacific Railroad. It was a revolt movement aimed at a monopoly-control situation."[16] Progressives, like the iconic Hiram Johnson

---

[12] Samuel E. Moffett, "The Constitutional Referendum in California," *Political Science Quarterly* 13, no. 1 (1898): 16.

[13] *Ibid.*, 16.

[14] *Ibid.*, 18.

[15] This phrase was used often by Progressives campaigning on behalf of their reforms. George E. Mowry, *The California Progressives* (Berkeley, University of California Press, 1951), 97.

[16] V. O. Key and Winston Crouch, *The Initiative and Referendum in California*

(R), who was a latecomer to the cause, believed the best way to reduce the monopolistic influence of the SPP was to delegate more power to ordinary voters. After Johnson was elected governor in 1910, largely on the platform of direct democracy, he stated his trust in the voters in his first inaugural address: "those of us who espouse these measures [IR&R] do so because of our deep-rooted belief in popular government, and not only in the right of the people to govern, but in their ability to govern."[17]

It is important to note how ballot-box budgeting related to direct democracy and the voters it would eventually empower. First, the corruption afflicting the capital did not primarily revolve around the public purse and how state money was dispersed, although there were some of these abuses. At the time of the Progressive movement, the "budget" was not the indispensable vehicle it is today for government power. The state collected little in revenue and had no formal, organized process for deliberating how resources should be allocated (see Chapter 2). The modern executive budget structure that we know today was not adopted until 1922, 10 years after the initiative process was adopted, and by an initiative (Proposition 12) we might add. Thus, there was little money to be abused and embezzled, or at least not the potential there is today. The corruption then took the form of vote-buying in the legislature that led to a lax regulatory environment that allowed the railroad monopoly and other favored business interests to prosper. However, by giving voters a greater role in governmental matters, an inevitable byproduct of democratizing government is ballot-box budgeting. Moreover, once the budget became a central function of government and the fiscal capacity to support a modern economy and welfare state emerged, budgeting through elections became more frequent. The perpetual mistrust of government, fueled by corruption at the beginning of the 20th century and subsequent episodes, and the widespread belief in popular sovereignty have led to the presumption that voters *should* weigh in on budgetary matters.

A second point about the Progressive push for direct democracy concerns the additional voting responsibilities placed on ordinary citizens. One complaint frequently heard today about direct democracy is the burden it places on voters to make an *informed* decision on ballot measures. Before its adoption, opponents of the initiative process raised similar concerns. However, when we consider the social class and status of reformers—middle- and upper-class professionals— they are the ones who could spare the time and would take the time to educate themselves on ballot measures. Lower, working-class people were less likely to have the time to devote to educating themselves about ballot issues or participate at all. This is not to suggest that Progressives intentionally sought to increase the influence of their own ilk, as their motivations appeared to be more principled and altruistic than self-interested, but one unintended consequence was that

---

(Berkeley: University of California Press, 1939), 423.

[17] Governor Hiram Johnson, *First Inaugural Address, 1911* (Sacramento: California State Library). Accessed June 7, 2013, at http://governors.library.ca.gov/addresses/23-hjohnson01.html.

middle- and upper-class voters, who tend to participate more, would have more influence over state policy.

The person most responsible for the initiative process in California, Dr. John Randolph Haynes, is a perfect example of this point. From the late 1890s until its adoption in 1911, Haynes was the most prolific advocate of citizen initiatives, holding numerous meetings up and down the state and gaining influential support from an extremely diverse coalition of groups, including labor, business, and newspaper editors. He was also extremely wealthy from his medical practice and real estate investments in the Los Angeles area, which allowed him to have the time to traverse the state advocating for reforms.

Early research indicated a fairly high level of ballot roll-off—that is, non-voting on certain propositions—depending on the specific issue that is still present in current elections.[18] Recent scholarship also shows that lack of knowledge and ballot language complexity lead to ballot roll-off.[19] Both of these factors impede the participation of lower-income and less-educated voters and contribute to a California electorate that has remained more white and upper class than the state as whole. The composition of the electorate, particularly on ballot measures, has yielded more fiscally conservative policies and ones that are less redistributive in nature than they might otherwise be.[20]

Overview of Ballot-Box Budgeting

Sources

Critics of ballot-box budgeting point to the frequent use of initiatives by sponsors to earmark state resources for pet programs and causes. However, as alluded to above, the legislature, and not the initiative, has been the primary source for ballot measures, including budget-related ones. Just as the legislature frequently referred measures to the ballot before the inception of the initiative process, it did so afterwards as well. In 1914 alone, voters were confronted with 48 measures on the ballot, more than half of which (27) were legislative referrals. Nine of these were fiscal legislative measures, while five were fiscally related initiatives. Over the entire history of the initiative process, 551 fiscal propositions have reached the ballot, *75 percent* of which were legislative measures. Fiscal propositions have represented a little less than half of all measures on the

---

[18] Key and Crouch, *The Initiative and Referendum*, Ch. VI; Allswang, *The Initiative and Referendum*.

[19] Shaun Bowler and Todd Donovan, "Information and Opinion Change on Ballot Measures," *Political Behavior* 16, no. 4 (1994): 411–35; Shauna Reilly and Sean Richey, "Ballot Question Readability and Roll-Off: The Impact of Language Complexity," *Political Research Quarterly*, 64, no. 1 (2011): 59–67.

[20] Of course, this does not mean that voters have not approved tax increases or program earmarks, but overall the tenor of approved measures has shifted state policy toward lower taxation levels and restricted the process for raising taxes at the state and local level.

Box 5.1. How Does California Ballot-Box Budgeting Compare to Other States?

California often receives national attention for its use of the initiative process under a presumption that the state is hyper-democratic. Is this true for ballot-box budgeting? Table 5.2 shows the percentage of California ballot measures with a fiscally related topic by source compared to other states. With the exception of popular referendums, California uses the ballot box to budget slightly more than all states combined. For instance, 31 percent of propositions in California have concerned fiscal topics, while 26 percent have for all states. The breakdown is roughly the same for total percentage of measures (41 to 35 percent). While California seems more likely to ballot-box budget, it is also not an extreme outlier in this regard.

Table 5.2 Fiscal Propositions Compared to All States

	Initiatives	Leg. Measures	Popular Refer.	All Props
California				
Fiscal	111	383	5	499
Total	355	819	46	1220
%	31	47	11	**41**
All States				
Fiscal	2428	4672	319	7419
Total	636	1930	62	2628
%	26	41	19	**35**

Source: National Conference of State Legislatures (NCSL) Ballot Measure Database.

Note: Fiscal Propositions include the categories of (1) budget, (2) bonds, and (3) tax and revenue. These data rely solely on the NCSL database and categorization. Thus, the California numbers here differ slightly from those reported elsewhere in this chapter.

ballot (46 percent), which indicates how budget-related matters have been the most frequent topic of measures placed before voters.[21]

---

[21] Several sources were used to compile a database of California fiscal propositions: the Ballot Measure databases at University of California Hastings Law School (available at http://library.uchastings.edu/research/online-research/ca-research.php) and the National Conference of State Legislatures (NCSL; available at http://www.ncsl.org/legislatures-elections/elections/ballot-measures-database.aspx); and California Secretary of State, *A*

Figure 5.1 shows the share of fiscal propositions by each source, either the legislature or the initiative, over the course of the 20th century. Legislative measures dominated the ballot until the 1980s when the share of initiative measures began to increase and legislative referrals began a steep decline. By the 2000s, the sources of fiscal measures were roughly equal, while initiatives far surpassed legislative measures in the early 2010s as the dominant source. These trends raise two important questions. First, why did legislative measures dominate much of the period and second, why did initiatives take over at the turn of the century?

The answers to these two questions lie in several factors that changed during each trend period. First, for a good part of the 20th century, partisanship was relatively low in the legislature, which allowed for more bipartisan agreement to reach the two-thirds vote requirement to place measures on the ballot. The partisan split between Democrats and Republicans reached extremely high levels in the 1980s, right about the time that fewer measures were referred to voters.[22] Another factor in the large share of legislative measures in the early decades was the legislature's response to the restrictive tax provisions embedded in the state constitution. Making minor changes to the tax code required constitutional amendments that were subject to popular vote. The vast majority of these measures granted tax exemptions to one class of individuals or another, such as military veterans, or to different types of organizations, such as public schools or churches. The structure of the tax system also underwent significant changes in the 1930s (see Chapter 3), which led to efforts to repeal those changes (e.g., income tax) or modify the tax rates under the new system.

Still a third factor in the prevalence of legislative measures was the strong, bipartisan push to build the state's infrastructure system to accommodate the rapidly growing population. The financing required to carry out this massive build-out relied on popular approval of numerous bond measures. As discussed further below, bonds have been, by far, the most frequent source of funding for fiscal propositions. Lastly, while the previous factors relate to the frequent appearance of fiscal *legislative* measures, another factor concerns the relatively low number of fiscal initiatives up until the 1980s. That is when certain interest groups, particularly public sector labor unions, became more active and influential in the initiative and legislative processes. More of these groups, including unions for teachers, law enforcement, and health workers, turned to the initiative

---

Study of California Ballot Measures, 1884–1993, (Sacramento: Secretary of State), January 1994. All official titles and summaries were read to code each measure according to whether it related to budgetary and fiscal matters and then whether its major provisions related to program spending (earmark), general taxation issues, the budget process, or were tax and expenditure limitations. NCSL has categorized all measures by similar categories, which we used as a benchmark, but they exclude some measures that are included here.

[22] For a discussion of partisanship in the California legislature, see Seth Masket, "It Takes an Outsider: Extralegislative Organization and Partisanship in the California Assembly, 1849–2006," *American Journal of Political Science* 51, no. 3 (2007): 482–97.

Figure 5.1. Sources of Fiscal Propositions by Decade

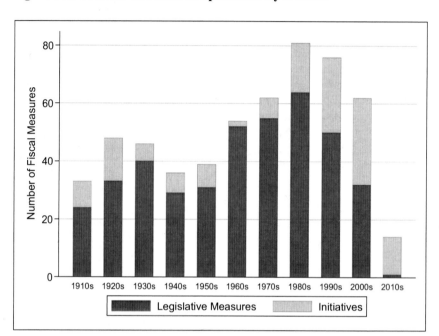

as a way to secure funding for their service areas. This strategy was probably a result of budget battles in the 1980s and 1990s and the huge reduction in property tax revenue from Proposition 13. Some argue that these end-runs around the legislature have led to an initiative process that functions as a "parallel legislature."[23] In addition, as opposed to the initial decades under the initiative process, when voters were not receptive to carve-outs for specific programs, efforts to earmark funding for programs through the use of the initiative became more successful in the 1980s. This inspired other groups to seek their own earmarks.

To explain the precipitous decline in legislative measures that began in the 1980s, we can look to the same factors that drove their dominance in earlier decades. A two-thirds vote to place measures on the ballot became more elusive as partisan lines drew more stark. The tax structure and exemptions became more solidified than they had been in previous decades. Despite recommendations from tax commissions and reform groups to modernize and update the tax system, a two-thirds majority became nearly impossible to muster for any serious constitutional amendments. The legislature did place some bond measures

---

[23] David McCuan and Stephen Stambough, *Initiative-Centered Politics: The New Politics of Direct Democracy* (Durham, NC: Carolina Academic Press, 2005).

on the ballot, mainly for new prisons and schools, but the state's budget problems prevented lawmakers from placing more ambitious infrastructure plans on the ballot as it had done in the 1950s and 1960s.

Types of Measures

Fiscal propositions can be categorized into four different types of measures. The first category and the largest is *earmarks*, which are propositions that dedicate existing or new revenue to a particular program, project, or service area.[24] These include bond measures that authorize borrowing for capital outlay projects and the infamous Proposition 98, which set aside a huge chunk of the budget for K-12 and community colleges. From 1911 to 2012, earmarks represented 52 percent of all fiscal propositions. We should note that this category includes propositions that either allocate or redirect general or special fund revenue or that create a new tax or fee to support specific spending.[25] The second category is *tax measures*, which are propositions that authorize new sources of revenue (but do not earmark it), grant tax exemptions or credits, change current tax rates, or repeal existing taxes. Until the last few decades, tax measures were the most common type of fiscal proposition (see Figure 5.2). Most of them were tax exemptions for various classes of individuals or groups and emanated from the legislature. They comprise 29 percent of fiscal measures.

The remaining two categories, *budget process* and *tax and expenditure limitations* (TEL), are a much smaller share of fiscal measures (16 and 3 percent, respectively) than the first two categories.[26] *Budget process* measures include those that modify the budget calendar, change voting requirements for fiscal and budgetary matters, and alter procedures or components within the state's budget system. For instance, Proposition 6 in 1946 converted the budget calendar to a one-year cycle, while Proposition 16 in 1962 effectively imposed the two-thirds vote requirement for the legislature to pass a budget. The appearance of budget process measures has remained fairly consistent since 1911 with a few surges in the 1970s and 2000s. Despite the national attention and antitax fervor that Proposition 13 spawned as an example of a *tax and expenditure limitation*, the number of these measures throughout the state's history has been relatively sparse (3

---

[24] Jackson refers to two definitions of earmark that are commonly used. One, used more often by the media and some political scientists, refers to pork-barrel spending. The second is drawn from the public finance literature and refers to designating specific taxes for a specific expenditure. The latter only includes earmarks from specific taxes and *not* from the general fund. The definition used in this chapter is similar to that used in the public finance literature, but also includes earmarks from the general fund. See Jeremy Jackson, "Tax Earmarking, Party Politics and Gubernatorial Veto: Theory and Evidence From US States," *Public Choice* 155 (2013): 1–18.

[25] This methodology reduces the number of propositions that thus fall under the tax measure category even though they create new revenue or change existing rates.

[26] Some of the ballot measures were categorized into more than one category, but represent a small number. They were coded this way when major provisions of the measure did not fall in mainly one category.

Figure 5.2. Fiscal Propositions by Type and Decade, 1960–2012

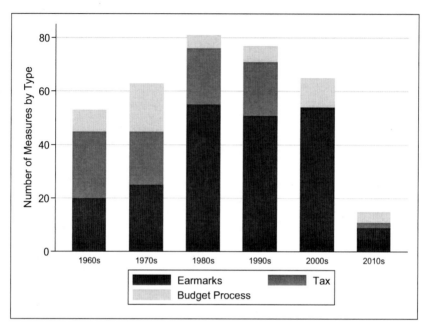

Note: Because there are relatively few TEL propositions, they are not shown here.

percent). We can define TELs as those propositions that cap a specific tax rate or authorize a formula to restrict the growth of revenues or expenditures. Although Proposition 13 led to a number of similar TEL ballot measures in other states, it did not unleash a surge of subsequent measures in California. Proposition 4, the Gann initiative, which instituted the state's appropriation limit (SAL), followed Proposition 13 in 1979, but, after this, few measures reached the ballot and those that did were mostly unsuccessful. In 1990, Proposition 111 loosened the spending restrictions to the extent that the SAL was no longer a factor in budget negotiations in the 1990s. Several governors have backed TEL measures that would limit state spending and increase executive authority to make mid-year budget cuts, but voters have rejected them. Governor Arnold Schwarzenegger's (R) proposals were spurned by voters in special elections in 2005 and 2009; both were rejected by more than 60 percent of the electorate.

The types of fiscal propositions voters encounter on the ballot have changed dramatically since the 1960s (see Figure 5.2). While tax measures, and to a certain extent, budget process measures, were quite common in the first half of the twentieth century, earmarks began to overwhelm all other types of measures in the 1970s and 1980s. By the 2000s, earmark propositions dominated the ballot and tax measures nearly vanished. The upward trend in earmarks was mainly driven by initiatives and bond referrals from the legislature, but in the 2000s, the legislature also placed a number of earmarks on the ballot to protect funding for local government and transportation and to redirect pots of money to shore up the general fund.

If 1978 was the watershed year for TEL propositions (Proposition 13 passed) across the country, then 1988 was the watershed year for *initiative* earmarks in California. Prior to 1988, the highest number of initiative earmarks on the ballot was three. Not only was the most consequential earmark ever, Proposition 98, on the ballot in 1988, but there were five others as well, including Proposition 10, which raised tobacco taxes and directed the revenue to health services and tobacco prevention. In the wake of 1988, another eight initiative earmarks appeared on the ballot in 1990, and the higher frequency rate became common in subsequent elections. Although most accounts point to 1978 as the genesis for the renewed interest in the initiative process as a potent tool of non-legislative policymaking, and there was a small surge in initiatives thereafter, 1988 appears to be a more pivotal point. What happened to set this initiative frenzy in motion?

As alluded to earlier, it is likely that the deep and widespread effects of Proposition 13 eroded funding for state and local government services enough to force program advocates (i.e., teachers) to seek funding protections outside of the normal legislative process. The spending limit imposed by Proposition 4, the Gann initiative, also played a role since it triggered a tax rebate and prevented funding increases for schools and other programs. Schrag points out that the sponsorship of Proposition 98 was a direct result of this tax rebate. "In response to Deukmejian's decision to refund the tax money, much of which would have gone to school support—and well before Proposition 71 failed—[Superintendent of Public Schools] Honig and the well-heeled California Teachers Association had spent $1.3 million to qualify" what would become Proposition 98.[27] Once it passed, other program advocates saw the initiative process as the only effective way to ensure funding support.

Who Is Behind Initiatives?

While the legislature is the source for about two-thirds of measures on the ballot historically, contrary to popular belief, no one group dominates among initiative sponsors. Early in the initiative era, political scientists V. O. Key and Winston Crouch remarked that "Virtually every type of interest-group has on occasion used the instrument."[28] This has remained the case in recent decades as well.

Then, as now, the initiative has also primarily been used as a tool to circumvent the legislative process when advocates did not attain their goals

---

[27] Peter Schrag, *Paradise Lost: California's Experience, America's Future* (Berkeley: University of California Press, 2004), 164.

[28] Key and Crouch, *The Initiative and Referendum*, 458.

through the legislative process or were on the receiving end of unfavorable policies. For instance, the legislature was well aware of widespread homeowner discontent over escalating property taxes in the late 1960s and 1970s prior to enactment of Proposition 13. Numerous bills were debated to grant homeowners taxpayer relief, but were usually thwarted by Democrats who wanted more income redistribution or Republicans who argued the bills did not do enough. By 1978, after two earlier failed initiative attempts, Howard Jarvis, the sponsor of Proposition 13, and his supporters were able to capitalize on homeowner frustrations with legislative inaction.

While no one industry or group has dominated sponsorship of ballot initiatives, the "average citizen" does not ordinarily make use of the process. Despite Progressive reformers envisioning this type of activism by ordinary citizens, money and organization have been the two major factors driving sponsorship. While some campaigns in the early years did qualify measures without them, paid signature-gatherers have been used since the first initiative campaigns. Nowadays, paid signature gatherers, under the supervision of petition management consultants, are essential to any modern initiative effort. Once sponsors have or raise around $2 million to support the signature qualification phase, depending on the type of measure and potential opposition, an effective campaign requires several million additional dollars, and sometimes up to tens of millions. The entire cost of initiative sponsorship is why initiatives tend to be out of reach for the average citizen.

Given the resources necessary for initiatives, sponsors tend to be labor unions, business groups, good government groups, and wealthy policy entrepreneurs. Ironically, elected officials have also been among the primary initiative sponsors. From 1966 to 1988, one-third of all initiatives were sponsored by elected officials.[29] Aspiring gubernatorial candidates or governors themselves have frequently been behind such initiatives, especially when the latter met resistance to their agenda in the legislature. Governors Reagan (R), Deukmejian (R), Wilson (R), and Jerry Brown (D - 2012) all sponsored or backed fiscal initiative campaigns. Threatening to use the ballot box as a way to secure budget priorities has become a regular feature of the budget dance between the governor and legislature. Schwarzenegger employed them with success early on in his administration, while Brown has similarly enjoyed some early success.

Although it is too early to tell if it is an increasing trend, several wealthy individuals played an active role in the initiative battles of 2012. Molly Munger, a civil-rights attorney and heir to billionaire Charles Munger, sponsored and bankrolled her own tax initiative (Proposition 38) that competed for attention and votes with Governor Brown's Proposition 30. Her brother, Charles Munger Jr., also a multimillionaire, spent over $35 million opposing Proposition 30 and supporting Proposition 32, a business-backed initiative to restrict political spending by labor unions and some businesses. Another multimillionaire, Tom

---

[29] Charles Bell and Charles Price, "Are Ballot Measures the Magic Ride to Success?" *California Journal*, September (1988): 380–81.

Steyer, a hedge fund manager and Democratic activist, "almost single-handedly paid for the entire Proposition 39 campaign." The proposition, which passed, generates $1 billion for the general fund by changing the tax formula for out-of-state businesses.[30] Overall, of the six fiscal propositions on the ballot in 2012, five were affiliated with significant funding or sponsorship from wealthy individuals.

Campaign Spending

Conventional wisdom would suggest that proposition supporters or opponents with the deepest pockets always prevail. We assume that these well-financed campaigns can purchase airtime on television and radio stations and mass distribute direct mailers with carefully crafted and tested messages. Initial research on the effects of campaign spending found that one-sided opposition spending had a significant impact on vote outcomes, but that one-sided support spending did not.[31] More recent research, however, suggests that the spending effect is roughly even for both sides, with a slightly stronger impact for opposition spending.[32] Additionally, spending in ballot measure campaigns exhibits a pattern of diminishing marginal returns; that is, at a certain point, each additional dollar spent produces fewer and fewer votes for the opponent or supporters. This type of pattern is not surprising because campaign spending in candidate races has demonstrated this effect for several decades.[33]

Overall, initiative measures tend to generate higher spending than legislative referrals. One recent study reported that from 1976 to 2004, supporters spent on average $3.6 million for initiatives, while opponents spent $2.4 million against them.[34] For legislative measures, the pro side averaged $478,406, while the con side spent $220,273. One possible explanation for the discrepancy in spending between initiative and legislative measures may be that potential opponents' concerns have been addressed by the time a bill surmounts the two-thirds vote threshold in the legislature. To reach this point, a bill for a constitutional amendment or bond measure must have a broad ranging coalition behind it. This was especially true when Republican votes were required to meet the

---

[30] "The Ballot's Millionaires and Billionaires," *Los Angeles Times*, November 5, 2012. Available at http://latimesblogs.latimes.com/california-politics/2012/11/the-ballots-millionares-and-billionares.html.

[31] See for example, Daniel Lowenstein, "Campaign Spending and Ballot Propositions: Recent Experience, Public Choice Theory and the First Amendment," *UCLA Law Review* 29, no. 3 (1982): 505–641; David Magelby, *Direct Legislation: Voting on Ballot Propositions in the United States* (Baltimore: The Johns Hopkins University Press, 1984).

[32] John M. de Figueiredo, Chang Ho Ji, and Thad Kousser, "Financing Direct Democracy: Revisiting the Research on Campaign Spending and Citizen Initiatives," *The Journal of Law, Economics, & Organization* 27, no. 3 (2011): 485–514.

[33] Gary Jacobson's *Money and Congressional Elections* is the seminal book on this topic. Gary C. Jacobson, *Money and Congressional Elections* (New Haven, CT: Yale University Press, 1980).

[34] de Figueiredo, Ji, and Kousser, "Financing Direct Democracy," 490.

two-thirds threshold. With little opposition spending, the measure's supporters do not need to spend as much to counteract the opposition's messaging. In some cases, there might not be *any* opposition. For instance, a bond package that emerged from the legislature in 2006 faced no registered opposition (Propositions 1B, 1C, 1D, and 1E). Furthermore, legislative measures may be initially popular with the public anyway, which is why lawmakers may be more receptive to them in the first place. On the other hand, since initiative measures require significant funding to qualify for the ballot (i.e., paid signature-gathering), it is likely that the sponsors also have the resources to mount a serious campaign in support of it and fend off potentially well-financed opponents.

The Role of Public Opinion
        The initiative and referendum have always been wildly popular with the public. In 1911, 76 percent of California voters supported the ballot measure to adopt them. Surveys of the 50 states reveal at least a majority in each state supports the initiative and referendum and, for many states, support is over 60 percent of the public.[35] According to a recent Public Policy Institute of California poll, 72 percent of Californians thought the initiative was a good thing for the state.[36] An overwhelming majority (79 percent) also believes that voters should make *some* budget decisions, while only 16 percent feel the governor and legislature should make *all* the decisions.[37] Despite the shortcomings of direct democracy, particularly California's version (discussed more below), the evidence is clear that citizen legislating is here to stay. Policymakers and government reformers alike realize this, which is why modifications to the initiative process have rarely been proposed in recent decades, as opposed to the first decades under the process.

        From the time an idea emerges for a ballot measure to the results on election night, concerns over public opinion are ever-present in ballot-box budgeting. Legislative and initiative measures are spawned from initial polling results showing a strong majority of the public in favor of a given proposal. For the 2006 bond measures mentioned above, Schwarzenegger capitalized on strong public support for infrastructure spending by pushing them in his state of the state speech and, in the process, rode their popularity to a second term. In another instance, public support for changing the two-thirds vote requirement to a simple majority had hovered in the mid-40s for years prior to its passage in 2010 (Proposition 25). An earlier measure to change to a lower threshold fell 16 percent short in 2004 (Proposition 56). However, after a decade of crisis budgeting and perpetual gridlock, public support began to hover around 50 percent and

---

[35] M. Dane Waters, *Initiative and Referendum Almanac* (Durham, NC: Carolina Academic Press, 2003), 477.
        [36] Public Policy Institute of California Statewide Survey, *Californians and Their Government* (San Francisco: Public Policy Institute of California, March 2013).
        [37] Public Policy Institute of California Statewide Survey, *Californians and Their Government* (San Francisco: Public Policy Institute of California, September 2012).

over in 2009 after a tumultuous budget year, signaling to advocates to strike while the iron was hot. Proposition 25 passed with 55 percent of the vote. In 2011, Jerry Brown doggedly pursued Republican votes to place a tax measure on the ballot because opinion polls showed that the public supported the *extension* of income and sales tax increases already on the books, while the same surveys showed support dropping off when *new* tax increases were proposed.

There is a widely held belief among polling experts and commentators that initial support for a ballot measure must be above 55 percent for the measure to have a chance to pass come election day. This is because historically support for a measure usually drops over the course of a campaign when voters learn more about the measure and the opposition campaign ramps up its critique of the measure. Polling evidence largely backs this belief. In Field Polls between 1978 and 2006, there were only three propositions out of 150 where the initial poll showed the measure behind, but the proposition went on to pass.[38] One of these cases occurred in 2004 when the legislature and newly elected Governor Schwarzenegger placed a $15 billion bond measure on the ballot to help close the budget deficit. In a January 2004 Field Poll, only 33 percent of respondents indicated support for Proposition 57, while 40 percent intended to vote no. In one of the largest and quickest swings in public opinion in state history, Schwarzenegger's action-hero status and initial popularity managed to turn the tide; 50 percent of respondents supported the measure by the end of February. It passed with an overwhelming 63 percent of the vote.

One challenge that ballot measure proponents face is voter awareness and knowledge of a given proposition. The main goal of a proposition campaign is to reach voters who will participate and cast a favorable vote towards their side. This objective starts with awareness of the measure. Surveys measure this by asking voters if they have "ever heard or seen anything about proposition x." Whether one answers this question in the affirmative depends on a number of factors. Generally, survey organizations only inquire about awareness for controversial and highly salient measures. At the individual level, awareness increases as income and education levels rise. The context of a given election also influences the level of voter awareness.[39] A midterm election, proximity to election day, opposition campaign spending, and the type of issue all impact voter awareness. Regarding types of issues, awareness is usually higher when propositions are intuitive to understand and tap into moral issues or civil rights and liberties topics.

Voter familiarity can range quite widely for different propositions. In budget-related propositions from 1956–2000 where survey respondents were asked about their awareness, the lowest level was 25 percent for Proposition 218 in

---

[38] Eugene C. Lee, "The Initiative Boom: An Excess of Democracy," in *Governing California: Politics, Government, and Public Policy in the Golden State*, ed. Gerald C. Lubenow (Berkeley: Institute of Governmental Studies Press, 2006), 145.

[39] Stephen Nicholson, "The Political Environment and Ballot Awareness," *American Journal of Political Science* 47, no. 3 (2003): 403–10.

1996, which changed voting requirements for local governments, while the highest level of familiarity (95 percent) was for Proposition 11 in 1982, which required a deposit for bottled drinks. Other measures that voters were most familiar with included the state lottery, Proposition 37 in 1984 (93 percent), and school vouchers, Proposition 38 in 2000 (88 percent).[40] We should note that the survey question asks about awareness and does not measure whether a respondent understands the proposition. With this in mind, the common link among the more familiar measures is the extent to which potential voters intuitively understand an issue (an easy issue) and whether it impacts their daily life.

Ballot Box Success

Most sponsors and supporters of ballot measures are concerned with the outcome of their efforts. We say "most" because some counterproposals are placed on the ballot to subvert other measures, potentially sinking both of them. Governor Brown and the legislature scrambled to produce a countermeasure to Proposition 13 in 1978, Proposition 8, hoping that if it did not pass, then at least both would go down. Those types of cases are more the exception than the rule. Sponsors usually do not undertake a political battle in the legislature or a costly public campaign unless they have some confidence that their measures will pass. For authors of legislative measures, their odds are relatively high for passage once the measure reaches the ballot, while initiative sponsors must prepare themselves for a much higher failure rate.

Overall, slightly less than 60 percent of fiscal propositions pass. However, the much higher passage rate for legislative measures of 68 percent is pulling the much lower 34 percent rate for initiatives up. These passage rates have remained stable over time and are usually attributed to two factors. First, proposed legislative measures go through a rigorous review and amendment process in the legislature before they are placed on the ballot. Bills with substantial flaws or fatal provisions will not likely make it past committee hearings or public scrutiny. Second, to secure the two-thirds vote necessary for referral to the ballot, a broad coalition of lawmakers and stakeholders must be assembled for legislative passage. Any substantial opposition may be avoided at this point by incorporating concessions or engaging in veiled bribery in the form of pork barreling or some other "policy benefit." The drafting of initiative measures is not subject to the same level of legislative and public scrutiny, which makes fatal flaws more likely. Even initiatives that pass are neutered by subsequent court decisions at the "adjudication stage" or state agencies undermining their intent at the "implementation stage" of the initiative process.[41] The threshold for legislative referrals thus ensures a high level of consensus and political support from key stakeholders, like legislative leaders, before they are subject to popular vote.

---

[40] *Ibid.*

[41] Elisabeth Gerber, Arthur Lupia, Mathew D. McCubbins, and D. Roderick Kiewiet, *Stealing the Initiative: How State Government Responds to Direct Democracy* (Upper Saddle River, NJ: Prentice Hall, 2001).

When we review the passage rates of fiscal propositions by source and type, it becomes clearer why initiative earmarks have been popular tools for sponsors in recent decades. Initiative earmarks have been approved at a much higher rate than other types of measures. Forty-one percent of initiative earmarks have passed, while budget process initiatives have passed at a much lower rate of 28 percent. Surprisingly, TEL initiatives have little success at the ballot box, as only two have ever been passed and those were the well-known Propositions 13 and 4 (Gann initiative). The approval rates for legislative measures do not vary much by type. All categories have a 50 percent or higher passage rate, with budget process measures passing at the lowest rate of 58 percent. (See Table 5.3.)

One variable that scholars have identified as important to the passage of fiscal propositions is the economy. Bowler and Donovan found that stronger economic conditions increase the likelihood that bond measures pass.[42] Apparently, voters feel more confident that the state can afford to borrow for infrastructure projects when economic conditions are healthy, perhaps akin to the wealth effect that can drive consumer spending when home equity values rise. On the flip side, a poor economy may provide the impetus for initiative sponsors to seek budget earmarks. Concerned with declining revenues from an economic downturn, an earmark is one way to secure more stable funding levels and perhaps even increase them.

Analysis and Implications

Much criticism has been directed at ballot-box budgeting and particularly the role of the initiative process in it. Direct democracy has been considered a threat to republican government because it usurps the powers of the legislative branch. For budgeting, the initiative adds a third party to the negotiations between the executive and legislative branches. Not only do policymakers have to consider the immediate priorities of their respective branches, but they also must consider whether to go to the ballot with certain budget solutions because of the constraints imposed by previous propositions. In this section, we analyze the impact of ballot-box budgeting on the state's budget process and the ability of the state to manage its budget effectively.

Earmarking

One of the most often debated topics concerning ballot-box budgeting is earmarking. As noted above, earmarking activity has surged in recent decades, removing revenue streams or some portion of them from the table each year in budget talks and specifying how much should be spent on certain programs and services. In effect, earmarking takes over part of the job that the governor and

---

[42] Shaun Bowler and Todd Donovan, *Demanding Choices: Opinion, Voting, and Direct Democracy* (Ann Arbor: The University of Michigan Press, 1998).

Table 5.3. Passage Rates for Fiscal Propositions by Source and Type, 1911–2012

Type	Leg. Measures % (N)	Initiatives % (N)	All % (N)
Earmark	74(155)	41 (35)	64(190)
Tax	65 (90)	17 (5)	57 (95)
Budget Process	58 (38)	28 (8)	48 (46)
TEL	75 (3)	14 (2)	28 (5)
Total	68 (286)	34 (50)	60 (336)

Note: N=Number passed.

legislature are supposed to do each year. Although commentators usually point to the initiative process as the culprit behind earmarking, the legislature's earmarking activity has been prolific, especially when we consider bond measures. Legislative earmarking can be just as consequential as that arising from initiatives—both limit the discretion of future policymakers and reduce options for addressing changing state priorities.

Proposition 98 is usually viewed as the archetypal initiative earmark that spawned the frenzy of subsequent initiative-driven carve-outs, but it was the culmination in a long line of education earmarks that set school spending levels. In 1920, voters overwhelmingly approved Proposition 16, which added kindergarten to the public school system, required a minimum of $30 in state per-pupil spending, and authorized higher county property taxes. Subsequent measures in 1944, 1946, and 1952 all received strong voter support and increased funding for schools. Proposition 3 in 1946 even set a minimum salary for teachers of $2,400 that is still enshrined in the constitution. Ironically, Proposition 98 received the lowest level of voter approval of any of the education earmarks that passed, barely slipping by with 50.7 percent. Aside from education, some success with transportation earmarks, and bonds, which have always enjoyed strong voter support, success with earmarks in other program areas did not really blossom until Proposition 98.

Researchers and practitioners have long debated the extent to which the state budget is "locked in" by earmarking.[43] In 1950, Winston Crouch remarked

---

[43] John W. Ellwood and Mary Sprague, "Options for Reforming the California State Budget Process," in *Constitutional Reform in California: Making State Government More Effective and Responsive*, ed. Bruce E. Cain and Roger G. Noll (Berkeley: Institute of Governmental Studies Press, 1995), 329–52; John Decker, *California in the Balance:*

that "California already has too much earmarking of funds and not sufficient flexibility in its state budget."[44] These claims, however, depend on what types of expenditures and revenues are included in the definition of earmarking. A more expansive definition of what is "locked in" leads to a higher estimate of earmarks, while a narrow definition yields a lower estimate. If we include caseload-driven programs in the tally, such as Medi-Cal and state prisons, then a high percentage of the budget is considered inflexible. In 1990, Winkler and Chapman, relying on estimates of the Legislative Analyst's Office, reported that "as much as 70 percent of the state's general fund budget is now statutorily or constitutionally earmarked for designated programs."[45] In a more recent study of voter-passed initiatives, Matsusaka concluded that about 33 percent of the state budget was cordoned off by such measures.[46]

What ultimately matters for budgeting purposes in this debate is how much discretion state policymakers are left with when all of these fiscal commitments, initiatives or otherwise, are taken into account. Since Matsusaka focuses only on voter initiatives, his accounting does not consider legislative measures, such as Propositions 172 and 42, which also permanently dedicate pots of money. Aside from voter-approved propositions, some federally supported programs require maintenance-of-effort spending commitments on the part of the state that also reduce discretion if policymakers wish to continue to receive federal funds. However, one important thing to remember about the source of earmarking, whether it be from propositions, caseload-driven programs, or federal requirements, is that those commitments imposed by propositions tend to be the hardest to modify because most changes are subject to voter approval. Policymakers can change the eligibility criteria for certain programs or withdraw from federal programs without voter approval.

Earmarking critics often focus their attention on the role of ballot-box budgeting for two reasons. First, in recent decades, proposition-related earmarks have been accumulating at a fast pace (see Figure 5.2). And second, their semi-permanent nature creates a "snowball effect" whereby the snowball, or total constraints, adds more and more layers as it moves from election to election. The accumulation of these constraints increasingly limits the policy options the governor and legislative leaders have to develop a budget plan each year. This

---

Why Budgets Matter (Berkeley: Berkeley Public Policy Press, 2009); John G. Matsusaka, "A Case Study on Direct Democracy: Have Voter Initiatives Paralyzed the California Budget," in *Book of the States* (Lexington: The Council of State Governments, 2010), 337-342; John G. Matsusaka, "Direct Democracy and Fiscal Gridlock: Have Voter Initiatives Paralyzed the California Budget," *State Politics and Policy Quarterly* 5, no. 3 (2005): 248–64.

[44] Winston W. Crouch, *The Initiative and Referendum in California*, (Los Angeles: The Haynes Foundation, 1950), 39.

[45] Donald R. Winkler and Jeffrey I. Chapman, "Earmarked Revenues and Fiscal Constraints," in *California Policy Choices* vol. 6, ed. John J. Kirlin and Donald R. Winkler (Sacramento: University of Southern California, 1990), 12.

[46] Matsusaka, "A Case Study."

became the primary complaint against earmarks particularly during the crisis budgeting era when state leaders were searching for options to close budget deficits.

Aside from limiting discretion, earmarks protect funding for programs that are potentially ineffective or are low priorities. Because policymakers know that earmarked funding will flow to its purpose no matter what they do, there is less incentive for them to rigorously evaluate these programs. Thus, legislators focus their review efforts on programs without protected streams of funding in order to divert that money to another cause.

One positive side of earmarking measures is that sometimes they create a *new* stream of revenue to support *new* program spending. For instance, the tobacco tax measures, Propositions 99 (1988) and 10 (1998), direct money toward health, tobacco prevention, and childhood development programs, but they also authorize new revenue to support these programs. This is in contrast to other measures, such as Proposition 49 in 2002, which dedicates funding to after-school programs, but does not authorize new revenue to support it. Earmarks with no new source of revenue only erode the capacity of the general fund to support existing programs and services. Some states avoid this by requiring new funding sources for new programs, often referred to as a pay-as-you-go provision, or PAYGO. When voters see new taxes coupled with program spending, they generally view these programs more favorably than new taxes not coupled to specific programs. This link provides some assurance to voters that their hard-earned tax dollars will not be wasted and potentially go to a program they despise. Better yet, if the funding goes toward a program the voter will benefit from (the benefits-received approach; see Chapter 3), he or she is likely to vote for it. In their studies of voting behavior on fiscal measures, Bowler and Donovan generally conclude that voters cast ballots with self-interest in mind, particularly if their geographic area will benefit from the program.[47] Unfortunately, earmark propositions are not always accompanied with a new funding source.

On the downside, earmarks, even with new sources of revenue, lead to piecemeal budgeting (described below) and deplete a potential revenue source that could be used to shore up existing programs or services or fund higher prioritized *new* programs. If voters are given more options for how that new source of revenue could be spent, they might not support the program specified in the proposition as much as another.

Loss of Budget Accountability

As discussed in Chapter 2, the chaotic and haphazard authorization of state spending at the turn of the 20th century led to the creation of the executive budget, widely regarded as a vast improvement in fiscal administration. It provided a single point of responsibility, the executive branch, for proposing and implementing the budget, and an institutionalized process for legislative review

---

[47] Bowler and Donovan, *Demanding Choices*, 104.

and modification. With these institutional roles, the traditional view is that the executive should bear the brunt of accountability for fiscal outcomes and, to a lesser degree, the legislature should be blamed as well. Ballot-box budgeting obscures this accountability in two ways. First, the initiative process adds a third "institution" and second track to the budget process. In a glaring contradiction, the public expects the governor and legislature to work out the budget each year since that is what they are sent to Sacramento to do, yet the public believes voters should make some of the big decisions. The governor and legislative leaders must then contend with the constraints imposed on them by previous propositions, such as special fund restrictions, high vote thresholds, and earmarks. In addition, whereas legislative review of the executive budget is intended to allow for careful scrutiny and analysis of the governor's proposals, the initiative, or second budgeting track, is not subject to this scrutiny nor are the sponsors held accountable for policies or programs authorized by the initiative. Instead, elected policymakers must put the remaining pieces of the budgeting puzzle together.

The second way ballot-box budgeting obscures accountability is similar to the first, but the legislature itself is to blame. For much of California's history the legislature has been the most frequent source of fiscal propositions. In recent decades, initiatives have overtaken legislative measures, but the latter still hamstring policymakers as well. In this case, legislators from decades or even a generation ago have referred measures to the ballot that affect budgeting in myriad ways. One of the most consequential examples is the two-thirds vote requirement to pass the budget that was on the books from 1933 until 2010. Its genesis was the Riley-Stewart amendment, a legislative measure that was subsequently modified by another "innocuous" clean-up of the constitution sponsored by the legislature in 1962. The combination of these two decisions tethered legislators to an extremely high vote threshold to pass the budget that eventually led to gridlock that lasted over half a century. Because of the high vote threshold, both the majority and minority party in the legislature had to approve annual budgets. As a result, each faction in budget negotiations (the governor, majority party, and minority party) blamed the other for poorly constructed budgets, which left lines of accountability unclear for voters.

Overall, both initiatives and legislative measures have reduced discretion on budgetary matters and instituted procedures that do not facilitate accountability. To induce greater accountability, the proposition-generated body of law would have to be unraveled so that a higher level of budget authority could be restored to the executive and legislative branches.

Piecemeal Budgeting

One of the major detrimental effects of ballot-box budgeting is that it violates one of the main principles of sound budgeting—prioritizing. As discussed in Chapter 1, the budget process allows policymakers to deliberate the state's funding priorities given available resources. When voters are presented with one or more fiscal measures at election time, each of these measures is evaluated within a vacuum; that is, voters must give an up or down vote without considering competing priorities. For instance, when voters were considering Proposition 184, the "three strikes" initiative, in 1994, the voting guide from the secretary of state's office did not point out that the measure would increase prison costs from higher incarceration rates *at the expense* of funding for state universities. In other words, with each proposition, voters are not explicitly confronted with the tradeoffs of their decisions and the zero-sum nature of budgeting. The same principle applies to tax-and-earmark measures such as Proposition 10 (tobacco tax increase) or Proposition 63 (income tax increase). Although both of these measures identified a funding source for their program expenditures, as opposed to a straight earmark, voters (or legislators) may have chosen to spend the revenue on other programs, besides childhood development (Proposition 10) and mental health services (Proposition 63). Voters make choices at the ballot box on these measures—in a yes or no sense—but they do not get choices between different programs and services.

The semi-permanent nature of approved measures also distorts the state's priorities over the short and long run. Once a funding priority is "locked in," this "priority" cannot be changed easily since any modification is subject to a popular vote. These priorities may not change from election to election, or even over several elections, but they are likely to change over a decade or longer, especially with the multitude of measures in the last few decades. In contrast, the process in the legislature allows lawmakers to choose *between* priorities and to *adjust* these priorities as needs and demands change.

The Competence of Citizen Legislators

From the very beginning, opponents of the initiative decried voters' ability to make sound judgments about major policy issues. "[T]he system of [direct democracy] is vicious and dangerous, affording an opportunity, as it does, of forcing a vote upon crude, ill-advised and possibly dishonest laws, which, through the ignorance or indifference of the voters, may become effective."[48] After a few decades of the initiative process, close observers writing in 1939 did not share this fear and opined that there was little difference in the decision-making capacity of ordinary voters and legislators. "The elector in his capacity as legislator listens to, and reads, arguments on measures and becomes about as well-informed concerning the general object of the initiative measure as the average member of the legislature is on most bills brought before that body."[49] Modern accounts of voter competence are not quite as optimistic in their assessments of voters' abilities, but they are also not as worrisome as some early opponents predicted.

---

[48] Henry Campbell, "The Initiative and Referendum," *Michigan Law Review* 10, no. 6 (1911): 431, quoted in Bowler and Donovan, *Demanding Choices*, 19.
[49] Key and Crouch, *The Initiative and Referendum*, 443.

Recent studies show that voters use the ballot pamphlet for information on measures and can make what appear to be informed decisions even when they lack detailed knowledge of particular measures. In the case of the latter, voters use cues from proponents and opponents to discern whether or not their views align with the intent of the measure. If an organization or person that the voter is familiar with and likes backs a proposition, then that voter will likely support the measure. At the same time, voters must resort to these information shortcuts because they may not fully understand the measure or even the summary of the measure in the ballot pamphlet, which is supposed to help voters. Magelby showed that the official description is the least readable part of the ballot pamphlet and that it required a third-year college student to understand it.[50] As we might suspect, educational background is the key factor behind how well informed a given voter is and whether consistent choices are made across different issues. Well-educated voters are more likely to use multiple sources beyond the ballot pamphlet to inform their decision, while less educated, nonwhite voters are more likely to cast confused ballots.[51]

The comparison between the average voter and legislator is probably not a fair one anyway. Legislators are elected and paid to study critical issues facing the state full time, whereas ordinary citizens, with their own full-time jobs and daily demands, do not have the time to educate themselves the way legislators do. The average citizen does not have the benefit of the deliberative process that occurs in legislative committees and on chamber floors that educates lawmakers on the merits of a proposal. Without access to and time for structured discussions, ballot measures place a considerable burden on voters if they wish to cast an informed decision. A big part of this burden arises from the complicated and confusing nature of ballot measures themselves, which are often poorly worded and misunderstood by the most seasoned policy analyst, and frequently overturned by the courts.

In a 1990 *Los Angeles Times* poll, 84 percent of respondents agreed that the average voter cannot make an intelligent choice.[52] Despite this general feeling among the public, the initiative process remains extremely popular with voters and is unlikely to change. Given this sentiment, it means that the deleterious effects of ballot-box budgeting can only be mitigated through reforms to the direct democracy process.

Reforming Ballot-Box Budgeting

Most of the efforts directed at curtailing the effects of ballot-box budgeting revolve around reforms to the initiative process rather than the legislative referral process. If indeed the goal is to limit ballot-box budgeting, then it is logical to look first to the main source of fiscal propositions, the legislature, for potential

---

[50] Magelby, *Direct Legislation*, 138.

[51] *Ibid.*, 137, 143.

[52] Simmons, "California's Statewide Initiative," 16.

solutions. However, its role in potential reforms is usually ignored. Such reform efforts may be fruitless because state constitutional and statutory law related to fiscal policy and direct democracy are so intertwined that it may be impossible to untangle without a constitutional convention. In addition, reform efforts may be extremely difficult because the initiative process is very popular with voters. Nevertheless, one potential way to limit ballot-box budgeting and address some of the deleterious effects discussed above would be to place bond approval authority solely under the province of the legislature and governor. Since bond measures have accounted for the lion's share of fiscal propositions, such a change would severely reduce the number of fiscal propositions on the ballot moving forward. It would also increase the legislature's responsibility and accountability for fiscal policy. Experienced legislators who are educated on such matters would be better positioned and prepared to decide long-term financial commitments of the state, compared to ordinary voters who are infrequently exposed to public discourse on the topic and do not have statewide perspective on budget priorities. Of course, it may be politically unfeasible to wrest control of borrowing authority from voters, particularly given the high levels of distrust in government.

To severely reduce ballot-box budgeting, the state could also prohibit or restrict tax changes and appropriations made through ballot measures. Eight of 24 states have similar provisions in their initiative process.[53] For example, Montana prohibits any appropriation by initiative, while Wyoming specifically proscribes earmarks and making or repealing appropriations. Some states also have PAYGO provisions, referred to earlier, which prevent appropriations through the initiative process without a new tax sufficient to cover the expenditure. These types of restrictions in California would likely drive down the number of measures approved by voters and prevent the deterioration of the general fund. Had one or more of these reforms been in place earlier in the state's history, crisis budgeting would have been less frequent and severe.

Conclusion

Since the late 19th century, ballot-box budgeting, to varying degrees, has been part of the state's political process. The legislature increasingly referred fiscal measures, mainly involving taxes, to the voters for their consideration even before the adoption of the initiative process. Once adopted, the initiative process moderately increased the number of fiscal measures on the ballot, but legislative referrals remained the primary source until the 1980s, when the transition to an initiative-dominant ballot began to emerge. Despite their widespread popularity and notoriety in California and elsewhere, initiatives pass at a far lower rate than legislative measures, although initiative success has been on the rise in recent decades.

---

[53] Waters, *Initiative and Referendum Almanac*, 18.

Ballot-box budgeting raises a number of concerns about effective budgeting and brings to light the dilemma inherent in an enhanced role for the public in democratic budgeting. Overwhelmingly, Californians consistently believe that they should make some of the state's budget decisions. However, citizens at the voting booth lack a statewide perspective on fiscal matters and are not exposed to the deliberative process that educates members of the legislature. Because of the accumulation of fiscal constraints and earmarks imposed on state policy-makers by voters, the governor and legislative leaders, in times of budget crisis, have few alternatives but to seek the input and imprimatur of voters for certain options. In 2009, when state leaders faced perhaps the pinnacle of crisis budgeting in the last century, they sought the approval of voters for five fiscal propositions to ease the budget crunch. Despite unusually high levels of bipartisan support in the legislature to place these measures on the ballot, all five were soundly rejected at the polls, as if voters were saying, "it's your job to fix the budget." But given the numerous constraints imposed at the ballot box, and the public's continuing desire to weigh in on at least some budgetary decisions, state policymakers may have to increasingly return to voters to keep the state's budget afloat.

Review Questions

1. How has ballot-box budgeting evolved over time and how has the role of the initiative process affected the budgeting capacity of state policymakers?

2. Why did legislative measures dominate ballot-box budgeting for a century and why did initiatives eventually become more predominant?

3. Why has earmarking become a popular tool for program advocates and budget stakeholders?

4. How does ballot-box budgeting help or hinder the ability of state policymakers to budget each year and plan for future state needs?

Additional Resources

UC Hastings Law Library Ballot Propositions Database

http://library.uchastings.edu/research/online-research/ca-research.php

The website has the most comprehensive database of ballot propositions with information on ballot pamphlets on all elections going back to 1911.

Initiative and Referendum Institute, University of Southern California

http://www.iandrinstitute.org/

The website has information on the history and procedures for initiatives and referendums and data on ballot measures for all initiative states.

Legislative Analyst's Office Ballot Proposition Database

http://www.lao.ca.gov/laoapp/

Their website includes fiscal analyses for all submissions and qualified ballot measures. The site also has a list of proposition-related publications and historical data on the source of measures.

Secretary of State's Ballot Measure Website

http://www.sos.ca.gov/elections/elections_j.htm

The site has comprehensive information on voting guides, election results, and historical information on all types of measures. It also has the status of pending measures.

Chapter 6

The Budget Environment:
The Media, Interest Groups, and the Public

> It's amazing how many conversations about the budget process with my Republican colleagues start with a mention of John and Ken.
>
> —Senate President Pro Temp Darrell Steinberg in 2011 referring to the John and Ken radio show in Los Angeles.[1]

> They didn't want to know what the bills said. The only question I was asked was, 'Where is CTA [California Teachers Association] on this?'
>
> —former state Senator and Education Committee chairwoman Gloria Romero referring to her colleagues about potential education reforms.[2]

In 2009, seeking to address a $40 billion deficit, the governor and legislative leaders negotiated a budget package that included a tax increase on sales and personal incomes and higher vehicle license fees (VLF). The package also authorized a special election in May to place a measure on the ballot (Proposition 1A) to extend these tax increases for another two years and adopt a new state spending limit. Voters roundly rejected this tax measure when 65 percent of the electorate opposed it. Just three years later, in 2012, Governor Jerry Brown (D) led an effort to place another initiative, Proposition 30, on the ballot to raise sales and income taxes to help close a $12 billion budget shortfall. That measure

---

[1] Quoted in John Diaz, "John and Ken Spread Fear and Loathing in Capitol," *San Francisco Chronicle*, March 26, 2011.

[2] Quoted in Michael Mishak, "California Teachers Assn. a Powerful Force in Sacramento," *Los Angeles Times*, August 18, 2012.

surprisingly passed with 55 percent of the vote even though a competing tax measure, Proposition 38, was expected to siphon off support for any tax increase.

Why did one measure to increase taxes fail and another pass a short time later? There are several reasons. In 2009, Governor Arnold Schwarzenegger (R) was nearing the end of his term and had been unsuccessful at turning the fiscal situation around, which led to low approval ratings and little influence with the public. The combination of a tax increase and a spending limit in the same measure made for strange bedfellows among normally opposed interest groups: some liberal groups opposed it because of the spending limit, while others supported the revenue increase. Some business groups opposed the tax increase, while others supported the spending limit. In addition, the effects of severe budget cuts had not hit the public yet as much as they would a few years later.

By the time voters considered Proposition 30 in 2012, these characteristics were largely reversed. Brown was in his second full year as governor and maintained a decent approval rating in the high 40s. Unions provided strong support for the measure, while business groups remained neutral on the sidelines, with a few even offering lukewarm support. After a few years of shortened school years, class reductions at colleges and universities, and other budget cuts, the public mood was more ripe for potential tax increases. From a broader perspective, we can see that the political environment surrounding these tax policy decisions was different in 2012 than it had been in 2009.

In this chapter, we examine the political environment in which budgetary policy is made by state policymakers and voters. We first focus on the media since it provides the primary link between the general public and government. The media functions as a conduit and filter of information that serves to frame the budget's status for the public. Reports of the effects of budget cuts on ordinary citizens or of egregious cases of government fraud or abuse form impressions in the minds of voters that influence their willingness to support or oppose various budget options. In the second section, we discuss the role of the public in fiscal policymaking and analyze public opinion on budgetary matters. To a certain extent, a shift in public sentiment can ease budget pressure as it did in 2012 or send state policymakers back to the negotiating table to come up with more acceptable policy alternatives. In the last section, we investigate the role of interest groups in the budget process and the pressure they bring to bear on budgetary objectives. The overarching question addressed in this chapter is how these components of the political environment shape budget outcomes.

The Media

The Project for Excellence in Journalism at the Pew Research Center tallies weekly the nation's top stories circulating on Facebook and Twitter. In May of 2009, the New Media Index reported that "the No. 1 story in social media was the California financial crisis and the voters' rejection of ballot measures designed to deal with the problem."[3] The fact that the California budget was the top news story from the index reveals two points about the nature of the current media environment and the state budget. First, it is not uncommon for the California budget to make national news. Unfortunately, during the recent crisis budgeting era, national news outlets, such as the *New York Times* or *Wall Street Journal*, consistently reported on the dire situation of the state budget. Second, the index report also emphasizes how the public is consuming and transmitting state news in new ways. In this case, the index indicated that much of the chatter came from conservatives crowing about the defeat of tax increases and the message voters were presumably sending to state policymakers. Here we describe the basic layout of the media landscape in more detail and how it relates to the California budget.

Media Landscape

The media landscape in California and the country has changed dramatically with the widespread use of the internet. Gone are the days when the average news consumer could rely solely on their morning newspaper or the local five o'clock television newscast. For policymakers, government workers, and political stakeholders, waiting for the next day's newspaper may put you a day behind unfolding real-time news. The one remaining constant in the media environment is that newspapers still serve as the main producer of news. While news-related websites and blogs pop on to the internet frequently, they largely rely on newspapers for investigative reporting and to generate the daily coverage of government and political activities.

To get a sense for the changing media environment, it is useful to divide these sources into two main types. Old media, which includes newspapers and major television networks (not cable), represents those news outlets which have an audience with a broad range of views. At one time, old media outlets dominated the airwaves because there were few alternatives and broadcasters were subject to the Fairness Doctrine, a federal law that required balanced viewpoints. New media is the second type and includes talk radio, opinion-based cable news shows, and the internet-based venues such as Twitter and Facebook. New media cater to a narrow segment of the news audience who share similar perspectives and political views. New media outlets have significantly increased with the expanding number of cable channels and widespread use of the internet.

The transition from an old media environment to one more rooted in new media is shown in Figure 6.1. It displays survey trends in primary news sources for California adults. Television has remained the primary source of news since

---

[3] "California's Budget Propositions Lead a Diverse Online Conversation," *PEJ New Media Index*: May 17-22, 2009, accessed May 28, 2014, at http://www.journalism.org /index_report/california%E2%80%99s_budget_propositions_lead_diverse_online_conver sation.

Figure 6.1. Primary News Sources for Californians

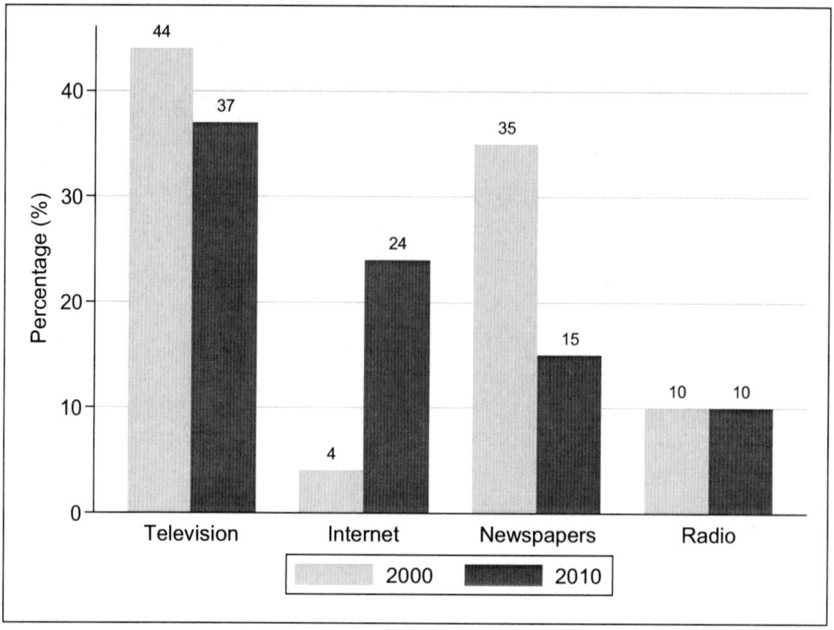

Source: Public Policy Institute of California Poll Database.

2000, but has lost ground to the internet. Newspapers have increasingly been replaced by the internet as a news source, while the use of radio has remained the same. In the case of newspapers, readers can access content at a newspaper's website, including the digitized daily edition, so the source is the same, but the method of transmission is different. Not represented in this figure is the growing use of social media by news outlets in the last five years. Many stories are now broken by Twitter, and some reporters live-tweet committee hearings, floor debates, and press conferences. The primary news sources are described more below.

Newspapers

As a result of the expanding use of the internet, the newspaper industry has been in a state of flux over the past decade. The cause of this flux has been the rapid decline in the reliance on printed newspapers and the print advertising revenue associated with it. This decline has put major newspapers and their owners on the brink of bankruptcy and left them struggling to survive. Even before the internet revolution, coverage of state government was minimal. Now only a few major state newspapers maintain bureaus in Sacramento with more than one reporter.

Despite the transition to a different vehicle, this has not changed the content of state news covered by newspapers, and the state budget has certainly remained one of the primary topics. Just as the budget cycle became a year-round activity, coverage of budget conditions has followed suit. It begins with the release of the governor's budget in early January and, depending on the state's financial condition, ends the year in December with gubernatorial proposals for mid-(fiscal)year cuts or early reports of the contents in the governor's soon-to-be-released January budget.

News and analysis of state politics, including the budget, is provided by newswires, such as the Associated Press (AP) and Reuters, and newspaper organizations located throughout the state. Some of these organizations with the largest readership include the *Los Angeles Times* (circulation—640,000), the *San Jose Mercury News* (530,000), the *Orange County Register* (285,000), the *San Francisco Chronicle* (210,000), and the *Sacramento Bee* (190,000).[4] Only the AP, *Los Angeles Times,* and *Sacramento Bee* have more than one full-time capital reporter. Some newspapers are members of media groups who share one or more capital reporters. The extent of coverage in newspapers depends on their audience and resources. The *Los Angeles Times* is the most widely read of any California newspaper and has the resources to offer more extensive coverage than other news organizations outside of Sacramento. The *Sacramento Bee* also provides comprehensive coverage because of its "home-field" advantage. The *Times* and the *Bee,* as they are commonly known, each have several reporters dedicated to capital coverage, usually including one whose main beat is the budget. Both also have columnists (Dan Walters at the *Bee* and George Skelton at the *Times*) who frequently comment on fiscal issues.[5]

The current trend among these news organizations is to offer blog-like news updates throughout the day or live tweet-breaking stories and then turn the higher profile stories into lengthier articles by the following day.[6] Smaller news organizations, without much of a capital presence, usually pick the top stories from the larger newspapers and the AP and run them in the following days. These smaller outlets also provide coverage of the local impact of state policy decisions with their own in-house reporters.

Aside from news coverage, newspapers also offer editorial content, such as candidate or ballot measure endorsements, that influence the budget environ-

---

[4] New Audit Bureau of Circulation, "Total Circulation for Newspapers," at http://www.auditedmedia.com/free-reports.aspx. The circulation data represent average Monday-Friday circulation as of September 2012.

[5] Much of the content in this section is based on discussions with Nicole Winger, Deputy Secretary of State, Communications, July 2014.

[6] The format of these blogs and news alerts has been in flux in recent years. As examples, the *Los Angeles Times* calls its blog site PolitiCal and features short news summaries throughout the day. The *Sacramento Bee* has the Capitol*Alert* blog, while the *San Jose Mercury News* has the Political Blotter blog.

ment. If an editorial board of a newspaper in a legislator's district takes a strong support or oppose position on a budget issue, the legislator is likely to take notice and it could sway his or her vote. In a similar vein, if several major editorial boards throughout the state draw attention to an issue, it can influence the actions of state leaders. Because of their influence on the public, elected officials, and political staff members, and interest groups sometimes proactively work editorial boards to cast a budget-related issue in their favor.

Television

Although television remains the primary news source for Californians, its coverage of state politics and government leaves a lot to be desired. Outside of the capital region, no local news stations maintain a state bureau. However, major broadcast networks (ABC, NBC, CBS, and Univision) have a capital bureau that shares stories with their local sister stations across the state. The Capitol Television News Service (CTNS), which provides original capital coverage, also distributes packaged news stories to subscribing local stations. Still, the lack of viewer demand for state political news leads to local newscasts that mainly focus on local issues, primarily crime, with some snippets of state coverage on major events, such as the State of the State address or significant budget developments. Although there was a temporary surge in television reporters stationed in the capital during the Schwarzenegger administration (2003–2011), the small amount of coverage is nothing new. A study in 1989 found that during "a typical television news hour, 2.9 percent of the time, or about 1 minute and 44 seconds, was devoted to state government."[7]

Political junkies seeking television coverage of state politics can tune into the California Channel, which is California's version of C-SPAN and provides 24-hour news and event coverage. The station is supported by local cable providers, and its access is limited to their subscribers, which does not reach the growing number of satellite television customers. However, those wishing to view budget hearings, floor sessions, or other events they cover can access California Channel's website (http://www.calchannel.com/).

Radio

Coverage of state politics and government on the radio suffers from the same structural impediment that afflicts television. The reach of local radio stations is limited by their broadcast signals and they are normally owned by or affiliated with a national media company. The news that local stations cover is primarily local with some interspersed national coverage. Exceptions to this generalization about local stations are National Public Radio (NPR) affiliates. The Capital Public Radio Network (CPRN) is a statewide news service operated by NPR affiliate Capital Public Radio in Sacramento. Its capital reporters provide "white label service" to dozens of stations throughout the state, which al-

---

[7] Quoted in John L. Korey, *California Government* (Boston: Houghton Mifflin, 2006), 27.

lows these stations to repackage the content and present it as their own. The California Report, produced by San Francisco-based NPR affiliate KQED-FM, also offers branded news segments about California politics and government that are carried by affiliates across the state.

Unlike major television broadcast networks, partisan talk shows dominate much of the programming on radio. These include locally produced shows, such as the Armstrong and Getty show in California, and nationally syndicated programs like Sean Hannity. The local shows include some coverage of state issues, but the opinions typically expressed by the hosts, their guests, and listeners are heavily partisan and ideological.

Internet

The internet occupies a unique place within the media world and politics in general. Unlike the other outlets, it further facilitates the dissemination of news content from the other three sources and allows these sources to supplement the news provided through their primary medium (radio, television, or newspapers). In addition, the internet also hosts news websites that exist only online (e.g., calpension.com). With this in mind, the internet serves four main functions in the political media arena. First, the internet allows the public to directly access government information and documents. Anybody with internet access can examine the Department of Justice's budget on the Department of Finance website or view policy recommendations from the Legislative Analyst's Office. Second, websites of newspapers and radio and television stations publish their original news stories and often complement these stories with additional ones and background information. The bulk of this additional material comes from newspapers. The home websites for these outlets thus provide a secondary access point for their customers.

Third, some websites act as news aggregators—that is, they compile news stories and columns from other websites, but do not offer their own original reporting or commentary. The Rough and Tumble website is the most prominent in California. Lastly, one of the burgeoning trends in internet media is the creation of commentary websites (blogs fall under this group) that offer their analysis and opinion, but do not usually generate original stories. It is fairly easy to start one of these sites since all one needs is a host server, but it is much harder to attract viewers if the commentators lack name recognition in the capital or statewide. The founders and contributors of more popular sites, such as CalBuzz (http://www.calbuzz.com/) and Fox and Hounds (http://www.foxandhounds daily.com/), usually are former state capital journalists, former executive and legislative staff, or long-time consultants and activists.

Media Effects and the Budget

After reviewing the media landscape in California, it is worthwhile to consider the impact of the media on the budget and its central players, the governor and legislators. The contents of the budget agreement each year are shaped by media coverage and how various courses of action are presented to the public and stakeholders. One way the media shapes public perceptions of the budget is through the anecdotal style of reporting, which focuses on stories that feature government programs and their impact on certain individuals. The "story" format may bring a more personal side to the issue, but the main subjects may not be representative of overall program beneficiaries. Journalists also have an incentive to highlight the most devastating consequences of budget cuts or tax changes because it will presumably attract more readers or viewers. A related factor in the media's impact is subject-centric reporting. This refers to how stories are sometimes reported in a vacuum that does not show the larger context of the budget and how policymakers must choose between competing policy priorities. For instance, the prison system has received a considerable amount of media attention for its overcrowding issues, lucrative prison guard salaries, and, at times, plush inmate living conditions. This disproportionate attention probably contributes to the mistaken belief that the prison system is the most expensive program area, when it fails to come close to the top two spending areas of K-12 education and health care. Since government programs and their impact are reported in isolation of one another, it is hard for the public to view these programs against competing priorities. This may be unavoidable because of the priming effect of the news on the public; that is, the media attention raises public salience of the issue. In this case, the media attention and importance attached to it translates into a belief that the prison system is the largest government program.[8]

Another frequent subject for the media is government waste and abuse. There is no question that the media play an indispensable role in ferreting out wasteful spending and fraud. Investigative stories frequently lead to further government inquiries and potentially prosecution. However, a major unintended consequence of this type of reporting is that the public is left with the impression that waste and abuse are rampant in government, when most independent reports show this is not the case. One such example of abuse occurred in 2012 when it was revealed that officials in the Department of State Parks maintained a large balance in one of their special funds that was previously undetected by executive and legislative budget staff. Top officials in the department claimed the pot of money was set aside to cushion the blow from potential budget cuts. A subsequent comprehensive investigation into other special funds demonstrated these were isolated incidents. While journalists might mention the isolated nature of these cases in their reporting, the public often believes these reported abuses are representative of what takes place on a regular basis in government. A 2014 poll

---

[8] Public Policy Institute of California Statewide Survey: *Californians and their Government*, (San Francisco: Public Policy Institute of California, May, 2014). Similar surveys are available in their searchable database at http://www.ppic.org/main/survAdvancedSearch.asp.

revealed that 48 percent of Californians think state government wastes "a lot" of taxpayer money.[9]

The media also has a tendency to highlight conflicts among policymakers and political parties that contribute to political polarization. For mainstream outlets (e.g., major newspapers, radio, etc.), part of this conflict bias is rooted in their goal of presenting a tory that includes two opposing viewpoints. On budgetary matters, stories may quote more extreme statements from either side that signal a lack of willingness to compromise, which may force the other side to dig its heels in deeper.

Nowhere is this conflict bias more evident than on partisan radio talk shows and websites. Studies at the national level indicate that dedicated followers of these outlets become more ideological (both conservative and liberal) over time, what researchers have termed a "polarizing effect."[10] This phenomenon is best exemplified by the John and Ken radio show popular in the Los Angeles area. Republicans who suggest any hint of supporting tax increases face the potential wrath of these talk show hosts and their dedicated listeners. In 2011, Republicans who "dared" to discuss a ballot measure for tax increases with Governor Brown appeared in images on the show's website with their heads on sticks. As reflected in the quotation at the beginning of this chapter, these tactics instill fear in Republican legislators, force them to think twice about any compromises, and lead to budget paralysis.

Overall, the media occupies a multifaceted role in the budget environment. Through various outlets, the media informs the public about the overall condition of state finances, lays out the options and tradeoffs that policymakers consider each year, and reports how the consequential decisions made affect state services and the average California resident. In the process, the media also influences the public's orientation and attitude toward government. The watchdog function of the media feeds into public cynicism concerning fiscal matters and impacts the feasibility of budget solutions available to state leaders. More partisan media outlets also reinforce ideological views that have increasingly pulled the Democrats and Republicans in opposing directions that have exacerbated severe budget problems.

The Public Role in Budgeting

Budgets are supposed to be a reflection of public values. State leaders should translate those values into funded priorities. In California, voters can also directly provide input on these priorities through ballot box-budgeting. In this section,

---

[9] Public Policy Institute of California, *Californians and Their Government* (San Francisco: Public Policy Institute of California, May, 2014).

[10] David A. Jones, "The Polarizing Effect of New Media Messages," *International Journal of Public Opinion Research*, 14, no. 2 (2001): 158–74; David A. Jones, "Partisan 'New Media' and Opinion Change, 2002–2004," *American Review of Politics*, 30 (2009), 1–16.

we discuss the role the public plays in the "regular" budget process (not through direct democracy) and the political environment this creates for decision-making.

For average Californians, their role is quite limited, although this is largely a reflection of their effort. For those constituents that expend the effort, they can have some influence over spending decisions. The most visible aspect of this influence can occur at budget subcommittee hearings in the spring each year. Depending on the topic and the stakes, the hearings can compete with the best drama shows on television. It is not uncommon for public witnesses to testify sobbing about the effects of a given budget decision, usually a program cut, on their daily lives. This testimony is intended to tug at the heartstrings of committee members, compelling them to reverse course on any proposed cuts. These types of "public displays" of support are often coordinated efforts by interest groups rather than individual citizens proactively expressing concern out of their own volition. Still, the testimony can be very effective, bringing home to legislators the real-world effects of their decisions. These testimonials can alter program reduction decisions, or, at the very least, delay the actual day of reckoning. In the latter case, really difficult cuts to health care or social service programs may then occur in Big 5 discussions or other stages where the public is not physically present.

Outside of the public venue of committee hearings, individuals may seek one-on-one meetings with key legislators to discuss budget matters, but, without much money or influence behind them, these meetings are not likely to be effective. On key decisions, however, legislative staff are probably tracking telephone calls, meeting requests, and emails and then briefing their member on the support and oppose tallies on a given issue.

While a very small segment of the public may actively participate in the budget process or contact a legislator, public opinion permeates the process. The public's mood can lay the foundation for budget discussions throughout the year and impact what policy options (e.g., tax increases, college tuition increases) are on and off the table. Rising costs of a particular state service, such as higher education, may preclude policymakers from program reductions, while general tax increases may be more acceptable to the public after years of severe cutbacks. Here we examine public opinion in more detail by reviewing survey trends and gaining a better understanding of how the public views the state budget. We also discuss how these views and attitudes influence budgetary decision-making.

Public Opinion on the Budget

Public opinion on the budget in California can be characterized in four ways. First, Californians' general attitude toward the state tracks closely with budget conditions (see Figure 6.2). When budget deficits are present and growing, survey respondents take a darker view of the direction of the state. Of course, the budget is not the sole factor behind this correlation; as discussed in

Figure 6.2. Projected Budget Conditions and Public Perception of State's Direction

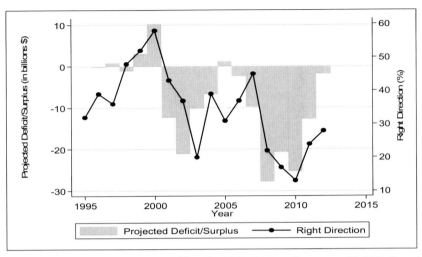

Source: Legislative Analyst's Office *Fiscal Outlook*, various years; Field Poll, various years.

Chapter 3, budget conditions are heavily influenced by the state of the economy. The public outlook is also a reflection of poor economic conditions that are likely hitting households hard. State government is one of the entities where the public can project its blame.

Second, state policymakers, especially the governor, receive a disproportionate share of the blame when budget conditions take a downturn and an inflated share of credit when the fiscal situation turns around. One study showed that in elections voters are most likely to take their wrath for budget deficits out on incumbent governors, while the legislature is not punished at all.[11] A review of approval ratings for the governor and legislature over the past decade or so largely bears this out. Although approval ratings for both the governor and legislature have moved up and down with the size of budget deficits (see Figure 6.3), the fate of governors has been tied closely to the budget outlook. The ratings for the legislature as a whole have been abysmal, but very few incumbent legislators have been unseated during this time.

Governor Gray Davis's (D) initial fumbling of budget deficits in the early 2000s was a primary reason for his fall in approval ratings and eventual recall in

---

[11] Jeff Cummins and Thomas T. Holyoke, "Electoral Accountability and Fiscal Policy in the U.S. States: A Reassessment" (presented at the Midwest Political Science Association annual conference, Chicago, IL, April, 2013).

Figure 6.3. Executive and Legislative Approval Ratings with Budget Conditions

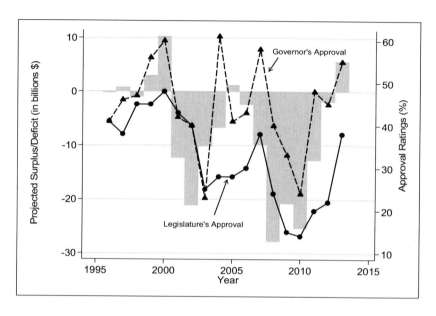

Source: Legislative Analyst's Office *Fiscal Outlook*, various years; Field Polls, various years.

2003. Schwarzenegger rode high approval ratings early in his administration, but they dropped after the budget continued to hemorrhage and he pushed an unpopular special election in 2005 to reform teacher tenure and pass a new state spending limit. Schwarzenegger's public standing recovered in time for his reelection in 2006, after an improving economy temporarily relieved the budget crunch. After calling several consecutive fiscal emergencies in his second term, he eventually left office with extremely low ratings. In 2011, Jerry Brown encountered somewhat lower approval ratings than when his predecessors assumed office, but his ratings began to improve when he announced an end to structural deficits in 2013.

Although policy decisions play a significant role in budget conditions, state and national economic trends are undoubtedly significant as well. On top of a volatile economy, policymakers also have to grapple with ballot-box budgeting, which can severely limit budgetary solutions. Despite the uncontrollable nature of these factors, the public does not discount them in approval ratings.

Third, the public's knowledge of the state budget is rather low. Despite 71 percent of likely voters indicating that they know "some" or "a lot" about how state and local governments spend and raise money, surveys consistently show that the public incorrectly identifies prisons as the top state spending area, even though K-12 education and health and human services are much higher.[12] Respondents fare better in polls that ask what the state's top revenue source is: a roughly even proportion indicates personal income and sales tax (the correct answer is personal income taxes, again, by far). However, close to 40 percent of the public still points to corporate taxes and vehicle license fees as the top source, even though both have been on the decline as a share of state revenue and each represents less than 10 percent of the general fund. Perhaps it is unfair to point out these gaps in budget knowledge; after all, studies of national public opinion dating back to the 1950s generally demonstrate that the public is poorly informed across the country.[13] Regardless, it leaves Californians ill-suited to evaluate the performance of state budget makers, and even more ill-equipped to make consequential budget decisions on ballot propositions nearly every election. Many other states do not have an initiative process where voters are making such decisions.

One last characteristic about public attitudes toward the budget is that they tend to be contradictory on policy preferences. When these preferences are untangled, the clearer picture comes down to this: the public wants more and better services, but does not want to pay the taxes to support them. On the spending side, with few exceptions, surveys show that respondents want to keep services that they personally might use and cut or eliminate services they do not use. This is particularly the case if respondents are likely voters, instead of all adults. The former usually have higher income levels and tend to be white so they are less supportive of social programs with low-income, minority recipients. Generally, voters favor spending more on police, fire, and education, and less on welfare, public housing, and government administration. These preferences have remained constant for decades.[14] When the state has faced the prospect of budget cuts, surveys have consistently revealed that education is the main area the public wants to protect, followed by health and human services, and higher education (see Figure 6.4).

On the revenue side, public support for taxes waxes and wanes with the target population. If proposed taxes are narrowly based and targeted toward a specific constituency, such as high-income earners or smokers, then there is likely to be majority support for measures. If the taxes are broad-based, such as general sales or income taxes, and likely to hit a large segment of the population, support generally plummets below majority support. For instance, Figure 6.5 shows strong support for raising the cigarette tax (77 percent favor it) and in-

[12] Public Policy Institute of California Statewide Survey: *Californians and their Government*, (San Francisco: Public Policy Institute of California, May, 2014).

[13] Michael X. Delli Carpini and Scott Keeter, *What Americans Know about Politics and Why It Matters* (New Haven: Yale University Press, 1996).

[14] Jack Citrin, "Do People Want Something for Nothing: Public Opinion on Taxes and Government Spending," *National Tax Journal* 32, no. 2 (1979): 113–29.

Figure 6.4. Areas Public Wants to Protect from Budget Cuts

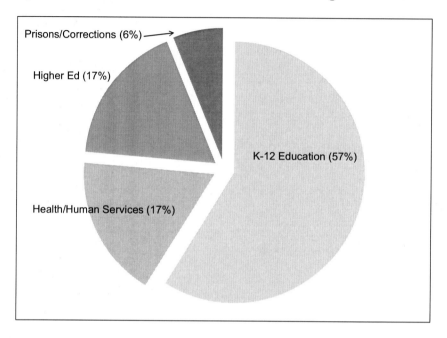

Prisons/Corrections (6%)

Higher Ed (17%)

K-12 Education (57%)

Health/Human Services (17%)

Source: Public Policy Institute of California Statewide Survey, January, 2013.

creasing the income tax on the wealthy (67 percent), but little support for raising income and sales taxes on everybody (67 percent oppose the income tax and 65 percent the sales tax).

During the crisis budgeting era, respondents were consistently asked about their preferences for closing budget gaps. Although a sizeable plurality (about 39 percent) indicated that it should be done mostly through spending cuts, a slightly larger 43 percent routinely preferred a mix of spending cuts and tax increases (see Cartoon 6.1).[15] About 13 percent opted either for mostly tax increases or borrowing.

What impact has public opinion had on budgetary outcomes in recent years? It is hard to say for sure, but major decisions have roughly matched public preferences. In the crisis budgeting era, policymakers turned to cuts more often than raising taxes, a direction that more than a third of the public indicated as their preferred solution. Keep in mind that projected budget deficits reached as high as $60 billion at their worst (2008) and remained in the $20 billion range for

---

[15] Public Policy Institute of California Statewide Survey: *Californians and their Government*, (San Francisco: Public Policy Institute of California, October, 2012).

Figure 6.5. Public Support for Different Tax Increases

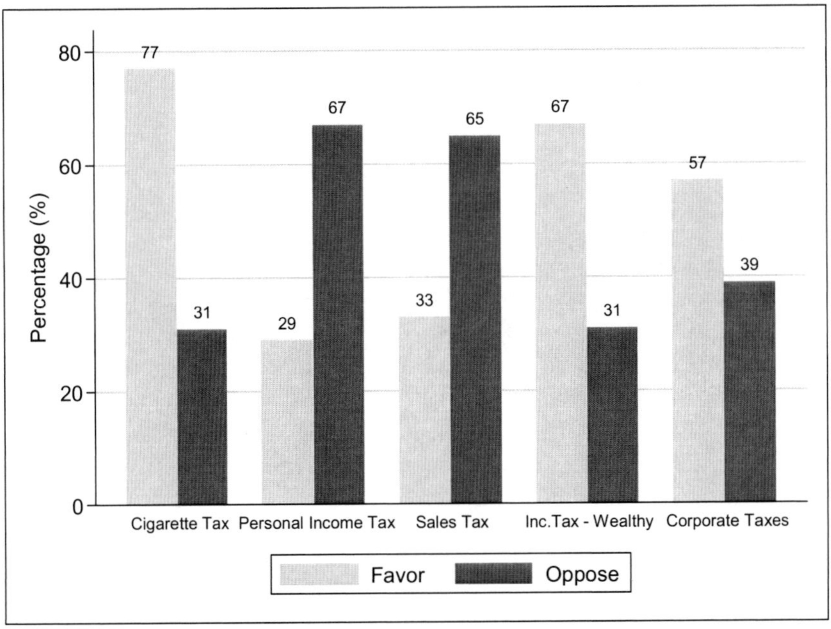

Source: Public Policy Institute of California various Statewide Surveys. January 2013: Cigarette tax and corporate taxes. October 2012: Personal income tax; sales tax; and income taxes on wealthy. Question asks whether you favor or oppose a given tax proposal.

much of that time. Actual year-end deficits never came close to those projections, while general tax increases were adopted only twice (2009 and 2012). When the budget situation improved in 2014, the legislature adopted the governor's proposal to pay down debt and build a reserve, which was favored by 57 percent of likely voters.[16]

With the chaotic nature of the budget process in recent decades and the bad press that has accompanied it, polls have frequently shown that the public thinks the budget system is broken. In 2009, the year before voters lowered the vote requirement to pass budgets by a simple majority, 80 percent of respondents felt that major changes were needed to the budget process.[17] This overwhelming negative perception of the process helped fuel the passage of the majority vote requirement for the budget. Despite several years of on-time budgets and the ebb of annual deficits, a clear majority of California voters in 2014 still thought the

---

[16] *Ibid.*, May, 2014.
[17] *Ibid.*, September, 2009.

Cartoon 6.1. Public Opinion on the Budget

Source: Tom Meyer.

budget situation was "a big problem."[18] This concern probably reflected residual feelings from the crisis budgeting era and the recognition that the state's finances were still not on firm ground.

The Polarized Public

The survey data we reviewed above captures statewide public opinion, but budget decisions made by legislators, in particular, are often made with their district constituencies in mind. Governors have a statewide constituency so their views are likely to be more moderate and coincide with statewide opinion. When facing budget deficits, the approaches of governors over the past several decades have usually been more balanced, in terms of considering both spending cuts and tax increases, than more partisan members of the legislature. Even Republican governors going back to Reagan, though reluctantly, have supported tax increases to address deficits. Public opinion in individual legislative districts, however, can be much different, both in liberal and conservative ways, from the aggregated statewide views reported in regular surveys. For legislators who wish

---

[18] *Ibid.*, May, 2014.

to incorporate district opinion into their decisions, surveys of this sort are virtually nonexistent. Instead, legislators must rely on the views of party supporters when state survey data is disaggregated

It is no secret that the political environment in California, like the rest of the nation, is very polarized. In Chapter 2, we discussed how party polarization in the *legislature* is a major factor behind budget gridlock. What is less known about California, however, is that extreme polarization also exists in the *electorate* and even more so than the rest of the nation.[19] "Thus, compared with other American voters, Californians over the past three decades have been stronger partisans, more loyal to their parties, and more consistent in their party preferences."[20] Similar to a legislature with more partisan representatives, stronger partisanship among the public also contributes to budget conflict. These partisan divisions emerge when we take a closer look at the fiscal preferences of each party's voters.

The cleavages between Republicans and Democrats are rooted in typical partisan preferences on fiscal issues. With few exceptions, Republicans are generally opposed to all types of tax increases and are less supportive of state programs. Democrats are usually supportive of most tax increases, although not all (e.g., sales tax for services), and favor a higher level of services (see Figure 6.6). Stark partisan contrasts exist, in particular, for certain types of taxes. For instance, Republicans and Democrats split sharply on raising income taxes on the wealthy. Democrats favor such a tax by nearly a 3-1 margin (80 percent of Democrats to 27 percent of Republicans). The same is true for proposals to raise corporate taxes (67 percent of Democrats to 21 percent of Republicans favor it). The only tax proposal where majorities of each party's voters favor an increase is on cigarette taxes (76 percent of Democrats and 58 percent of Republicans).

The partisan differences in opinion between Democrats and Republicans only contribute to a highly charged budget environment. Hyperpartisan voters reinforce a feedback loop with their elected representatives that exacerbates the polarization. Voters demand, and legislators espouse, fiscal rigidity that fortifies the schism between the parties. Hence, alternatives to spending cuts are nonstarters for Republicans, while Democrats are more reluctant to cut spending, especially for social programs. Legislators from both parties fear that giving ground to the other side will jeopardize their support from partisan voters and allied interest groups.

While the polarization in the electorate has increased over the last several decades, as discussed elsewhere, reforms are already in place that should help diffuse polarization in the legislature and the electorate should not be too far behind. Nonpartisan redistricting and the top-two primary have the potential to produce more moderate legislators. Moderate legislative candidates appealing to voters from both parties may help break the partisan ties between representatives

---

[19] Gary Jacobson, "Partisan and Ideological Polarization in the California Electorate," *State Politics and Policy Quarterly* 4, no. 2 (2004): 113–39.

[20] *Ibid.*, 118.

Figure 6.6. Partisan Fiscal Preferences

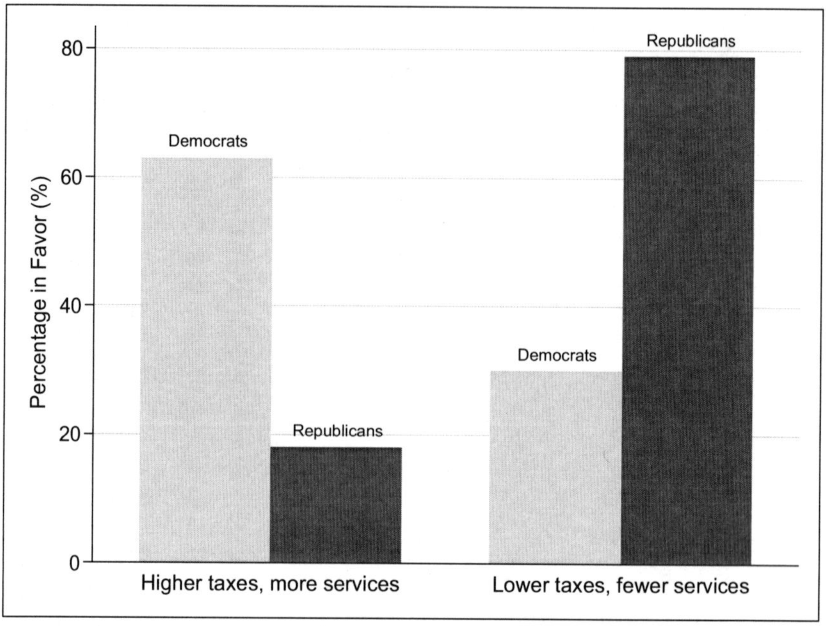

Source: Public Policy Institute of California Statewide Survey, January, 2014.

and their constituents. Aside from these reforms and an abrupt about face for the ideological direction of each party, there are few other tools to lessen the polarization in the electorate.

The Third House

If the public's role in budgeting is more subtle and indirect, then interest groups, or the "third house," as they are sometimes called, occupy a more direct and overt role in state budgeting. Interest groups constantly maneuver, fight, and compete to benefit from the public trough. In this case, the trough is over $200 billion in federal, state, and local dollars that flow through the state budget process each year. Some close observers would say that interest groups and their army of lobbyists and "government affairs" staff pull most of the strings in the state capital. Long-time journalist Dan Walters and former lobbyist Jay Michael offered this account in 2002:

> It would be fair to say that 200 to 300 of the 1,200 registered lobbyists, the cream of the crop, routinely and reliably call the shots on at least 80 percent of the issues coming before the Legislature and play major roles in the outcome of

decisions in other governmental or political forums, such as administrative agencies and the initiative process.[21]

State legislators would, of course, deny such claims, but one statistic supports the observation above. In *Capitol Weekly's* annual list of the "Top 100" most influential unelected people in California politics, more than half are lobbyists and executive staff of interest groups.[22] While much of their participation in the budget process is visible during testimony at committee hearings, lobbyists, or legislative advocates, also work behind the scenes to secure benefits and funding for their associations and clients.

Types of Interest Groups

It should be noted that not all interest groups and their various representatives "work" the state budget. Many interest groups, particularly ones advocating for profit-driven industries (i.e., financial, restaurants, etc.), concentrate their efforts on the policy process, where they support or oppose bills that might advance or retard their economic goals. Thus, certain types of "interests" attempt to influence the budget and the distribution of funding. Here we discuss those groups that are most active in the budget process. Many observers would agree that the most influential type is *public sector groups*, which includes labor unions and local government entities. Labor unions, in particular, are widely regarded as the most powerful and include the California Teachers Association (CTA), the California Correctional Peace Officers Association (CCPOA), and the Service Employees International Union (SEIU). Union clout increased significantly in the late 1970s when Governor Brown signed a bill authorizing collective bargaining for state employees. This allowed unions to negotiate their contracts with the executive branch, giving them significant input over salaries, health and retirement benefits, and general working conditions.

Another branch of public sector groups includes local public agencies at the city, county, and district level and the numerous entities that pool their influence in associations. Nearly every city, county, school district, and special district has at least one lobbyist working the halls in Sacramento to improve their piece of the budget pie; many have multiple lobbyists pushing their agendas. Not only does each government entity have lobbyists representing its own individual interests, but most also are dues-paying members of statewide or regional associations. "Voters, and the broader public, often reflect the negative stereotypes of lobbyists flowing from reformers and the media. In part, this popular view of lobbyists and their activities reflects an ignorance that just about everyone di-

[21] Jay Michael and Dan Walters, *The Third House: Lobbyists, Money, and Power in Sacramento* (Berkeley: Berkeley Public Policy Press, 2002), 5.

[22] "Capitol Weekly's Top 100 List," *Capitol Weekly*, August 20, 2013, accessed May 29, 2014, at http://capitolweekly.net/capitol-weeklys-top-100-players-unelected-california/.

rectly or indirectly employs lobbyists through their taxes to local governments and schools, their labor unions and/or their trade associations."[23] A few of the associations that many government entities belong to are the League of California Cities, California State Association of Counties (CSAC), the California School Boards Association, and the Association of California Water Agencies (ACWA). Local government agencies seeking favorable funding allocations or appropriations for specific projects may use a two-pronged approach by directing their own lobbyist to advocate on their behalf and persuading their association to push the item as well.

A second type of interest group can be referred to as *social welfare groups*. These organizations seek to influence policymakers on specific policy areas, such as health care, welfare, or children's issues. They may be comprised of a network of health care clinics or providers, local foster care agencies, or are the umbrella organization for numerous local chapters located throughout the state (e.g., United Way). Some of these associations include the California Children's Institute, Health Access, California Health Care Foundation, and the County Welfare Directors Association. Although these types of groups may work with public sector groups on specific issues or may have members from public agencies, their focus is usually more on one budget area rather than the cross-cutting concerns of public sector groups.

Another type of interest group that is active on budget issues is *economic groups*. The goal of this type of group tends to be different than those types discussed above. Economic, or business groups, place more emphasis on the revenue side of the budget than the spending side. These groups, such as the California Chamber of Commerce, the California Business Roundtable, and the California Manufacturers Association, seek tax policies and a regulatory scheme that are conducive to a strong business climate. These groups may attempt to squelch tax increase efforts or expand favorable business tax breaks, such as empowerment zones or manufacturing equipment credits. Although their main concerns may be tax policies or the regulation of businesses, they also have secondary concerns with the education system and infrastructure, since an educated workforce and efficient transportation system help their businesses thrive. In addition, their opposition to higher taxes has not been categorical. With the state facing large budget deficits, some of these business groups have remained neutral on tax increases or even indicated lukewarm support for them. The absence of an all-out war from these groups against Brown's Proposition 30 tax initiative in 2012 probably contributed to its passage.

Tricks of the Trade

Interest groups and lobbyists employ numerous tools and tactics to pursue their goals. The following are those commonly applied to the budget in order to

---

[23] Michael and Walters, *The Third House*, 3–4.

secure increased funding allocations, grants, pork, and other favorable policy treatment.[24]

Contract Negotiations

Perhaps the most lucrative tool, and consequential for budgeting purposes, is collective bargaining over state worker contracts. Annual salary and benefit costs for state workers total over $20 billion and represent about 11 percent of total state expenditures (see Figure 6.7). There are 21 bargaining units that the governor's administration directly negotiates with periodically on salary, benefits, and other employment conditions. The most contentious issue is invariably salaries—both their size and scope (who they apply to)—particularly during tight budget conditions. When employee contracts expire, with more set to expire, salary and benefit terms determined in the earlier expiring contracts usually set a precedent for subsequent contract negotiations. As discussed in Chapter 4, this ripple effect had dire consequences for public pensions when retirement formulas for public safety workers spiraled upward as agencies sought to compete for personnel through more generous formulas. In the last decade, negotiations with bargaining units have revolved around salary cuts, the number of furlough days, and increased retirement contribution rates in order to help address budget deficits.

Personal Contact

Personal contact is the type of activity that gives lobbying its name. Lobbyists congregate outside of legislative chambers or in hearing rooms so that they can pull a lawmaker aside or send a message to them via legislative staff. Interest group representatives frequently meet with legislators in their offices to make their case for a particular item. Prior to term limits, legislators and lobbyists often hung out together in capital bars and restaurants, blurring the lines between business and socializing. Some lobbyists even have unparalleled access to meetings with legislative leaders and the governor. In 2011, final details of the budget were hammered out with the governor and "three of the most powerful people in state government: the Assembly Speaker, the Senate leader—and Joe Nuñez, chief lobbyist for the California Teachers Association."[25] Nuñez later delayed a plan to fill the budget deficit with rosy revenue assumptions and secured a no-layoff clause for teachers. In 2009, the CTA's presence in budget talks was felt even when they weren't in the room. Susan Kennedy, Governor Schwarzenegger's chief of staff, received a text that read, "Don't go there," referring to offering school districts more funding flexibility. "Democrats in the

---

[24] These are based on strategies outlined in Michael and Walters, *The Third House*, Chapter 3.

[25] Mishak, "California Teachers Assn."

Figure 6.7. State Worker Salaries as Percentage of Total State Expenditures, 1980–2012

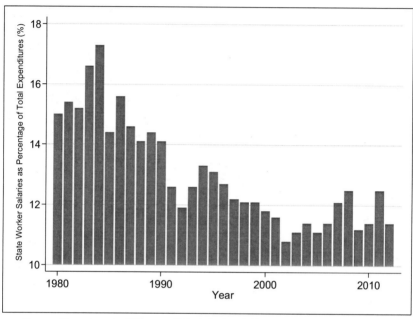

Source: Department of Finance, Schedule 4 and Chart B.

room, Kennedy fumed, were emailing Nuñez real-time updates on the budget talks. "It was almost as if CTA had a seat at the table."[26]

Ballot Box Strategies

Another important tool for interest groups is the ballot box—both the actual use of initiatives and the mere threat of them. We have already discussed the far-reaching implications of the actual use of initiatives for the budget process, such as Proposition 98. According to Michael and Walters, "Sometimes the threat of an initiative will break the stalemate or achieve a [budget] compromise."[27] One such example occurred in the Davis administration when he reluctantly agreed to increase education funding after the powerful California Teachers Association was set to submit signatures for a ballot measure that would mandate higher per-pupil spending.

---

[26] *Ibid.*
[27] Michael and Walters, *The Third House*, 43.

Campaign Contributions

A more subtle way for interest groups to influence the budget is through contributions to candidates' campaigns. It is subtle because contributors cannot specify what the purpose is, but it is understood by the officeholder and interest group that it will "help" keep their interests in mind. Elected officials will usually say that contributions do not influence their votes, but that is because they risk prosecution for corruption if they indicate otherwise. This is where public sector unions can flex their muscle over their public sector agency cousins (individual cities, counties, etc.) and social welfare groups. The latter two do not have the pools of member dues that provide resources for political contributions. In the 2012 election cycle, public sector unions were the largest campaign contributor by industry at $93 million. This figure is unusually high because unions shelled out significantly more than usual to fight Proposition 32, which would have gutted their main source of campaign funding—union dues. Still, they are usually among the top 10 in spending. The California Teachers Association alone spent $35 million, 33 of which was used to fight Proposition 32. The rest of the contributions were targeted towards union-friendly Democrats, who help protect education's share of the budget.

Grassroots Mobilizing

One technique of lobbyists that is evolving with new technology is grassroots organizing. This is intended to galvanize legislative constituents, recipients of state or local services, and anybody else who might be in the crosshairs of a budget decision that may sway legislators. In the "old" days, interest groups organized letter writing campaigns, coordinated phone calls to legislative offices, and contacted key legislative donors to "persuade" legislators to "support" the group's position. With the advent of new technologies, there are now numerous ways to orchestrate "legislative alerts." Email, Facebook, and YouTube all offer inexpensive ways of communicating with, organizing, and rallying effected constituents. For example, to thwart an oil severance tax that would have earmarked funding for state universities in 2011, the Western States Petroleum Association and oil companies employed a combination of old and new grassroots tactics. "The group [also] commissioned a study showing the economic impact of the industry, produced slick videos for YouTube and touted its positions on blogs and in newspaper opinion pieces. It sent out "issue alerts" to get workers to write to their legislators."[28] Busing hundreds of college students, teachers, or nurses to Sacramento for Capitol step rallies and to fill legislative offices has become commonplace in recent budget battles. Some deep-pocketed groups like the CTA can afford to augment the grassroots efforts with other ways to open legislative ears. "In addition to paying a team of seven in-house lobbyists, the CTA wined and dined elected officials and their staffs and helped cover travel and lodging costs as hundreds of teachers converged on Sacramento

---

[28] Patrick McGreevy, "Lobbying of Legislators Sets Record" *Los Angeles Times*, March 6, 2012.

for a 'week of action' on the budget crisis. . ." in 2011.[29] Normally, it is easier for member-based groups, such as labor unions, to turn out a crowd for budget hearings or rallies, but some industries facing a major policy change may be able to turn out numbers as well. In the oil severance tax case, industry groups packed a legislative hearing with oil workers brandishing shirts that said "Save Our Jobs."[30]

Procedural Maneuvering

Since few people in Sacramento understand the state budget process, knowledge of where to insert an appropriation or kill an unfavorable issue can be very effective. A savvy lobbyist might target members of a budget subcommittee or reach out to staff writing the budget bill and numerous trailer bills. Toward the end of the budget season, when the pace becomes more frenetic, inserting an appropriation earmarked for a client (city or county) or placing favorable funding criteria in a trailer bill may go unnoticed. Even if it does come to light, a legislator or staffer may not want to cross the lobbyist's client or raise the ire of a colleague.

Litigation

The court system is a frequent arbiter of disputes between the state and various labor unions, local government entities, and taxpayer protection groups who feel aggrieved by budgetary policy. These lawsuits are filed based on the plaintiffs' view that the state violated state and/or federal law. In recent years, topics have revolved around procedural authority during budget standoffs, state worker furloughs, reducing worker pay to the minimum wage, cuts to education, health, and social welfare programs, and special fees. Some of the most costly lawsuits the state has faced in recent years involve inmate conditions at state prisons. The Prison Law Office, a nonprofit law firm specializing in prison litigation, has filed several high-profile lawsuits that challenged prison overcrowding and the provision of health care. In response, federal judges have appointed high-paid receivers to oversee the mitigation of these problems. The cost to the state runs into the billions of dollars and is one reason prison costs have skyrocketed over the last decade.

Interest Group Influence on the Budget

The impact of interest groups on the state budget permeates the process from beginning to end. It starts before the governor even releases the budget in January, when interest groups, their lobbyists, and any other surrogates they can rustle up flood the governor's office and legislative staff with requests for funding and special consideration. As alluded to above, the most influential lobbyists can even be involved at the highest level of final negotiations at the end of the

---

[29] *Ibid.*
[30] *Ibid.*

process. In between these time points, lobbyists pursue every opportunity to expand the policy benefits their organization or clients already receive and create new ones.

One question about interest groups that has been raised by observers of state politics is whether their influence has grown in recent years. There is no doubt that interest groups have played a central role in policymaking in California for some time, particularly when it comes to the state's fiscal structure. One need only remember that a crusading Howard Jarvis harnessed homeowner wrath over escalating property taxes with Proposition 13 in the 1970s and turned state and local finances on their head.

A strong argument can be made that interest group influence grew after the adoption of term limits. Once thought to sever the ties between legislators and lobbyists, there is evidence that term limits make legislators more reliant on lobbyists and their more detailed knowledge of policy issues.[31] When veteran legislators with years of policy expertise and institutional memory are termed out of office, they take that knowledge and expertise with them. New legislators can no longer turn to these veterans for voting cues. Instead, lobbyists fill this knowledge vacuum. Research suggests that states with term limits encounter more budget problems and posits that interest group fiscal pressure was partly to blame.[32] Even so, it is difficult, if not impossible, to measure the entire effect of how interest groups may distort lawmakers' decisions on the budget and other matters.

One way to think about the fiscal effects of interest groups is to separate them into "spending groups" and "tax-cutter" groups. Spending groups, such as labor unions and social welfare advocacy groups, primarily seek to encourage more state spending in their respective areas. Education, health care, and law enforcement groups all seek to ratchet up spending, usually under the guise of providing better public services, but group members can also benefit substantially from funding increases in the form of salary and benefits. Although we just as well might characterize these groups as tax-and-spend, the reality is that the "tax" part is usually off the table in California. This is because of the various restrictions on the adoption of new taxes, such as the two-thirds vote necessary in the legislature. These groups, who otherwise would be advocating more responsible fiscal policy by seeking to balance their pro-spending ways with new revenue, mainly focus their efforts on higher spending, without as much concern for where the resources come from.

In contrast to spending groups, tax-cutter groups are usually concerned with keeping the tax burden low by reducing taxes and fees. This category of groups does not just apply to taxpayer protection groups, such as the Howard Jarvis

---

[31] Christopher Mooney, "Lobbyists and Interest Groups," *in Institutional Change in American Politics: The Case of Term Limits*, ed. Karl Kurtz, Bruce Cain, and Richard G. Niemi (Ann Arbor: University of Michigan Press, 2007) 119–33.

[32] Jeff Cummins, "The Effects of Legislative Term Limits on State Fiscal Conditions," *American Politics Research* 41, no. 3 (2012): 416–41.

Taxpayers Association or the California Taxpayers Association, whose sole purpose is lower taxes. It also applies to many business groups who view tax levels as already too burdensome and strongly oppose any additional tax increases. This includes groups such as the California Retailers Association whose members would be hit by broad-based sales taxes and groups, such as the Western States Petroleum Association, that might be affected by more targeted tax increases, such as one on oil extraction. This does not mean that all of these groups categorically oppose any increases in tax levels, although some do. But, on the whole, these groups resist tax increases and seek additional tax breaks as much as possible.

At first pass, it might seem as though we can neatly line these groups into liberal and conservative groups and that their primary targets are Democrats and Republicans, respectively. However, while this is largely true, there are notable exceptions as some party members advocate issues normally associated with the other party's groups. For instance, in response to consistent criticism about the state's low-ranking business climate, Democrats have become more supportive of regulatory and tax relief. Some tax loopholes, such as the Hollywood film credit, are primarily Democrat-driven. Republicans have grown wary of cuts to K-12 education and college tuition increases because suburban schools and middle-class constituents are impacted. It is also not unusual for these groups to make campaign contributions to both parties. Law enforcement unions occupy a gray area of the traditional partisan lineup because Republicans have been strong advocates of cutting crime, while Democrats are traditional union allies. So while spending and tax-cutter groups may seem to fall along typical partisan lines, their affiliations with each party are not as exclusive as we might think.

One detrimental outcome of interest group behavior for fiscal policy is the feedback loop that occurs between policy benefits and campaign contributions. This mostly applies to spending groups, and labor unions in particular, but it can apply to tax-cutter groups to a lesser extent. It works like this for labor unions. The group donates campaign cash to the governor, legislative leaders, and many rank-and-file members, usually of the ruling majority party, but it could be both parties. The governor and legislature agree to funding increases for state prisons and schools. This allows more teachers or prison guards to be hired, who then become dues-paying members of the CTA or CCPOA. The unions can then use the incoming dues to lavish more campaign money on policymakers and the cycle continues.[33]

For tax-cutter groups, the mechanics are generally the same. Business groups donate to legislators' campaign accounts, which makes legislators more supportive of tax breaks that will improve the bottom line for businesses. More profits then allow these businesses and corporations to give money to officeholders. The links here are more tenuous than for labor unions, but the concept is the same. Contributions beget policy benefits beget contributions.

---

[33] The general idea for the feedback loop is based on Michael and Walters, *The Third House*, 72.

In the aggregate, the opposing forces of the spending and tax-cutter groups create a fundamental tension in the alignment of spending and revenues. Each side pulls the state's balance sheet in different directions. When persistent imbalances occur, as they did in the 2000s, each type of group pressures policymakers to protect its interests. Spending groups dig their heels in on spending and tax-cutter groups do the same on tax levels. Because of the popular appeal of tax cuts to Democrats and Republicans, tax cutters even managed to secure cuts when severe deficits were present. As legislators come to depend on interest groups and their deep pockets for the means to their next elective office, the narrower fiscal interests of these groups take precedence over the state's overall interest in a balanced budget.

Conclusion

Budget decisions are influenced by the political environment in which they are made. Policymakers face intense pressures from the public and interest groups to make decisions that will benefit their constituents. In recent decades, this environment has made it harder for the state to deal with significant fiscal challenges. The public's understanding of budget issues has never been strong and matters have only been made more complicated by the creative financing that policymakers used to stitch and patch budgets together during the crisis budgeting era. Newspapers have generally been an indispensable source in explaining these complicated matters and highlighting the impact of budget decisions on ordinary Californians. However, newspapers are losing ground to internet sources that are more partisan and engage in less investigative journalism. This trend will reduce the amount of more objective budget information available to the public and hurt the media's watchdog role.

For interest groups, the budget stakes are high. As budget conditions have become more volatile in recent decades, it has only intensified longstanding battles over taxing and spending. It is easier to claim a piece of a growing pie, but it is much harder to when that pie is shrinking, or just not growing as fast as it once did because of a deteriorating revenue base. This has led to a mad scramble for interest groups and their lobbyists to capture what policy benefits they can, often at the expense of sound fiscal policy.

Review Questions

1. How has the media landscape changed in recent decades and how does this impact budgeting?

2. Explain how the public influences budgeting. Does the budget reflect public attitudes about budgeting?

3. How do interest groups strain the state budget process?

Additional Resources

Rough and Tumble

http://www.rtumble.com/

The site provides daily snapshots and links of news articles related to California politics from newspapers, blogs, and radio.

The Field Poll

http://field.com/fieldpollonline/subscribers/

The site has summaries of statewide public opinion polls dating back to the mid-1990s.

Cal-Access, Secretary of State's Office

http://cal-access.ss.ca.gov/

The site provides access to a database for campaign contributions and lobbying activity in California.

Chapter 7

Operating in the Red:
Deficits, Debt, and the Elusive Balanced Budget

> The 42 billion dollar deficit is a rock upon our chest and we cannot breathe until we get it off. It doesn't make any sense to talk about education, infrastructure, water, health care reform and all these things when we have this huge budget deficit.
>
> —Governor Arnold Schwarzenegger's (R)
> 2009 State of the State Address

When is a budget ever really balanced? Who has "authority" to determine whether projected revenues and expenditures are balanced? What seem like straightforward questions have increasingly taken on more complicated answers in California's budget process. These questions rose to the fore in the budget battle of 2011. Democrats in the legislature, operating under the new majority vote rule, passed what they claimed was a "balanced budget" by the constitutional deadline of June 15 and sent it to Governor Jerry Brown (D), only to have him veto it because he said it was not actually balanced. State Controller John Chiang (D), citing his authority as the state's bookkeeper, then intervened and announced that the legislature's budget was about $2 billion short of penciling out. Fearing their salaries were in jeopardy, thanks to Proposition 25, legislative Democrats quickly adopted a patch to cover the budget hole, at the same time they were publicly questioning the controller's self-declared authority. The governor signed the 2011–12 budget a few days later, bringing the year's budget drama to a close, but the episode raised fundamental questions about the state's budget procedures and rules, especially given the constitutional mandate to adopt a balanced budget.

A state court later ruled that only the legislature has the power to determine whether a budget is balanced, answering the second question posed above. However, the question of whether a budget is ever really balanced remains unanswered. Policymakers can employ numerous tricks to align proposed revenues and expenditures for the coming year or even to close out the previous year's balance sheet in the black. Interfund borrowing, unrealistic revenue assumptions, and spending deferrals have become commonplace in budgetary decision-making in California and many other states. Such maneuvering and manipulation of accounting for public resources and expenditures are intended to maintain the illusion of sound fiscal management when the conditions are suspect, to say the least, and may even be dire.

In this chapter, we explore California's experience with deficits and debt and the efforts of policymakers to avoid budget imbalances. We start by discussing the question of balance and reviewing various types of deficits. We then examine budget rules that California and other states have adopted to slow government growth or avoid budget deficits. California was among the forerunners in enacting tax and expenditure limitations (TELs), however it is not considered a model state for other rules, such as balanced budget requirements (BBRs) and budget stabilization funds (BSFs). Before embarking on an in-depth analysis of the crisis budgeting era in the 2000s and beyond, we provide an overview of the state's history with boom and bust cycles. Prior to the 1980s, periods of crisis budgeting were short-lived, with the exception of the 1930s. Starting with the 1980s, these crises became more frequent and severe culminating in the second crisis budgeting era. We trace the roots of this era and explain how it is different than earlier episodes of budget stress. Finally, we conclude by looking at the state's use of debt as a financial management tool.

The Balance Question

Balance is a central value when government entities, or even individuals, are managing their finances. As long-time budget expert Irene Rubin observes, "Budgets have to balance. A plan for expenditures that pays no attention to ensuring that revenues cover expenditures is not a budget."[1] Capturing what balance is, however, is not so obvious—expenditures are a constantly moving target—which means reconciling expenditures with revenue depends on a point in time. For the federal government, identifying anticipated deficits is not as important since it does not face balanced budget requirements like states and local governments do. However, even with BBRs, when states run out of money, they have options to keep government running. California, like other states, routinely borrows money on a short-term basis through RANs—revenue anticipation

---

[1] Irene Rubin, *The Politics of Public Budgeting* (Washington, DC: CQ Press, 2014), 4.

notes—and RAWs—revenue anticipation warrants—to smooth out cash-flow gyrations.[2] When coffers have run completely dry, the state has issued IOUs to vendors, which can be likened to the state creating its own currency, something prohibited by the federal constitution.

To begin to address the balance question, we examine different types of budget deficits in order to lay the groundwork for a more in-depth discussion of crisis budgeting in California historically and during the crisis budgeting era. As discussed in Chapter 1, the basic definition of a deficit is straightforward—it occurs when expenditures exceed available resources over a given time period. However, the time period used, the magnitude, and the recurring nature of the shortfalls vary for each type of deficit, indicating the severity of the fiscal problem. For instance, a one-time or operational deficit may be short-lived and disappear the very next year, while a structural deficit may last for five or more years, akin to what occurred in the early 1980s.

To recap, the three types of deficits in order of severity are operational, cyclical, and structural. Operational deficits are temporary in nature, usually last about a year, and are the result of a revenue or expenditure shock or both. A mild recession could drag down revenues or an unexpected increase in program caseloads could boost expenditures for a year or so, but they are fairly easy to address. Cyclical deficits are a symptom of the business cycle and occur periodically when a recession sets in. They may last two to three years and normally diminish as the economy recovers. Policymakers can "paper over" both operational and cyclical deficits by resorting to accounting gimmicks, such as accelerating revenue streams (e.g., tobacco settlement proceeds), deferring spending until the subsequent fiscal year, or by borrowing from special funds. Surpluses from previous years can also help fill in operational or cyclical deficits. Most of California's deficits prior to 2001 were operational or cyclical in nature. Structural deficits are the most severe and occur when expenditures consistently exceed revenues on a long-term basis. They signify more fundamental problems with the state's tax base, mix of taxes, and long-term spending commitments.

Yet another type of deficit that occurs, but that is usually not treated with the same level of concern as those above, is a cash deficit. This is where receipts flowing into the state treasury from various revenue sources do not keep pace with the disbursement of expenditures. These cash-flow issues emerge because expenditures on a monthly basis have a fairly stable pattern to them, while some revenue sources yield lump sums at certain dates in the fiscal year (i.e., April for income taxes). The state controller handles these cash-flow problems by moving money between the general fund and hundreds of special funds, borrowing from these special funds in accordance with their statutory authority, and using the RANs and RAWs mentioned above. During the crisis budgeting era, in addition to the structural deficits, the state routinely encountered cash deficits of up to

---

[2] RANs are short-term loans that must be paid back within the fiscal year and are more common than RAWs, which can be paid back in the next fiscal year and usually cost more.

$10 billion at the end of the fiscal year.[3] These cash-flow problems reached their peak in 2009 when State Controller John Chiang issued IOUs for the third time in the state's history (1933 and 1992 were the others). Aside from these cash-flow emergencies, it is generally acceptable for governments to manage cash deficits, as long as budget deficits or excessive short-term borrowing costs are not present.

Another important characteristic of budget deficits is whether they are projected versus actual deficits. A projected deficit is when estimated expenditures exceed estimated revenues and is an assessment of the budget's future conditions. Both the Department of Finance (DOF) and the Legislative Analyst's Office (LAO) provide budget projections at several points during the fiscal year (see Chapter 2 for a budget timeline). Although both agencies conduct longer term projections, the focus of the agencies, legislature, and budget observers is the amount of the deficit (or surplus) incorporating the remaining current fiscal year (wherever that may be in the budget calendar) and the coming budget year (See Figure 7.1). Depending on the type of deficit forecasted, this may or may not spur the governor and legislature into some remedial action. Throughout much of the crisis budgeting era, policymakers took few actions mid-year to avert these projected deficits, hoping that better economic conditions would be just around the corner.

While projected deficits afford some time for budget makers to avoid fiscal shortfalls, actual deficits signify that the government has failed to balance its books at the end of the fiscal year. For several reasons, actual deficits tend to be rare events. Since 1950, California has registered only 12 actual deficits over 60 plus years, despite its notorious reputation for them.[4] From 1983 to 2010, 17 states recorded an actual deficit in one or more years. One of the primary reasons for this rarity is the accounting maneuvers that elected officials employ. Elected officials try to avoid the actual recording of a deficit as much as they can.[5] However, this also means that if a deficit is recorded, then it is probably more severe than the actual number shows, particularly if it lasts more than one year. For instance, early in the crisis budgeting era, an actual deficit occurred only in 2001–02, but voters also approved a $15 billion bond (Proposition 57) to cover ongoing deficits, which masked a severe structural deficit (See Figure 7.2). In other states, such as Arkansas, they always avoid a deficit because they have a BBR that automatically reduces total expenditures to the level of resources anticipated for that year.

---

[3] The state controller issues monthly reports on general fund cash-flow conditions. Available at http://www.sco.ca.gov/ard_state_cash_summaries.html.

[4] Historical data on revenues and expenditures comes from Department of Finance, Chart A, (available at http://www.dof.ca.gov/budgeting/budget_faqs/information /#SummarySchedules/) and the *California Statistical Abstract*, various years (Sacramento: Department of Finance).

[5] Robert Bifulco, Beverly Bunch, Willicam Duncombe, Mark Robbins, and William Simonsen, "Debt and Deception: How States Avoid Making Hard Fiscal Decisions," *Public Administration Review* 72, no. 5 (2012): 659–67.

Figure 7.1. LAO Projected Surpluses/Deficits, 1995–2013

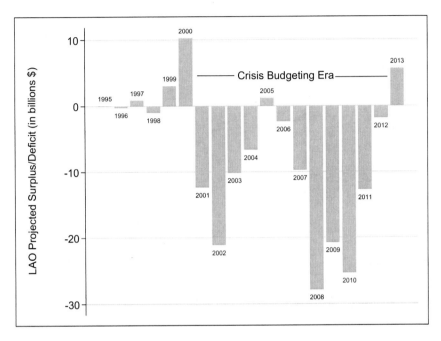

Source: Legislative Analyst's Office (LAO) *Fiscal Outlook*, various years. Year is year report was published. Amount represents total current and budget year deficit/surplus.

The Fiscal Toolbox

When budget deficits begin to occur more frequently, policymakers and stakeholders typically turn to the procedures and process as a way to mitigate the causes of deficits and stave off future shortfalls. The executive budget movement in the early 20th century is a prime example of how the process can become a target for reform efforts. In California, the 1922 reforms stabilized the dysfunctional legislative process until the state's financial conditions were overwhelmed by the tumult of the Great Depression. After the crisis budgeting era of the 1930s, California's finances stabilized for the most part and only encountered sporadic budget imbalances until the 1980s. As government spending grew rapidly in the 1960s and 1970s, conservative politicians and activists began to question the pro-growth budget mentality. The pro-growth mentality was so endemic by the 1960s that even conservative Republican icon Governor Ronald Reagan could not harness the state's unyielding growth. During his administra-

Figure 7.2. Actual Surpluses/Deficits, 1975–2013

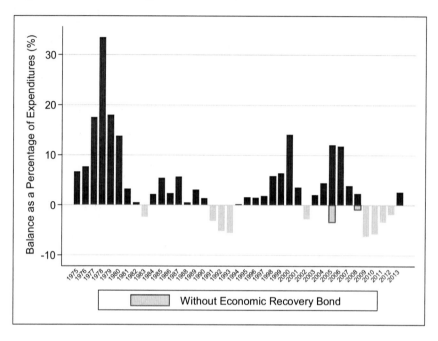

Without Economic Recovery Bond

Source: Department of Finance, Chart A. Year:1975=1974–75.

tion, spending grew by 14 percent annually, eclipsing even his liberal predecessor, Pat Brown (D).[6]

To combat the spending growth, activists such as Howard Jarvis and Paul Gann believed constitutional rules were the best way to stop the runaway spending. By galvanizing resentful and outraged homeowners with Proposition 13, Jarvis set in motion an antitax movement that swept across the country with the purpose of limiting the expansion of government. Not only did more states seek to place constitutional and statutory caps on tax sources, but they also employed these rules to ensure budgets were balanced.[7] Here we examine three types of rules that California and other states employ to limit government growth and remain in the black.

---

[6] Department of Finance and the *California Statistical Abstract*.

[7] Mikesell notes that many broad, sweeping tax revolt initiatives, akin to Proposition 13, were unsuccessful in the immediate wake of 13. Instead, the tax revolt movement was characterized more by piecemeal changes than wholesale revisions. See John Mikesell, "The Path of the Tax Revolt: Statewide Expenditures and Tax Control Referenda since Proposition 13," *State and Local Government Review* 18, no. 1 (1986): 5–12.

Tax and Expenditure Limitations (TEL)

One popular way that states have attempted to slow the growth of government is through tax and expenditure limitations. There is no common definition for a TEL, but the basic goal is to reduce the growth of government by imposing caps or restrictions on either revenues, expenditures, or both. In addition, TELs are viewed by some as a way to prevent budget deficits by curbing excessive spending before it outpaces sustainable revenue growth. They have been enacted by citizen initiatives or through the legislature and are either statutory or constitutional amendments. TELs can be broken down into two categories: mechanical and procedural. *Mechanical TELs* set an overall spending limit or cap a particular tax rate, such as for property taxes.[8] *Procedural TELs* require a supermajoritarian vote in the legislature to raise taxes or to exceed the overall spending cap.[9] Most discussions of TELs revolve around mechanical limits that lay out a formula for how much expenditures can grow from one year to the next. The formulas use one or more of the following factors to determine the growth ceiling: personal income growth, population growth, inflation, and/or expenditures as a percentage of total personal income. Some require that expenditures cannot exceed 95 to 99 percent of projected revenue. Proposition 13, the most well-known TEL, has both mechanical and procedural components to it since it stipulates a rate cap on property taxes and a two-thirds vote requirement for raising taxes at the state and local level. Proposition 4, commonly known as the Gann limit, is considered a mechanical TEL because it imposes an overall spending cap. Although not commonly regarded as a TEL, the Riley-Stewart ballot measure, adopted by voters in 1933, included an overall spending limit provision that was, for all intents and purposes, California's first tax and expenditure limitation.

Currently, 30 states have some type of mechanical TEL, while 15 states have a procedural TEL. The adoption of state TELs exploded in the late 1970s and again in the 1990s. Several states, including California twice, attempted to enact new TELs in the 2000s, but were unsuccessful.[10] By all accounts, Proposition 13 is considered the watershed moment in the spread of TELs across the nation. The Proposition 13 movement itself was rooted in escalating property taxes in the 1960s and '70s that reached a crescendo right before voters considered Proposition 13 on the ballot in the June 1978 primary.[11] Like many Ameri-

---

[8] The definition of TELs varies by study. Some studies refer only to tax rate reductions and growth caps as TELs, or what we have termed mechanical TELs here, while others expand the scope to include vote thresholds that must be met to increase taxes or spending growth beyond the cap, or what we term procedural TELs. Thus, we use the more expansive definition of TELs.

[9] Daniel R. Mullins and Bruce A. Wallin, "Tax and Expenditure Limitations: Introduction and Overview," *Public Budgeting & Finance* 24, no. 4 (2004): 2–15.

[10] Bert Waisanen, "State Tax and Expenditures Limits—2010," National Conference of State Legislatures, accessed September 12, 2013, at http://www.ncsl.org/research/fiscal-policy/state-tax-and-expenditure-limits-2010.aspx.

[11] Jack Citrin, "Proposition 13 and the Transformation of California Government,"

cans, Californians had been facing overall tax levels that were rising faster than their incomes in the 1970s due to stagnant economic growth. Aside from a desire to cut the property tax burden, in California and across the country, there was widespread distrust in government and a belief that government spending was wasteful and inefficient.[12] "On the eve of the vote on Proposition 13, fully 38 percent of the California electorate believed that state and local governments could provide the same level of services as previously with a 40 percent reduction in their budget."[13] The overwhelming success of Proposition 13 led antitax crusaders Howard Jarvis and Paul Gann to push an overall spending limit in 1979 in the form of Proposition 4.

From a macro perspective, TELs were also a response to a long-term trend of pro-growth budgeting. Strong economic growth in the decades prior to the passage of Proposition 13 in 1978 allowed all levels of government to fund large infrastructure projects, enlarge public school systems, and expand the safety net for low-income and poor families. With consistent revenue growth, policymakers had an easier time budgeting, as they could bicker over where to direct new revenue rather than where to cut. When economic growth in the 1970s stagnated due to oil shortages, but home values continued to rise, homeowners, in particular, shouldered an increasing share of the cost of government through higher property taxes. Without sharing in the benefits of economic growth that they had enjoyed before, government spending became a target. Tax and expenditure limits were a way of hitting that target.

Effectiveness

The major question concerning TELs is whether they are actually effective at constraining government expenditures. The evidence of effectiveness is quite mixed and depends on the type of TEL examined.[14] Although less scholarly attention has been devoted to procedural TELs that require a legislative supermajority to raise taxes, the evidence is more consistent that they reduce state spending. On the other hand, mechanical TELs only appear to work when they are adopted through a citizen initiative or have strict growth formulas that exempt few types of expenditures.[15] In the case of the latter, a strict formula sets a hard ceiling for states, while the lack of exemptions makes it harder for policymakers

---

California Journal of Politics & Policy 1, no. 1 (2009): 1–9.

[12] *Ibid.*

[13] Jack Citrin, "Do People Want Something for Nothing: Public Opinion on Taxes and Government Spending," *National Tax Journal* 32, no. 2 (1979): 115.

[14] Thad Kousser, Mathew D. McCubbins, and Ellen Moule, "For Whom the TEL Tolls: Can State Tax and Expenditure Limits Effectively Reduce Spending?" *State Politics and Policy Quarterly* 8, no. 4 (2008): 331–61; Michael J. New, "U.S. State Tax and Expenditure Limitations: A Comparative Political Analysis," *State Politics and Policy Quarterly* 10, no. 1 (2010): 25–50; Waisanen, "State Tax and Expenditures Limits—2010."

[15] Sharon N. Kioko, "Structure of State-Level Tax and Expenditure Limits," *Public Budgeting & Finance* 31, no. 2 (2011): 43–78; New, "U.S State Tax."

to circumvent the ceiling. The TABOR (Taxpayer's Bill of Rights) limit approved by Colorado voters in 1992 is often regarded as a model TEL because studies indicate that it actually restricted spending growth whereas TELs in other states have not. However, voters loosened the TABOR cap in 2005 because many Coloradans believed that it was eroding state services.

The buyer's remorse experienced in Colorado is not uncommon, as California voters relaxed the Gann spending limit in 1990 through Proposition 111. Originally, the state appropriations limit (SAL), or overall spending cap, adopted under Gann was adjusted each year for population growth and inflation and exempted certain items, such as local government subventions and debt service. State spending did not bump up against the limit in the early1980s, but exceeded it in 1986–87, triggering a $1.1 billion rebate to taxpayers the next year.[16] The California Teachers Association, resentful that the excess revenue did not go to school spending, sponsored Proposition 98 to secure their budget allocation and stipulate that schools receive a portion of any future excess revenues. Proposition 111 adopted a more generous index of growth factors, exempted more categories of spending (e.g., capital outlay and natural disaster funding), and split excess revenues between schools and taxpayers if there were two years of excess revenues. After revenues grew rapidly in the late 1990s, state spending exceeded the cap in 1999–2000 by $1 billion, but did not trigger the excess revenue provisions because the excess lasted only one year. In the second crisis budgeting era, the SAL played no role in budget discussions because the slack, or difference between the appropriations limit and actual appropriations, grew wider from two economic recessions.[17] In 2013–14, state spending was $18 billion below the limit.[18] Kioko reported that the average slack as a percentage of actual appropriations for states with similar types of TELs was 36 percent from 2009–2011, which indicates that overall spending caps frequently do not constrain spending.[19]

Although conservatives frequently tout the merits of new stronger spending limits as a tool to prevent deficits and constrain the size of government, California voters have not warmed to the idea of further limits. Voters soundly rejected two such proposals pitched in 2005 and 2009 by Governor Schwarzenegger. Sponsors of procedural TELs that target certain revenue sources have been more successful as evidenced by the passage of Proposition 26 in 2010. It subjected more types of fees to the two-thirds vote requirement to raise them. Overall, voters' attitudes have remained surprisingly consistent regarding tax and spending limits since the original adoption of Proposition 13. On the one hand, voters

---

[16] Legislative Analyst's Office, *State Appropriations Limit* (Sacramento: Legislative Analyst's Office, 2000).

[17] Kioko, "Structure of State-Level Tax."

[18] Department of Finance, Chart L. Accessed October 18, 2013, at http://www.dof.ca.gov/budgeting/budget_faqs/information/.

[19] For California in 2013–14, the slack as a percentage of actual appropriations would be calculated as follows: (1) state appropriations limit ($90 billion) - actual appropriations ($71 billion) / actual appropriations ($71 billion) = 27 percent.

usually support procedural TELs that impose higher vote thresholds to raise tax-es.[20] On the other hand, they generally oppose *new* mechanical TELs that tighten overall spending limits.

Budget Stabilization Funds (BSF)

Another tool states employ to address budget deficits is budget stabilization funds, or rainy-day funds. These are essentially savings accounts to support the general fund that can be tapped when state expenditures exceed revenues within a fiscal year. They usually have a deposit rule that requires a certain percentage of general fund revenue to be deposited in a reserve account until an overall tar-get percentage has been met (e.g., 5 percent). Withdrawal rules vary by state and may require gubernatorial or legislative approval or stipulate a statutory formula to authorize withdrawals from the account. Rainy-day funds gained traction in the late 1970s and early 1980s as a way to stabilize volatile budget conditions, particularly after the 1974–75 and 1980–82 recessions.[21] Currently, 48 states have reserve accounts.[22] California adopted its version of a BSF, the Special Fund for Economic Uncertainty, in the 1980 budget act.[23] It added another fund, the Budget Stabilization Account, in 2004 under the Schwarzenegger-backed Proposition 58. Deposits were made for two years before the state again encoun-tered enormous fiscal imbalances, leaving the rainy-day fund dormant through-out the crisis budgeting era.

Research on the effectiveness of BSFs at shoring up state fiscal conditions has found that they work, but it depends on the structure of the funds. The struc-ture refers to the stringency of the deposit and withdrawal rules and to the size of the target balance level. Structures with statutory formulas that set aside a certain amount of revenue each year and that make it hard for the legislature to override these fund transfers generate stronger balances and provide a better cushion against economic downturns. On the back end, withdrawals that are triggered by estimated shortfalls or revenue/economic benchmarks instead of legislative or gubernatorial discretion stand the best chance of helping states weather fiscal stress.[24] In addition, Douglas and Gaddie found that the presence

---

[20] There are, of course, exceptions to this generalization. One important one is Prop-osition 39, which was passed in 2000 and lowered the vote threshold for local school bonds to 55 percent.

[21] Gary A.Wagner and Russell S. Sobel, "State Budget Stabilization Fund Adoption: Preparing for the Next Recession or Circumventing Fiscal Constraints," *Public Choice* 126 (2006): 177–99.

[22] National Association of State Budget Officers, *2008 Budget Processes in the States* (Washington, DC: National Association of Budget Officers, 2008), at http://www.nasbo.org/publications-data/budget-processes-in-the-states.

[23] Department of Finance, "Manual of State Funds," at http://www.dof.ca.gov/accounting/manual_of_state_funds/index/documents/0374.pdf.

[24] Yilin Hou, "Budget Stabilization Fund: Structural Features of the Enabling Legis-lation and Balance Levels," *Public Budgeting & Finance* 24, no. 3 (2004): 38–64; Sobel

of multiple rainy-day funds also reduces the severity of budget imbalances.[25]

Some research has also looked at the optimal size of BSFs to determine whether a certain balance level should be targeted to soften the blow of revenue shocks. A common rule of thumb in public finance has always been that policy-makers should shoot for a fund balance equal to 5 percent of annual expenditures, but there is nothing "magical" about this number.[26] Studies suggest that some states may need to carry a fund balance near 15 percent based on the magnitude of historical revenue shortfalls.[27] California, for instance, experienced an unprecedented $19 billion drop in revenue in 2009 that would have required a BSF balance of 19 percent of the previous year's expenditures to fill the gap.

In 2014, voters passed a new rainy-day fund that Governor Brown and the legislature had placed on the ballot. It sets a target balance level of 10 percent, which is an improvement over the 5 percent level in the Proposition 58 BSF, and requires annual deposits based on capital gains revenue and 1.5 percent of general fund revenue. Half of the deposited funds are also slated to pay off previous state debt, which reduces the reserve amount available for future budget shortfalls. When the next recession hits, we will gain a better idea of whether this new rainy-day fund will soften the blow of budget cutbacks that occurred in previous recessions.

Balanced Budget Requirements (BBR)

The most direct way that states can adopt procedures to attempt to avoid budget deficits is through balanced budget requirements. These are statutorily or constitutionally authorized rules that require revenues to meet or exceed expenditures upon submission or approval of a budget or by the end of the fiscal year or biennium. In most states, they are intended to apply to states' general fund accounts since these are the largest sources of spending and are subject to the most political discretion.[28] In some states, balanced budget provisions also apply to

---

and Wagner, "State Budget Stabilization Fund"; James W. Douglas and Ronald Keith Gaddie, "State Rainy Day Funds and Fiscal Crises: Rainy Day Funds and the 1990–91 Recession Revisited," *Public Budgeting & Finance* 22, no. 1 (2002): 19–30.

[25] Douglas and Gaddie, "State Rainy Day Funds."

[26] The 5 percent figure can be traced back to an interview in 1978 with an executive from Standard & Poor's Corporation, a bond rating agency. For more background, see Yilin Hou, "Budget Stabilization Fund: Structural Features of the Enabling Legislation and Balance Levels," *Public Budgeting & Finance*, 2004.

[27] Philip Joyce, "What's So Magical about Five Percent? A Nationwide Look at the Factors That Influence the Optimal Size of State Rainy Day Funds," *Public Budgeting & Finance* 21, no. 2 (2001): 62–87; John C. Navin and Leo J. Navin, "The Optimal Size of Countercyclical Budget Stabilization Funds: The Case Study of Ohio," *Public Budgeting & Finance* 17, no. 2 (1997): 114–27.

[28] Hou argues that many BBRs are not explicit about their exclusive application to general fund accounts and that many could reasonably be interpreted to apply to special funds as well. However, in practice, it is commonly understood by budget officials and

Cartoon 7.1. Balanced Budget

Source: Tom Meyer.

education funds. Special funds are often governed by legal provisions that restrict their spending to only their designated purposes. Like the other fiscal rules discussed above, the stringency of BBRs varies by state, which also influences their impact. Unlike other fiscal rules, however, they have a much longer history in the budget processes of the states and have not exhibited adoption patterns as distinctive as the other rules. Many states adopted BBRs in the late 1800s up through the mid-1900s. All states except Vermont have some form of balanced budget requirement.

BBRs can apply to different stages of the budget process (i.e., submission or approval) and can trigger required policy actions when a deficit is anticipated within the fiscal year. The most common balanced budget rules in order of stringency from least to most are the following (number of states with each in brackets): (1) the governor must submit a balanced budget [44]; (2) the legislature must pass a balanced budget [41]; (3) the governor must *sign* a balanced budget [37]; and (4) a deficit *cannot* be carried over into the next budget period [43]. California enacted its first BBR in 1922 when it institutionalized the executive budget process and required the governor to submit a balanced budget. As the weakest of the BBRs, it did little to prevent budget imbalances, particularly in

policymakers that these rules are intended to apply to the general fund. There have also been no court challenges to such a practice.

the 1980s and '90s. Confronting an enormous deficit and considering a $15 billion loan to cover it in 2004, voters backed a requirement that the governor must sign a balanced budget. Although it does not fall under the four common BBR categories, Californians also authorized fiscal emergency procedures as part of the Proposition 58 reform package (see Chapter 2 for a more detailed discussion).

Much scholarly attention has been devoted to the impact of BBRs on budget solvency and fiscal outcomes. There is fairly consistent evidence that they reduce spending levels, boost year-end balance levels, and increase the likelihood of a budget surplus.[29] In most studies, stringent BBRs have stronger effects than less stringent ones or the latter do not have significant effects at all. In a recent study, Campbell and Sances showed that states with strong BBRs confronted smaller budget gaps than those with weaker ones during the Great Recession from 2009 to 2011.[30] Other research suggests they improve state credit ratings and reduce debt levels, and that states with strict BBRs respond more quickly to projected deficits.[31] Overall, balanced budget rules seem to produce positive fiscal conditions and outcomes. While California no longer has the weakest rule, it is too early to determine whether its recent "upgrade," requiring the signing of a balanced budget by the governor, can yield the positive results seen in other states. The state may need to consider another upgrade to a no deficit carry-over rule in order to optimize its chances of fiscal stability.

Boom and Bust in Historical Perspective

For most of the first decade of its existence, California ran deficits to support the few services the state offered. This is not surprising since a fledgling state must establish its tax structure and collection methods before it can begin to receive revenue. Once it emerged from this early period of deficits, California had few instances of budget imbalances and avoided any severe fiscal crises until the 1930s.[32] The state mainly relied on the property tax, as did local governments,

---

[29] Henning Bohn and Robert P. Inman, "Balanced-Budget Rules and Deficits: Evidence from the U.S. States," *Carnegie-Rochester Conference Series on Public Policy* 45 (1996): 13–76; Yilin Hou and Daniel L. Smith, "Do State Balanced Budget Requirements Matter? Testing Two Explanatory Frameworks," *Public Choice* 145 (2010): 57–79; James Poterba, "Balanced-Budget Rules: Budget Institutions and Fiscal Policy in the U.S. States," *American Economic Review* 86 (1996): 395–400; Daniel L. Smith and Yilin Hou, "Balanced Budget Requirements and State Spending: A Long-Panel Study," *Public Budgeting & Finance* 33, no. 2 (2013): 1–18.

[30] Andrea Louise Campbell and Michael W. Sances, "State Fiscal Policy During the Great Recession: Budgetary Impacts and Policy Responses," *The Annals of the American Academy of Political and Social Science* 650 (2013): 252–73.

[31] Shanna Rose, "Institutions and Fiscal Sustainability," *National Tax Journal* 63, no. 4 (2010): 807–37.

[32] California Assembly Interim Committee on Revenue and Taxation, *A Resume of California's Tax Structure, 1850–1955* (Sacramento: Assembly Interim Committee on

until 1910 when this source of revenue shifted exclusively to local governments and the state turned to the public utilities gross receipts tax as its primary source. In fiscal year 1902–03 the state ran a one-time deficit of $1.5 million, which was equivalent to 10 percent of state expenditures, and then encountered another small deficit of $266,000 in 1909–10. Although voters approved an overhaul of the state's tax structure in 1910, these deficits were not the impetus behind the reforms. Redistribution of the tax burden was the driving factor.

The state's first severe fiscal crisis was caused by the Great Depression in the 1930s when the "financial solvency of the State government was almost destroyed."[33] The magnitude of the deficits revealed a tax system that was wholly inadequate for such devastating social upheaval. Beginning in 1933, the state plunged into deficits that were around 10 percent of expenditures and that did not let up until 1941 when national war efforts began to ramp up.[34] In terms of its severity and length, this crisis budgeting era was comparable to the one that began in 2001. Deficits were ongoing, and the state was forced to issue IOUs when it ran out of cash. In some ways, it was worse for California residents because the social safety net we know today was in its infancy at the state and federal level.

Three major factors helped pull the state out of its fiscal and economic crisis. First, as mentioned elsewhere, California overhauled its tax structure with the passage of the Riley-Stewart amendment in 1933. As a result, two new major tax sources were adopted: the personal income tax and the sales tax. Both taxes were particularly responsive to economic growth and accelerated revenue growth more than if the previous tax structure was left in place.[35] Second, California was a major beneficiary of Franklin Roosevelt's New Deal programs, which helped to stimulate the state economy. The Conservation Corp, Public Works Administration, and other programs all operated in California, significantly increasing the workforce, and resulting in upgrades to national and state parks and the construction of major infrastructure projects, such as the Central Valley Project (water). Third, the beginning of World War II brought a huge surge of people and defense dollars to the state. The population influx and the presence of the defense industry bolstered the economy so much that by the time an Assembly Committee on Taxation issued its recommendations in a 1947 report, it noted that "revenues are flowing into the state treasury in quantities be-

---

Revenue and Taxation, 1956).

[33] *Ibid.*, 43.

[34] The exact size of deficits is hard to pin down. Both the Department of Finance and state controller report figures, but they are not directly comparable. The state also operated on a two-year budget cycle, but numbers were often reported for fiscal years. The cumulative shortfall over this period was in the range of $145 million. Those figures reported here are very rough estimates.

[35] James E. Hartley, Steven M. Sheffrin, and J. David Vasche, "Reform during Crisis: The Transformation of California's Fiscal System during the Great Depression," *The Journal of Economic History* 56, no. 3 (1996): 657–78.

wildering to the imagination."[36] In a little over a decade, California had experienced its first bust to boom cycle.

After the conclusion of World War II, the state largely managed to avoid any serious financial problems until the early 1980s. Buoyed by consistently strong national economic growth, the California economy benefited greatly from the defense industry that was expanding as a result of the Cold War and from the newly emerging microchip industry in Silicon Valley. Americans and immigrants flocked to the Golden State in search of the American dream in a warm, Mediterranean climate. The state's fiscal situation prospered from the rapidly expanding population and economy, which produced strong revenue growth. From 1950 to 1980, general fund revenue grew 13 percent a year, on average.[37] The robust economic and revenue growth provided favorable financial conditions to expand the university systems, the network of roads and highways, and build the infrastructure to support the growing population.

This does not mean the state did not experience any fiscal stress at all. Economic recessions in the 1950s, '60s, and '70s all temporarily disrupted the expansion of government, but the downturns and the associated revenue declines were short-lived. The state encountered small deficits in 1950, 1953, and 1971, all below 5 percent of state expenditures. When budget imbalances were projected, approval for tax hikes could more easily be attained than it could in the 1980s and later, particularly because tax increases only required a simple majority vote in the legislature. Even with the lower vote threshold, partisanship in the legislature was low, and Republicans frequently supported tax increases. Upon entering office in 1967 and encountering a substantial budget deficit, Governor Ronald Reagan (R) proposed and passed the largest tax increase in state history up to that time.

The pro-growth orientation permeated public budgeting and allowed incrementalism to flourish during this time. Budgets were expected to grow, not contract, and if the resources were not there, the governor and enough legislators were willing to support tax increases. This pro-growth budgeting environment was not unique to California. The federal government and the rest of the states, with the possible exception of the South, largely subscribed to this practice. Aaron Wildavsky and Naomi Caiden described the incrementalist approach this way: "Because there was agreement on most programs, these constituted a base that was generally considered untouchable. For the most part, differences centered upon small departures from the base, rather than the program itself."[38]

Although the 1970s continued to see government growth, signs of pullback and retrenchment were beginning to emerge. A major factor in the early trans-

---

[36] Assembly Interim Committee on State and Local Taxation, *Report of Assembly Interim Committee on State and Local Taxation* (Sacramento: Assembly Interim Committee on State and Local Taxation, 1947), 21.

[37] Department of Finance and *California Statistical Abstract.*

[38] Aaron Wildavsky and Naomi Caiden, *The New Politics of the Budgetary Process* (New York: Pearson Education, Inc. 2004), 66–67.

formation of public sentiment, and eventually the positions, if not views, of policymakers, was the economic malaise of this decade. High inflation increased
the costs of government growth and forced policymakers to bring in more revenue if they wanted that growth to continue. Property taxes acted as a catalyst for
the changing public sentiment because they grew rapidly in the 1970s, doubling
from one year to the next in some areas, while these increases were also visible
to taxpayers. Once homeowners received their property tax bill, they could easily compare it to the previous year's. Other major taxes like sales were less
transparent since they were extracted incrementally with each purchase. Although legislators realized the growing public discontent with property taxes, and
tried unsuccessfully to grant relief, Democrats, in particular, were reluctant to
reduce the flow of revenue into government coffers. In addition to the brewing
tax backlash, increasing public perceptions of government waste and inefficien-
cy signaled a changing attitude toward government in general. Slowing economic growth and high inflation yielded small real income gains for Californians
that also contributed to their dissatisfaction. Austerity and retrenchment politics
were emerging on the fiscal scene and displacing the pro-growth orientation to
budgeting. California was not alone in this current of change. Prior to the passage of Proposition 13, the tax revolt was already underway in some states and
just arriving in others, but California came to symbolize the nascent austerity
approach.

Within the first few years after the Proposition 13 tax revolt, California experienced its first severe boom-to-bust cycle, which ushered in a period of crisis
budgeting not witnessed since the Great Depression. Part of what fueled Proposition 13 was a $20 billion plus reserve that state policymakers were sitting on
(see Figure 7.2) prior to passage in 1978. This pot of money helped ease the
blow for local governments from a significant hit to their main revenue source.
However, the drawdown of this reserve also made it harder for the state to cope
with the dramatic slowdown in revenue growth instigated by the 1980–1982
recession. In the 1970s, California enjoyed a *14 percent* average annual revenue
growth rate. From fiscal year 1980–81 to 1982–83, the average dropped to less
than 6 percent. In addition to the dramatic decline in the rate of revenue growth,
the Reagan administration cut federal aid to states, resulting in a $2 billion loss
for California. Crisis budgeting mode kicked into high gear in the 1981–82
budget year when projected shortfalls in the range of $1 billion began to surface.
Legislators, unaccustomed to fiscal restraint, approved temporary fixes that only
led to the need for more solutions before the year's end. To make fiscal matters
worse, in the June 1982 primary, voters considered propositions to eliminate the
gift and inheritance tax and permanently index income tax rates for inflation.
Combined, these measures would reduce annual revenue by about $1 billion
(about $2.5 billion in 2014 dollars). By May of 1982, the Department of Fi-
nance, anticipating that the tax propositions would pass (which they did), esti-

mated a $3.3 billion deficit by the end of the 1982–83 fiscal year, which represented over 2 percent of annual expenditures.[39]

Governor George Deukmejian (R) and legislators eventually whittled the deficit down through a series of small measures, but they were not enough. The state ended the year with a general fund deficit of $521 million. It marked the first time California ended a fiscal year with a deficit since 1970–71, a period of 12 years. Although the state began to climb out of its budget doldrums in the mid-1980s, this previously rare bout with crisis budgeting would be symbolic of what was to come with more intensity and frequency. A contemporary account captures the essence of state budgeting during this period and portends what would become a common pattern:

> In order to achieve a formally balanced budget, there has been resort to expedients—one-time ad hoc taxing and spending measures—which provide no lasting basis for sustained   financial capacity. In fact, a real annual budget cannot be produced at all; instead, the budget is made and remade throughout the fiscal year in a desperate game of catch up to make the figures come out even at the end.[40]

The respite from budget stress would be short-lived. Despite a strong economy, the state encountered another sizeable fiscal imbalance in April 1988 when it looked like California would end the year with a $1 billion gap. This time the economy was not to blame; instead, budget staff attributed the looming shortfall to tax legislation that sought to align the state tax code with new federal reforms. The state's tax conformity legislation did not generate the revenue that was anticipated.[41] Governor Deukmejian, a strong opponent of tax increases, proposed to close the gap with a combination of spending cuts and revenue adjustments. The latter consisted of further tax conformity modifications and a freeze on the indexing of income tax rates. Although technically the freeze on indexing did not constitute a tax increase in the traditional sense, the proposal was pilloried by the media and, surprisingly, by Democrats, who claimed the governor was backtracking on his previous opposition to tax increases. Some Republicans and Democratic leaders supported his proposal, but they were not enough to neutralize the damage from those Republicans and taxpayer groups that portrayed it as a tax increase. Despite many Democrats later announcing their support for the revenue adjustments, Deukmejian withdrew the proposal. The budget gap was closed with a combination of expenditure reductions and additional tax conformity changes.

The 1988 budget episode showcased two characteristics of the crisis budgeting environment. First, it demonstrated that the antitax orientation towards

---

[39] Naomi Caiden and Jeffrey I. Chapman, "Constraint and Uncertainty: Budgeting in California," *Public Budgeting & Finance* 2, no. 4 (1982): 118.

[40] Caiden and Chapman, "Constraint and Uncertainty," 118.

[41] Russel Gould, "Surviving a Revenue Collapse: Shortfall and Recovery in California," *Public Budgeting & Finance* 10, no. 4 (1990): 64.

budget deficits was becoming more entrenched among the public and Republicans. This was different from earlier decades when governors, such as Pat Brown and even Ronald Reagan, could usually rely on public and Republican support for raising taxes when the budget situation turned dire. As the chief deputy director for the Department of Finance, Russell Gould observed, "In the current political environment, one can expect exhaustive scrutiny of any revenue proposal whether a proposal truly constitutes a tax increase or not."[42] Second, the antitax sentiment meant that one of the primary tools government has available to address fiscal problems was largely off the table. From this point forward, in only the most dire circumstances would the governor or legislative leaders float the idea of raising taxes.

The 1990–91 recession would present state policymakers with their toughest budget test since the Great Depression. Unlike the early 1980s' recession, the state did not have an enormous reserve to cushion the blow. In addition, several other significant economic and policy factors set the stage for structural deficits for the foreseeable future. Even before the recession, the seeds of California's economic decline were sown. The downsizing of the defense industry hit California particularly hard, as 18 military bases were closed and 162,000 related jobs disappeared from 1988 to 1993.[43] Not only would the downsizing affect the resiliency of the state economy to respond to recessions, it would be a permanent drag on long-term growth. War spending, after all, is what helped pull the state out of its first crisis budgeting era in the 1930s, and military programs had remained a mainstay of the economy ever since.

A second related issue concerned the intentional and unintentional deterioration of the tax base. The intentional part was a result of the elimination and modification of certain types of taxes, such as the inheritance tax and the adoption of new tax expenditures (see Chapter 3), at the hands of both voters and policymakers alike. The unintentional deterioration occurred from the transition to a more service-oriented economy that was not subject to the sales tax. Both of these developments inhibited revenue growth and contributed to the long-term misalignment of revenue and expenditures.

In terms of policy changes, the adoption of Proposition 98 in 1988 reduced policymakers' discretion over how to resolve budget problems and accelerated the practice of earmarking. In addition, with the imposition of term limits in 1990, the legislative environment was destabilized as legislators and their staff jockeyed for their next career move. These changes made the legislature more ill-equipped to deal with budget crises.

The fiscal emergency greeted new Governor Pete Wilson (R) as he entered office in January 1991. The state faced a $1.9 billion gap in the current year that was projected to grow to $7 billion by the end of the budget year (1991–92). By June, the estimated gap grew to $14 billion, the largest in state history. Two

---

[42] *Ibid.*, 70.

[43] Jeffrey I. Chapman, "California: The Enduring Crisis," in *The Fiscal Crisis of the States*, ed. Stephen D. Gold (Washington, DC: Georgetown University Press, 1995), 106.

weeks into the 1991–92 fiscal year, the governor approved a budget package of expenditure and revenue changes, including a major increase in sales and income taxes. The package was not enough to avoid the red in 1991, and year-end deficits would persist for another two years. Gridlock over the budget situation culminated in 1992 when the budget act was not finalized until September 2, two months into the fiscal year.

By the mid-1990s, this episode of crisis budgeting began to subside and, once again, an economic boom rescued the state from the fiscal abyss. Fueled by the explosion in the creation of software and internet-based companies, in what became known as the dot.com boom, California and the rest of the country enjoyed some of the strongest economic growth in recent decades. By 2000, the state unemployment rate dipped below 5 percent, while it reached 4 percent nationally, levels not reached in a generation. State coffers overflowed with revenue, particularly from capital gains taxes related to the stock market run-up. In one year alone, fiscal year 1998–99 to 1999–00, general fund revenue grew by an astonishing *23 percent*. Instead of the governor and legislators battling over where to cut spending, they feuded over what to do with the largesse: new programs or tax cuts. Budget gridlock, however, continued, even under the best of financial circumstances, as budgets were not finalized until a month and a half into the fiscal year.

The dot.com boom came to an abrupt end in June 2000 and, with it, the prospending ways that policymakers had become accustomed to over the previous five years. The economic good times only masked the festering structural problems underlying the state's fiscal system. The deterioration of the tax base was further accelerated by numerous tax breaks approved on bipartisan votes that seemed routine as revenues flowed in. These loopholes would be more difficult to reverse when budget conditions began to hemorrhage. At the same time, spending measures were approved under the assumption that the revenue surge would continue. These myopic decisions set the stage for a fiscal disaster that, with the next recession, was just around the corner.

Examining the Crisis Budgeting Era (2001–2012)

Until the 1980s, episodes of crisis budgeting were few and far between. When deficits arose, they were usually quickly dealt with in a bipartisan fashion. With the crisis budgeting period in the early 1980s, these episodes became more frequent and severe so that by the 2000s, crisis budgeting became the norm. Here we discuss budget conditions under the crisis budgeting era and trace the roots of its existence.

To contextualize the precarious nature of the state's finances, it is useful to examine statistics on its fiscal health. The transition from boom to bust was made official in November 2001 when Legislative Analyst Elizabeth Hill projected a $12 billion deficit by June of 2003. Just one year earlier, her office had forecasted a $10 billion surplus for the upcoming budget year (2001–02). The abrupt turnaround in the state's financial picture was a direct result of the dot.com demise and the 2001 recession that was amplified by the September 11 terrorist attacks. In seven out of the next eight years, the LAO's annual *Fiscal Outlook* reported a projected deficit (See Figure 7.1). In virtually every one of these reports, the long-term forecast—that is, beyond the upcoming budget year—showed a structural deficit in the range of $10–20 billion. That represented more than 10 percent of total general fund expenditures at the time.

As mentioned earlier, projected deficits are just that—projected until economic conditions change and policy actions are adopted. In other words, they can come to fruition if policymakers do not act or if economic conditions do not improve. In this case, policymakers engaged in enough fiscal legerdemain to keep *actual deficits* low or avoid them altogether in the early 2000s. California sustained only a $2.1 billion deficit in 2001–02. However, while temporary spending and revenue measures kept the looming fiscal disaster at bay, the $15 billion deficit bond passed by voters in 2004 headed off potential insolvency. The finger-on-the-dike approach worked for now, again, but only temporarily.

As if on schedule, the mid-decade economic resurgence that had occurred in the 1980s and 1990s appeared again and provided a brief respite from the dire budget conditions and carried Governor Schwarzenegger into a second term in 2006. Under improved economic conditions and perhaps fiscal delusions, Schwarzenegger even pitched the idea of California adopting a new universal health care system in 2007. Once again, such ambitions would prove short-sighted, as the state's fiscal condition was still precarious, a housing collapse was underway, and the Great Recession would begin in late 2007. The next two years would be marked by a continuous fiscal emergency.

Despite only "officially" recording two year-end deficits in the 2000s, budget conditions were much worse. If we exclude the revenue from the $15 billion deficit bond to plug budget holes, four years would have registered deficits (See Figure 7.2). In the 2000s, only nine other states recorded a budget deficit even with the effects of the Great Recession. If we look at the structural gaps during the entire crisis budgeting era, the state recorded four consecutive years of deficits from 2009 to 2012. Questions about the state's fiscal conditions became more frequent and some commentators compared California to Greece as it teetered on the brink of insolvency halfway around the world.

Tracing the Roots of Crisis

Revenue Roots

If we take a cursory glance at Figure 7.2, there is a clear demarcation line between fiscal conditions prior to 1980 (or thereabouts) and after. If we go back further in time, this does not change the picture. The most obvious factor we can attribute this dividing line to, as many scholars have, is the adoption of Proposition 13. California's actual deficits and structural gaps became more frequent and deeper in the post-13 era. Proposition 13 not only cut property tax revenue in half, but it also made the entire state's fiscal system more reliant on volatile tax sources. The state then picked up the tab for local government and school district losses. Recent research concludes that the fiscal consequences of shifting away from a stable funding source like the property tax are not unique to California. "Our results suggest that states, in response to tax limits, are building a revenue system that puts them on a budgetary roller coaster with huge swings between the apex of the coaster's climb and the nadir of its fall."[44]

Another clearly significant revenue factor that contributed to the crisis budgeting era was the rate of general fund revenue growth. In the three decades prior to 1980, average annual revenue growth was above *10 percent*. This rate was just under 10 percent in the 1980s, but it dropped to a much lower average of 4 percent in the 1990s and 2000s (see Figure 7.3 for this trend). This rate is barely enough to keep pace with inflation and population growth at moderate levels, let alone respond to emerging needs.

The obvious question about this trend is what accounts for it. We have already discussed many of these factors in previous chapters so we will only briefly mention them here. First, policymakers and voters have both approved tax policies that have eliminated revenue sources outright (inheritance tax), reduced rates (car tax), or downsized the tax base. The sales tax base is also naturally deteriorating from the lack of sales tax on services and the increase in e-commerce.

One other factor should be noted about the pattern of revenue growth. In the 1990s and 2000s, California had slower economic growth rates than in previous decades. The real growth rate in the 1990s and 2000s was around 2 percent, while it was in the 3–4 percent range in the decades prior. This slower economic growth rate also occurred at the national level, particularly in the 2000s when it averaged 1.8 percent, so it cannot be attributed to California's economic environment. However, the slower economic growth in these decades did drag potential revenue growth down with it.

Spending Roots

Although the average rate of general fund spending growth prior to the crisis budgeting era was slower than earlier decades, spending commitments based on caseload, retiree benefits, and federal obligations continued to increase budgetary pressures. Despite popular notions to the contrary, overall general fund spending has not been excessive in the last few decades. In fact, in the 1990s, the decade prior to the crisis budgeting era, and in the 2000s, during the era, average spending rose around 5 percent per year. This contrasts sharply with average annual spending increases near 10 percent or above in the 1980s and prior. Still, as detailed in Chapter 4, some areas, such as infrastructure (bonds) and prison spending, have risen much more rapidly than others. Both of these trends are driven by public sentiment since voters must approve bond issues and

---

[44] Matthew D. McCubbins and Ellen Moule, "Making Mountains of Debt Out of Molehills: The Pro-Cyclical Implications of Tax and Expenditures Limitations," *National Tax Journal* 63, no. 3 (2010): 619.

Figure 7.3. Annual General Fund Revenue Growth, 1950-2013

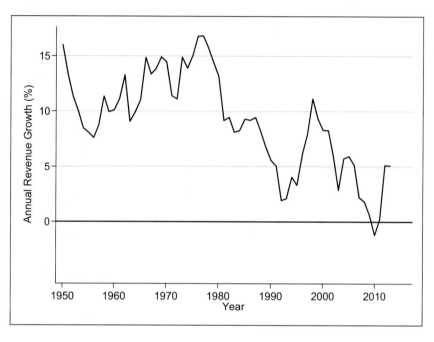

Source: Department of Finance, Chart A
Note: The line is a 5-year moving average of the percentage change in general fund revenue.

the general public has long subscribed to a "lock 'em up" mentality that has greatly expanded the size and cost of the prison system.

Long-term commitments to state pension and retiree health care plans have also increased the state's financial obligations. The most notorious of the commitments was made in the late 1990s when policymakers agreed to more generous pension benefits. Since these benefits fall under constitutional contract rights, they are difficult for policymakers to retract. The state's retiree health care obligations are even more pressing because there is no funding set aside to meet these future obligations as there is with pensions. While these obligations remain a relatively small share of the overall budget pie, their raw amounts are rapidly growing and eating up a larger share.

California's spending is also significantly influenced by federal government programs and policies. These include federal matching programs such as Medi-Cal and CalWorks, which require a state funding match in order to receive federal funding. The sharing arrangements create a spending floor if the state wishes to avoid losing its federal match and reduce spending options available to policymakers. When the state has attempted to reduce reimbursement rates to medical providers under the Medi-Cal system, the changes have been delayed or rejected by federal courts. With the largest number of undocumented immigrants in any state prison system, California has continuously sought full reimbursement from the federal government for their incarceration, but the actual reimbursements usually fall several hundred million dollars short.

Thus, in numerous ways, the state must meet spending obligations that emanate from the federal system of government.

Great Recession

The Great Recession was devastating economically and fiscally enough in and of itself, but it also amplified the structural gap between revenues and expenditures that already existed. The structural gap was there because lawmakers had only approved temporary fixes for the problems that emerged in the early 2000s. The Great Recession further pulled the revenue trend line down and pushed the spending line up. The housing market collapse in 2006–07 sent property tax revenue plunging and increased the state's share of K-12 funding, not to mention that it eventually pushed many cities and counties in California toward the brink of insolvency.

Two additional effects of the recession make prospects for a strong economic recovery, and, therefore, a brighter long-term budget outlook, doubtful. First, it accelerated a trend of income inequality that had been rising for decades. Researchers reported that the wealthiest one percent of Americans took in 95 percent of the income gains in the wake of the recession, which signaled that the prosperity from a recovery was not reaching the middle- and lower-income groups.[45] Gains in income in previous recoveries were more widely shared between income groups, and there is evidence that economic growth could be stunted by the lopsided gains. Second, the Great Recession was caused by a financial crisis. After studying financial crises over the last six centuries throughout the world, Reinhart and Rogoff concluded that economies take an average of 10 years to recover from such catastrophes. If so, in the case of the United States, strong revenue growth from a robust economy is unlikely. Of course, this was not the experience of the American economy after the Great Depression, which is also considered a financial crisis, because the California budget entered one of its healthiest eras.

Institutional Roots

The crisis budgeting era was also the culmination of a number of other institutional trends that have mostly been instigated by voters. As chronicled in Chapter 5, ballot-box budgeting has always influenced fiscal decision-making,

---

[45] Dylan Matthews, "How the 1 Percent Won the Recovery," *Washington Post*, September 11, 2013, accessed November 15, 2013, at http://www.washingtonpost.com/blogs/wonkblog/wp/2013/09/11/how-the-1percent-won-the-recovery-in-one-table/.

but its presence dramatically increased in the 1980s. The practice of earmarking, in particular, has grown exponentially in recent decades and severely constrained the budget process. The "snowball effect" of ballot measures means that policymaker discretion over spending is incrementally reduced with each measure adopted. During the 2000s, policymakers operated under more constraints than they did in either of the shorter crisis budgeting periods of the 1980s and 1990s.

One of the biggest institutional changes in the state's history was the imposition of term limits in 1990. This shortened the political outlook of legislators and made temporary budget patches more attractive. Legislators no longer had an incentive to be concerned about the long-term condition of state finances. These effects are exacerbated in states with the strictest term limits, such as those adopted by California in 1990.[46] Term limits were not in effect in the 1980s' crisis and were not yet implemented in the 1990s' crisis, although, in the latter case, legislators were starting to depart office in response to them.

California also had a perfect storm of procedural constraints that handicapped policymakers more than any other state. These budget institutions, as they are sometimes called, were either not effective at preventing deficits or required unusually high thresholds to approve budget solutions. The most significant, of course, was the two-thirds vote requirement to pass a budget, which lasted until 2010. The two-thirds threshold to raise taxes was more easily reached during the 1990s' crisis, but virtually impossible during the early part of the crisis budgeting era. Not until the state faced a $60 billion deficit in 2009 did enough Republican legislators agree to raise them. When those tax increases expired in 2011, Brown could not round up one Republican vote to extend them.

As mentioned in earlier sections, none of California's budget rules have been effective. The Gann limit has a huge gap between the limit and actual spending, while the state's balanced budget rule has been among the weakest. The state's rainy-day fund never had sufficient revenue to reduce the severe effects of budget deficits.

In sum, California's budget institutions have either been among the weakest at preventing budget disasters or make it very difficult for the state to respond to them. The majority vote budget rule should help reduce these issues, but when voters adopted it by passing Proposition 25 in 2010, they simultaneously tightened up the restrictions on tax and fee increases. Some of the budget rules mentioned above would not have been as problematic if the legislature were not as polarized as it has been in recent decades. This meant that Republicans and Democrats during the 2000s' crisis voted more in lock-step with their respective parties than they did in earlier crisis periods. The related partisan component that also contributed to the 2000s' crisis was divided government. Although he

[46] Jeff Cummins, "The Effects of Legislative Term Limits on State Fiscal Conditions," *American Politics* Research 41, no. 3 (2013): 417–42; Jonathan Day and Keith Boeckelman, "The Impact of Legislative Term Limits on State Debt: Increased Spending, Flat Revenue," *Politics and Policy* 40, no. 2 (2012): 320–38.

was considered a RINO (Republican in name only), Republican Governor Schwarzenegger stuck to the party line on taxes and blamed Democrats for the state's free-spending ways. If Democrats continue to dominate statewide offices as they are expected to, divided government may subside as a factor in future crisis budgeting episodes.

Why This Crisis Was Different

The length and persistence of the recent budget crisis begs the question of what was different about this era when compared to previous bouts with crisis budgeting. To fully appreciate the severity of the crisis, it is perhaps most useful to compare it to the first crisis budgeting era in the 1930s. The conditions in both eras were similar in many ways, but also different in some important ways. First, both eras experienced ongoing deficits driven by structural mismatches between revenues and expenditures. However, gridlock was not present during the 1930s' crisis, while it was constant in the recent crisis era. There are a number of reasons for this difference—the two-thirds threshold to pass a budget, coupled with higher levels of partisanship in particular—but the overarching factor is that there was more consensus about how to respond to the crisis. Legislators in the 1930s coalesced behind an overhaul and modernization of the tax system to generate more revenue. The Riley-Stewart amendment was the vehicle for the later adoption of a new sales and income tax. No serious legislative consideration of a tax overhaul occurred in the wake of the 2000s crisis era or in either of the earlier crises in the 1980s and 1990s. Ironically, the state is now facing a similar problem with its tax structure that it did in the 1930s—it is disconnected from an economy in transition.

Although we discuss prospects for a tax overhaul in more detail in Chapter 9, it is important to note here that a significant catalyst in the 1930s' overhaul was voters' disposition toward support for higher taxes. Voters then did not share the antitax sentiment that is omnipresent today in public discourse and even spurned several attempts to overturn the adoption of the new income tax. It is unlikely that the visceral reaction to tax increases witnessed today will turn around anytime soon and move back in the direction of more receptivity to them.

Another significant difference between the recent crisis and the 1930s' one was the absence of Proposition 13. Property taxes were the primary source of revenue for local governments and schools and reduced the financial obligations of the state in supporting both. As portrayed in Figure 7.2, budget conditions after the passage of 13 suffered and became more volatile. Numerous other budget-related measures have also been approved since 13, which have made the budget more of a jigsaw puzzle than it was in the 1930s.

Borrowing and Debt

A common tool for aligning revenues and expenditures during a fiscal year and over time is debt management. As mentioned at the outset of this chapter, California frequently uses short-term borrowing instruments—RANS and RAWS— to manage cash flow throughout the year. Policymakers and voters also approve long-term bonds to fund major infrastructure projects, such as dams, highways, and office buildings. Certain types of borrowing are considered acceptable and prudent financial practices, while other types, such as for operational costs, are not.

There are three main types of bonds that the state issues and each has its own process for authorization. The first type are bonds that are supported by the general fund and include general obligation (GO) and lease-revenue bonds. General obligation bonds are backed by the state's taxing power, require a two-thirds vote in the legislature, and must be approved by voters. They represent the majority of bonds issued. Lease-revenue bonds are paid by state agencies (mainly from the general fund) who lease facilities to conduct their operations. They only require a majority vote in the legislature and do not have to be approved by voters. They also draw a higher interest rate because they are not guaranteed.

Two other types of bonds are traditional revenue bonds and budget-related bonds. Traditional revenue bonds are paid from streams of funding generated from the use of the completed project, such as toll bridges. A special type of bond financing emerged in 2004 when voters approved Proposition 57, which authorized the state to borrow $15 billion to cover the general fund budget deficit. Proposition 57 carved out a portion of the sales tax to pay back investors.

Working with the governor's administration, the state treasurer handles the issuance of bonds and oversees their payments. For GO bonds, once approved by voters, the legislature must appropriate funding in the annual budget act. The Department of Finance then estimates the cash necessary for carrying out the projects and, with the treasurer, determines the amount of bonds to be sold. The treasurer is responsible for selling the bonds to investors based on a certain interest rate and time period for repayment.

Along with market forces, a big contributor to the interest rate demanded by investors is the state's credit rating. The credit rating of California and other government entities is set by three credit rating agencies—Standard and Poor's, Moody's Investors Services, and Fitch Ratings. The rating represents an indicator of the state's likelihood of defaulting on its debt and is based on the state's financial health, including its level of existing debt and whether a budget deficit is present or projected. Lower credit ratings signal to investors that an issuer has a higher risk of default. California's credit ratings remain among the lowest of any state in the nation. In 2014, Standard and Poor's rating for the state was A, Moody's was Aa3, and Fitch's was A.[47] This means that California must offer a higher interest rate to attract bond investors and that the state ends up paying a

---

[47] The ratings are available at http://www.treasurer.ca.gov/.

higher price overall for infrastructure projects. According to the Legislative Analyst's Office, for a 30-year bond, the state pays close to $1 in interest for every $1 borrowed.[48] Once bond proceeds are obtained, the state deposits the money in bond funds, which are then allocated by the legislature and governor over one or more years. Bondholders then receive their payments on principal and interest from the general fund (if it is a general fund supported bond).

What Are the State's Debt Levels?

Like tax burdens, we can evaluate debt levels to determine their overall financial burden. One way to examine the debt burden is to look at the amount of bonds approved and issued. As of 2014, the state has approved about $128 billion, which is less than the total amount of state spending (general and special fund) for fiscal year 2013–14.[49] Of this total, $75 billion has been issued or sold to investors.

Rather than look at overall debt levels, a more important indicator, and one that rating agencies pay attention to, is the debt-service ratio. This ratio is similar to a debt-to-income ratio that lenders assess for potential homebuyers. The debt-service ratio represents the percentage of annual revenues (usually general fund) that must be used to make bond payments to investors and cannot be used for other budgetary purposes. Generally, a debt-service ratio around 5 percent is viewed as acceptable, although there is no official standard. A ratio around 10 percent or higher may concern credit rating agencies and may result in a downgrade of status. The state's debt-service ratios from 1979 to 2013 are presented in Figure 7.4. For much of this time period, the ratio hovered well below 6 percent. It approached 6 percent in the years of the Great Recession, but has fallen in the last few years

When Does Bond Financing Make Sense?

Financing expensive infrastructure projects through borrowing is generally considered an acceptable practice. It is similar to the purchase of a house or taking out student loans for a college degree. Potential homebuyers or students cannot afford the cost of a house or education all at once, but do benefit from the purchase over a long time period and perhaps for the rest of their lives. Infrastructure projects are often too expensive to pay off in a single year. To do so would mean severely cutting funding for other core services. With most infrastructure projects, user benefits are intergenerational since users will be able to use a highway, water from a dam, or an educational institution over many de-

---

[48] When the amount is adjusted for inflation, the state pays about 30 cents for every $1 borrowed. California Secretary of State's Office, "An Overview of State Bond Debt." *Voter Information Guide.* (Sacramento: Secretary of State, November 4, 2008).

[49] Approved debt does not include debt retired or completely paid off. The total approved debt for California's history would be much higher if that were included.

Figure 7.4. Debt-Service Ratio, 1979–2013

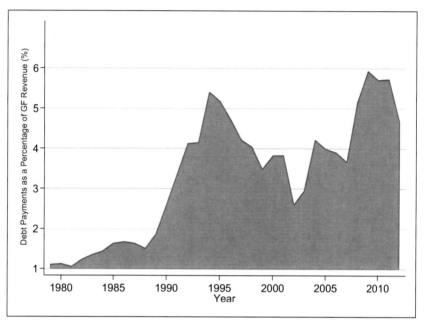

Source: Department of Finance, Charts A and K-3.
Note: Does not include unsold but authorized bonds.

cades. Since several generations of users will benefit, then it seems reasonable to spread the costs of the project among different users. For some types of projects, this could be a period up to 30 years, which is a common maturity time for GO bonds. Mikesell notes that the "fundamental rule of debt policy is: do not issue debt for a maturity longer than the financed project's useful life."[50]

Using bonds to finance operating deficits for ongoing programs and services is generally not advisable for states. Borrowing to cover ongoing deficits is a signal of a larger problem with the state's fiscal structure. The revenue system is not adequate for the service demand or the state is spending at a pace that its revenue capacity cannot maintain. Even though California borrowed $15 billion to cover ongoing programs in 2004 with the passage of Proposition 57, state leaders all agreed that this was not a good way to run the state. The main objection to deficit financing of this sort is that the state ends up paying significantly more with interest charges than it normally would under pay-as-you-go financ-

[50] John L. Mikesell, *Fiscal Administration: Analysis and Applications for the Public Sector* (Boston: Wadsworth, 2011), 640.

ing and this would continue to be the case for such ongoing programs. On the other hand, the construction of infrastructure projects is temporary in nature, frequently between one and five years, so their construction costs eventually end.

Deficit financing at the federal level is not viewed as negatively because the federal government is held responsible for economic growth and, at times, it is appropriate to borrow money to revitalize consumer demand. A relatively small ongoing deficit to gross domestic product ratio also does not negatively influence the federal government's credit rating as running a deficit does for states.[51]

The Debt Outlook

Although traditional measures of California's debt load such as the debt-service ratio are not cause for concern, other forms of borrowing and debt are. The most immediate concern is the wall of debt that has accumulated from spending deferrals and covering general fund deficits with special fund revenue. Estimated at $30 billion in 2013, Governor Brown proposed a multi-year plan to pay down this debt. Despite claims that the state began operating in the black in 2013, one could argue that the state is still in the red since this outstanding debt is owed for operating expenses. Again, this depends on how and when we define the term balance.

Other forms of borrowing and debt are more long-term in nature and not as "official" as other types. We have already discussed the state's unfunded long-term obligations for state worker pensions and retiree health care benefits in Chapter 4. Some believe that these obligations should be counted in official tallies of the state's debt. When they are, estimates put total state debt in the range of $500 billion to $1 trillion, or nearly *half* of the state gross domestic product.[52] Much of the state's future obligation in this case will hinge on whether courts allow *future* benefits of *current* employees to be reduced by initiatives or policymakers.

The other unrealized long-term debt is the state's infrastructure needs. A combination of factors contributes to California's growing need for infrastructure investment. First, much of the state's infrastructure investment was made between the 1950s and 1970s. The educational institutions, roadways, and other

---

[51] In 2011, Standard and Poor's downgraded the federal government's credit rating because the president and congressional leaders failed to adopt a long-term budget plan to address increasing debt levels. While the federal government frequently ran deficits in the past and had growing debt, both reached historically high levels at this time. The downgrade, however, did not affect interest rates on long-term Treasury bonds. The other two rating agencies, Moody's and Fitch's, did not change their rating, which contributed to the null effect on interest rates. See Dennis Cauchon, "Federal Credit Downgrade Could Trickle Down to States," *USA Today*, August 9, 2011, at http://www.usatoday.com/news/nation/2011-08-08-state-debt-downgrade_n.htm.

[52] Dan Walters, "California Could Owe $1 Trillion," *Sacramento Bee*, May 12, 2013.

capital projects supported by this funding have been deteriorating for decades and have forgone normal maintenance and repair because of budget conditions. Thus, these structures are in a more dilapidated condition than they would otherwise be. Second, the state's population grows annually by 400,000 people. To accommodate the population increases, the state must build more schools and universities, roadways, and water storage facilities, among other projects.

The Department of Finance is required by law to submit annually a five-year infrastructure plan with identified funding sources. The Department ceased publication of the report in 2008 because of its onerous workload and the state's financial condition, but resurrected it in 2014. The 2014 plan identified $65 billion in deferred maintenance needs that Governor Brown would focus on over the next five years. The amount reflected years of infrastructure neglect that occurred in the crisis budgeting era. The plan does not identify the funding needs for *new* infrastructure projects that the state may need to undertake to accommodate the growing population.

In 2012, the American Society of Civil Engineers (ASCE), which periodically conducts infrastructure needs assessment for government, assigned California a grade of C for its infrastructure conditions and planning.[53] This was a slight improvement from their 2006 assessment, when the state received a C-. However, the more staggering statistic to emerge from the report was their estimate of $65 billion that the state needs to spend *annually* to significantly improve conditions. Keep in mind that the general fund budget for 2013–14 was around $100 billion. The annual funding could come from a variety of sources (i.e., federal and local too) besides the general fund, but the comparison is still an indicator of the enormous needs of the state.

Conclusion

With the exception of the 1930s, California's budget crises were relatively minor and sporadic prior to the 1980s. Cyclical deficits in the 1980s and 1990s turned into persistent structural deficits in the 2000s that ushered in the second crisis budgeting era. Unlike the first crisis budgeting era, no significant modernization of the state's tax system has been undertaken to meet rising spending demand.

Because of its unique characteristics and notoriety, one would think that California is alone in its persistent budget struggles, but this is not the case. As mentioned throughout the chapter, California does have characteristics that make it more prone to fiscal stress, but many states have encountered similar problems, particularly during economic downturns. In 2010, in the aftermath of the Great Recession, Campbell and Sances report that 48 states had budget gaps. Although California had one of the largest, its neighbors, Nevada and Arizona, had similar-sized gaps when using standardized measures.[54]

---

[53] The report is available at http://www.ascecareportcard.org/.

[54] The gaps are relative to the size of each state's budget. Campbell and Sances,

Many of the issues that contributed to California's crisis budgeting era plague other states as well. Those that followed California in cutting their property taxes have faced a destabilization of their revenue system that makes them more vulnerable to budget deficits. Like California, other "states and localities are confronted by challenges in their revenue systems, including heightened voter resistance to tax increases and tax structures that fail to capture growth in important sectors of the economy [i.e., services]."[55] Similarly, polarization among the parties is a national phenomenon that makes compromise difficult and quick responses to fiscal problems unlikely.

Just as California has been the symbol of fiscal dysfunction, it has also been a beacon for political reforms that reverberate across the country. Both policymakers and voters have shown cracks in the antitax attitudes that have driven policy decisions over the last few decades. Governor Brown led a successful effort in 2011 to subject Amazon.com and other e-commerce vendors to sales taxes, while voters raised sales and personal income taxes in 2012. These incremental steps to modify the tax system, along with spending reductions, are unlikely to be sufficient for California to avoid future budget crises.

Review Questions

1. What are the three types of budget deficits and explain how they apply to California's budget history?

2. What fiscal tools does the state have in place to prevent budget deficits and excessive spending? How would you rate their effectiveness?

3. What conditions characterize California's two crisis budgeting eras? What factors contributed to California's most recent crisis era?

4. Describe and analyze the state's borrowing practices and management of debt. How will California's debt load impact the budget process in the future?

Additional Resources

State Treasurer's Office

http://www.treasurer.ca.gov/

The website has press releases, reports, and statistics on the management of the state's debt.

"State Fiscal Policy."

[55] Robert B. Ward and Lucy Dadayan, "State and Local Finance: Increasing Focus on Fiscal Sustainability," *Publius: The Journal of Federalism* 39, no. 3 (2009): 455.

National Conference of State Legislatures

http://www.ncsl.org/research/fiscal-policy/state-budget-procedures.aspx

The website provides summaries and data on budget rules in the 50 states, including information for balanced budget requirements, tax and expenditure limitations, and other budget procedures.

Chapter 8

Top-Down Budgeting: Understanding Local Budgeting in the State System

> Over 4 million of our fellow citizens have sent a message to City Hall, Sacramento and to all of us. The message is that the property tax must be sharply curtailed and that government spending, wherever it is, must be held in check. We must look forward to lean and frugal budgets.
>
> —Governor Jerry Brown (D), June 8, 1978,
> two days after Proposition 13 passed

Prior to the passage of Proposition 13 in 1978, local governments retained a considerable amount of discretion over their fiscal affairs. The governing bodies of counties, cities, school districts, and special districts all maintained the ability to set their own property tax rates—one of their main sources of revenue. This fiscal autonomy allowed government entities to meet the service demands of their residents, avoid budget deficits, and remain relatively independent from policymakers in Sacramento. However, this authority was a two-edged sword as homeowners eventually became disgruntled with rapidly rising property taxes, sometimes doubling from one year to the next. Proposition 13 brought this fiscal autonomy to a climactic end. Not only did this initiative cut in half the amount of property tax revenue flowing to local governments at the time, it also severely restricted their ability to raise revenue from nearly *any* source.

In previous chapters, we have focused on how the state budget process and fiscal authority have been increasingly constrained over time, but the straitjacket around local governments is tighter. Sitting on a sizeable budget surplus in 1978, the state came to the rescue of local governments when many entities saw their revenue cut in half. All local jurisdictions were affected, but some, like counties, were affected more than others because the property tax was a greater source of

231

revenue for them. With the benefit of hindsight, the state rescue of local government can be viewed as both a blessing and a curse. On the positive side, it helped fill in the budget holes punched by Proposition 13 and transition local governments into their new fiscal circumstances. But on the negative side, it centralized authority over local revenue sources in Sacramento, leaving local governments at the mercy of the state's annual budget imbroglio.

In this chapter, we examine the complex relationship between state and local government in California. We focus on counties and cities because they are the main general government entities at the local level. We start with a brief description of local government autonomy and how it has evolved over time in response to significant policy developments and the state's encroachment on their powers. To get a sense for how counties and cities budget in a state-dominant system, we provide an overview of the typical local process and fiscal structure. We then turn our attention to how direct democracy at the state and local level influences the local budgeting process. In the final section, we discuss how local governments manage their finances under fiscal constraints and in the wake of the Great Recession.

Evolution of State-Local Fiscal Relations

Although it is common to treat the relationship between the state and local government as a bilateral one, this oversimplifies the connection between the state and different local jurisdictions. The financial condition of counties has been more closely tied to the state than that of cities, which operate more independently in the state-local system. This divergence in state dependency can be traced back to two factors. First, cities were originally granted more authority than counties to manage their affairs under the 1879 constitution. Among these powers was the ability to adopt a charter to govern their affairs, which provided more autonomy, or home rule, than cities subject to the general laws of the state.[1] Subsequent amendments to the state constitution extended this charter authority to less populated cities. Counties can adopt their own charters as well, but this does not grant them much additional authority. It primarily gives them more discretion over the number and selection of countywide elected officials. "Compared to cities, counties—general or charter—are far more circumscribed with regard to what policy areas they can address, such as raising taxes or other forms of revenue, and the state can mandate that counties perform many state functions."[2] Second, both counties and cities became more disentangled from the state in 1910 when separation of sources was adopted. This made property taxes an exclusive source of revenue for local government and forced the state to

---

[1] Max Neiman, "Local Government: Designing and Financing the Cities and Counties, in *Governing California: Politics, Government, and Public Policy in the Golden State*, ed. Ethan Rarick (Berkeley: Berkeley Public Policy Press, 2013), 338.

[2] *Ibid.*, 337.

rely on other tax sources. This change was based on the principle that revenues generated locally should be used to support local services only. "Taken together, the establishment of charter cities and the separation of sources provided a measure of autonomy for local governments."[3]

After 1910, counties and cities embarked on different paths of autonomy that were influenced by the services they provided and their separate roles in a multi-layered system of government. This eventually led to starkly different levels of reliance on property tax revenue. As government at all levels grew to meet the service demands of a modern society, cities assumed a role that fostered their financial independence from the state, while counties increasingly administered programs supported by state and federal aid. Cities became the primary provider of utility services, such as water and sanitation, which became a large component of city expenditures. These services were supported with user charges and fees set and controlled by cities. With the onset of the Great Depression, welfare programs were assigned to counties and funded with federal and state subventions. Subventions to cities also grew in response to Great Society spending in the 1960s and 70s, but remained a small share of their overall revenue picture by the time Proposition 13 passed in 1978. However, for counties, subventions became the primary source of their overall revenue and property taxes represented two-thirds of their own-source revenue. For cities, property taxes were only 16 percent of their own-source revenue by 1978.[4]

Proposition 13 Transforms State-Local Relations

Prior to Proposition 13, local governments set their property tax rates to meet the revenue needs of their particular jurisdiction, in what Steven Sheffrin refers to as a *budget-based system*.[5] After two failed attempts to reduce property taxes, Proposition 13 tapped into the growing discontent over skyrocketing property tax bills in the 1970s that reached its peak right before the vote on Proposition 13. First and foremost Proposition 13 was an effort to reduce the property tax burden. Those local governments that relied more on property taxes were in line for a harder impact. Thus, property-tax dependent counties received the brunt of the effects, while cities, with a more diversified revenue base, had more mild consequences. Once the state stepped into rescue local government finances, it only made the counties more dependent on intergovernmental aid.

If Proposition 13 had only cut the property tax, its fiscal effects might have been more bearable for local (and state) government. Instead, Proposition 13

---

[3] Fred J. Silva and Elisa Barbour, *The State-Local Fiscal Relationship in California, A Changing Balance of Power* (San Francisco: Public Policy Institute of California, 1999), 5.

[4] *Ibid.*, 29.

[5] Steven M. Sheffrin, "Rethinking the Fairness of Proposition 13," in *After the Tax Revolt: California's Proposition 13 Turns 30*, ed. Jack Citrin and Isaac William Martin (Berkeley: Berkeley Public Policy Press, 2009), 126.

struck a second blow at the fiscal autonomy of local governments. First, it stripped local governments of an essential component of fiscal autonomy—the ability to set their own property tax rates. In a *rate-based system*, budget decisions would be based on projected revenue and not the other way around.[6] Second, Proposition 13 transferred authority over the allocation of property tax revenue to the legislature. After much debate, legislation (SB 154, 1978) was enacted to divvy up the revenue in each county according to the pre-Proposition 13 distribution. This decision had the effect of rewarding those jurisdictions that had imposed higher tax rates just prior to Proposition 13 and permanently allocating smaller shares to those that did not. AB 8 (1979) would later modify the allocation formula, but the die had been cast: the property tax was once again a *state tax*. Third, Proposition 13 severely constrained other revenue raising options. It initially prohibited the use of general obligation bonds and subjected all local tax increases (not fees or user charges) to voter approval.

Beyond the immediate constraints, Proposition 13 also indirectly laid the groundwork for the further erosion of fiscal autonomy over the long term. Similar to the state level, earmarking would dictate how a growing share of local government budgets would be spent. This earmarking has been driven by two sources: (1) ballot-box budgeting at the local and state level; and (2) state policy decisions. Since county supervisors and city councils can no longer authorize tax increases on their own, measures are placed on the ballot in cities and counties to dedicate a tax to a specific spending area, such as public safety or transportation. Statewide measures have also been placed before voters to dedicate some portion of the sales or income tax to support local programs and services (e.g. Proposition 63 for mental health programs). In some cases, state policymakers use these tax measures to replace funding streams that the state has co-opted from local agencies. For instance, when the state shifted property tax revenue from counties and cities to schools in 1992 and 1993 through the Educational Revenue Augmentation Funds (ERAF), lawmakers placed Proposition 172 on the ballot to direct increased sales taxes to local law enforcement. In effect, the state exchanged one discretionary local government revenue source for an earmarked source. On top of that, counties and cities lose about $5 billion annually on the exchange.[7]

At the same time that Proposition 13 reduced much of local governments' unilateral authority to raise revenue, it also unintentionally made the fiscal situation of counties and cities more volatile because their fortunes are more closely tied to the state's unstable revenue sources. Property taxes are the most stable source of revenue for state and local government. In fact, even when recessions occur, the eventual drag on property tax revenue, if it is present at all, lags behind other major revenue sources, such as income and sales taxes. This gradual slowdown in property tax revenue allows governing bodies to plan better and

---

[6] *Ibid.*, 126.
[7] Michael Multari, Michael Coleman, Kenneth Hampian, and Bill Statler, *Guide of Local Government Finance in California* (Point Arena, CA: Solano Press, 2012), 49.

adjust to economic downturns. However, because the state backfilled the loss of property tax revenue with aid from its more volatile sources, the planning and budgeting environment from one year to the next became more uncertain for counties and cities. Not only would this aid depend on healthy growth in income tax revenue, it would also depend on the generosity of state policymakers each year, who frequently contend with their own financial problems.

Budgeting at the Local Level

The budget process at the local level varies considerably across the state. State law prescribes the format and process for counties (Government Code 29000), but no similar such law exists for cities. The budget process in cities depends on the form of government: (1) strong mayor or (2) council-manager. All cities and counties follow the proposal-review-adoption format in one form or another that is common in public sector budgeting. In strong-mayor cities, the process is executive-dominant. The city manager, appointed by the mayor, oversees the budget development process with the mayor's priorities in mind. In counties and council-manager cities, the process is legislative-dominant because there is no elected executive equivalent to the strong mayor. The city manager, who answers to the entire city council, and the county executive, appointed by the board of supervisors, direct the budget processes. In both counties and cities, departments and agencies develop and submit their baseline budgets and new funding requests to the finance or budget office. In strong-mayor cities, the mayor makes final decisions over department budgets and then presents the final proposed budget to the city council for its modification and approval. In the legislative-dominant counties and cities, the city manager or county executive makes final budget decisions before presenting the spending plan to the council or board of supervisors for adoption.

Depending on the jurisdiction, there is also wide variation in the budget display format (i.e., line-item versus performance), length of public hearings process, the budget cycle, and the level of conflict. As we might assume, these characteristics typically vary according to the population and budget size of the particular jurisdiction. Counties and larger cities generally conduct their public budget hearings over a two-month span in May and June, while smaller cities may need just a few weeks or even one meeting to formally adopt their budget. Although counties are required to have annual budgets, some cities operate on a two-year cycle. Larger cities, such as San Diego and San Francisco, have independent budget analysts that make recommendations to the legislative bodies similar to the Legislative Analyst's Office at the state level.

In strong-mayor cities, budget clashes over fiscal matters can occur between the executive (mayor) and legislative (council) branches, akin to what occurs at the state and national level. In a few of the largest cities, mayors have line-item veto powers that can be overridden by supermajoritarian votes of the council.

This is fairly common in the largest cities throughout the United States.[8] For counties, conflict over the budget may occur among supervisors and between supervisors and countywide elected officials. In Fresno County in 2010, for example, the sheriff filed a lawsuit against the board of supervisors for rescinding layoff notices the sheriff had sent to 69 correctional officers. In a case with statewide implications, a superior court later ruled that the board had violated the sheriff's constitutional and statutory authority. These instances of conflict mainly erupt in highly populated jurisdictions, while, in contrast, there may be little conflict in the more numerous counties and cities with smaller populations. The stakes are not as high where budgets are smaller; they tend to move through the adoption process more smoothly.

When the state is in crisis budgeting mode, the same vagaries of the state process afflict local budget processes. The budget calendar used in county and city processes becomes subject to the lurching decision points of state policymakers. It is not uncommon for local governing bodies to adopt two different budgets—one prior to the passage of the state budget and another one once the final state budget is approved. When budget gridlock was present, the final county or city budget might not be adopted until August or September. And again, because counties rely more heavily on state aid, they were more impacted by a state process constantly in flux. Cities, however, did have to adjust to significant policy changes that affected their financial situation, such as the dissolution of redevelopment agencies and the diversion of vehicle license fee (VLF) revenue. Local governments have attempted to protect their revenue streams from raids by state policymakers (Proposition 1A in 2004), but legislators seem to always find ways to circumvent these protections.

When it comes to decision-making, local budgeting differs from the state process in two major ways. First, a relatively small portion of county and city total revenue is considered discretionary each year. For counties, on average, about 75 percent of their revenue is on autopilot and beyond the control of county boards. For cities, about 65 percent of their revenue is tied to a particular service, leaving 35 percent for discretionary purposes each year. Second, while ballot-box budgeting has become a significant component of state budgeting, it is required at the local level if a jurisdiction seeks to raise tax revenue. In contrast, the state legislature can raise taxes on its own if it can muster the two-thirds vote to do so. County boards and city councils do not have such authority. These local governing bodies can still adopt some fees and charges by a majority vote, but user charges for services such as water and trash cannot exceed the cost of providing the service. Thus, a key component of budgeting at the local level—raising tax revenue—*requires* the participation of voters.

To get a sense for the budget situation at the local level, it is useful to look at the breakdowns of revenue and expenditures for counties and cities. Figure

---

[8] Irene Rubin, *The* Politics *of Budgeting: Getting and Spending, Borrowing and Balancing* (Thousand Oaks, CA: CQ Press, 2014), 89. In California, this includes Los Angeles, San Diego, San Francisco, Long Beach, and Fresno.

8.1 shows a comparison of the revenue sources for counties and cities statewide. Several points related to the discussion above appear in stark relief. First, counties rely on property tax for more than 20 percent of their total revenue, while cities rely on it for 8 percent. Second, charges and fees, which local governing bodies have the authority to set, comprise the largest share of revenue for cities (45 percent), but, for counties, only make up 13 percent of their budget. Third, the figure clearly illustrates the dependent nature of county finances; 58 percent of their revenue comes from intergovernmental aid.

Figures 8.2 and 8.3 show the breakdown of statewide county and city expenditures by function. As is readily evident, both types of jurisdictions spend the largest share of their budgets on public safety (33 percent for counties and 26 percent for cities). This is where their spending patterns diverge however. Counties spend their next largest share on public assistance programs (31 percent), while cities' second highest spending category is public utilities (21 percent). For counties, the third largest share is spent on health and sanitation (19 percent), followed by general government, public ways and facilities, recreation and education, and debt service. Cities' third largest spending area is transportation (16 percent), followed by health, general government, community development, and culture and leisure. These spending breakdowns also illustrate how counties are more vulnerable than cities to budgetary pressures during economic downturns. Demand for public assistance and health care increases during recessions and they represent the second and third largest areas of county spending. The second largest area for cities is public utilities and poor economic conditions do not put as much spending pressure on utilities as they do for human services.

Ballot-Box Budgeting Required

One of the major impacts of Proposition 13 was that it *required* greater public participation in local budgeting by mandating voter approval of tax increases and spending from dedicated revenue sources (i.e. special taxes); in effect, it democratized decision-making over taxes and—to a more limited extent— spending. This aspect of Proposition 13 is different than the state level where lawmakers can still raise taxes on their own and judiciously refer tax increase measures to the ballot. For local elected officials, the voter approval stipulation has led to a different approach to the normally controversial topic of taxes: they frequently turn to the ballot to raise revenue for their jurisdiction more so than state elected officials.[9] This likely occurs for several reasons. First, the voter approval requirement provides political cover because local officials cannot be accused of increasing taxes on their own. Second, these taxes can be linked to

---

[9] Andrew D. Green, Max Neiman, Shel Bockman, and Barbara Sirotnik, "Public Support for Transportation Sales Taxes in California: A Two County Assessment," *California Journal of Politics and Policy* 5, no. 4 (2013): 652.

Figure 8.1. City and County Revenue by Type

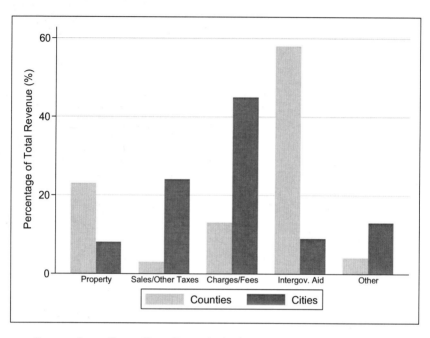

Source: State Controller, *Cities Annual Report, 2010–11*; *Counties Annual Report, 2011–12*.

specific services, which reduces the perception of wasted government resources or taxpayer dollars going to undeserved causes. Third, it reinforces the notion of local control since tax dollars will stay in the local region and the benefits will be more readily apparent.

The approval process for local legislative referrals has become fairly complicated, as statewide propositions subsequent to Proposition 13 have modified voter requirements. The approval requirements vary by the type of tax (see Table 8.1). General taxes, which support general purpose spending, and property assessments require a majority vote of the governing body. Special taxes, which earmark revenue for specific purposes, and general obligation (GO) bonds require a two-thirds vote by the governing body. General taxes then require approval from a majority of voters, while special taxes and GO bonds require approval from two-thirds.

Aside from local legislative referrals, voters may also encounter local budget-related *initiatives* at election time, but they are not the increasingly dominant force they are at the state level. Proposition 218, passed in 1996, clarified the voter approval requirements for ballot measures and laid out a distinct process

Figure 8.2. City Expenditures by Type, 2010–11

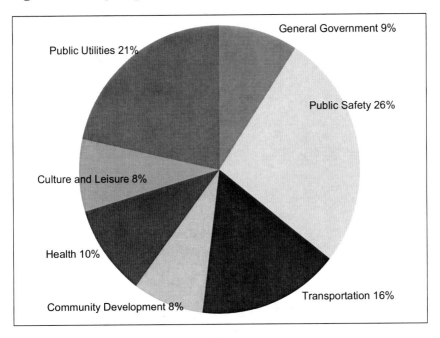

Source: State Controller, *Cities Annual Report*.

for local tax initiatives. It limited the signature requirement for tax initiatives to no more than 5 percent of the votes cast in the last gubernatorial election in that jurisdiction, the same as for statewide statutory initiatives.[10] Tax initiatives also only require a majority vote for approval. In a study of local initiatives from 1990 to 2000, Gordon found that 72 percent of city initiatives and 64 percent of county initiatives qualified for the ballot, rates much higher than we see at the state level. Approval rates were also higher than the state level, as 50 percent of city initiatives passed, while 57 percent of county initiatives did.

Types of Local Budget-Related Measures
From 2000–2012, there were a total of 3,248 county and city measures on the ballot.[11] The number of measures surged in even-numbered election years,

---

[10] For an explanation of the signature threshold requirements in cities and counties, see Tracy Gordon, *The Local Initiative in California* (San Francisco: Public Policy Institute of California, 2004), 7–18.

[11] Data for ballot measures was taken from the California Elections Data Archive (CEDA) at Sacramento State University. Available at http://www.csus.edu/calst/cal_studies/CEDA.html.

Figure 8.3. County Expenditures by Type, 2011–12

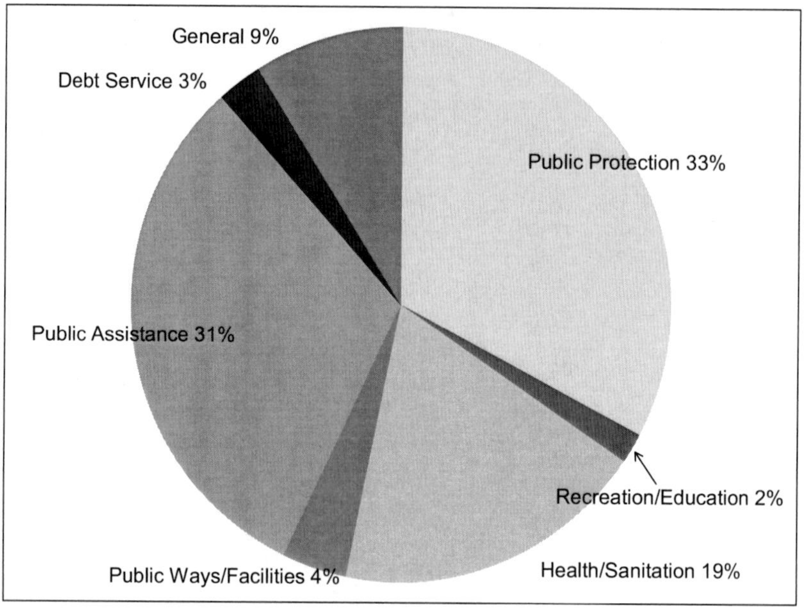

General 9%
Debt Service 3%
Public Protection 33%
Public Assistance 31%
Recreation/Education 2%
Public Ways/Facilities 4%
Health/Sanitation 19%

Source: State Controller, *Counties Annual Report.*

usually in the range of 3–400 measures, and dropped into the low 100s in off-year elections. Around one-third (1,118 measures) of these measures were tax-related and the vast majority of them were placed on the ballot by elected governing bodies. In fact, of all measures on the ballot in any given year, only a very small portion of them are initiatives and those typically deal with land use or governance issues.[12] In contrast with the state level, few ballot measures authorize bonds (< 3 percent) or modify the budget process (< 2 percent).

As Figure 8.4 shows, the most frequent type of tax to appear on the ballot is the sales tax. In the 12-year period, there were 288 sales tax measures, followed closely behind by hotel taxes (transient oriented taxes—TOT) with 254, and utility taxes (i.e., water, cable, etc.) with 218 measures. Property-based taxes (e.g., parcel taxes) are fairly common and appear more often than business taxes or miscellaneous taxes. We might assume that local officials would shy away from referring broad-based taxes to the ballot, such as sales or utility taxes, since they would affect everyone in the community, but this is not the case. Instead,

---

[12] Gordon found a similar pattern with initiatives in the 1990s. See *The Local Initiative*, 24–25.

Table 8.1. Revenue Approval Process for Counties and Cities

Revenue Type	Governing Body Approval	Voter Approval	Examples
Taxes General (unrestricted)	General law cities: 2/3 Charter: majority	majority	General purpose
Special (earmarked)	majority	2/3	Public safety, transportation
Fees	majority	none	Water, sewer, trash, development impact
Property assessment	majority	majority (affected property owners)	Roads, street lights
General obligation bonds	2/3	2/3	Facilities

Source: Legislative Analyst's Office, *Calfacts 2013*.

revenue-generating capacity seems to trump potential public resistance to these taxes.[13] Public opinion surveys also support this strategy because respondents are somewhat open to sales tax increases, but less inclined to support property tax increases. Local officials are also more likely to place general taxes on the ballot, which have lower voter approval requirements than special taxes and are presumably aware of the higher passage rate for general taxes. On the other hand, hotel taxes place the burden on a popular target: visitors from out of town. In recent years, these potential taxpayers have become a more frequent target of local policymakers.

Passage rates of particular types of taxes shed some light on the choice of tax measures placed before voters (see Figure 8.5). Of particular note overall, and a major reason for the fairly high frequency of tax measures on the ballot, is

[13] Kim S. Reuben and Pedro Cerdán, *Fiscal Effects of Voter Approval Requirements on Local Governments* (San Francisco: Public Policy Institute of California, 2003), 73; Mark Baldassare and Christopher Hoene, *Local Budgets and Tax Policy in California: Surveys of City Officials and State Residents* (San Francisco: Public Policy Institute of California, 2004).

Figure 8.4. Local Tax Measures by Type, 2000–2012

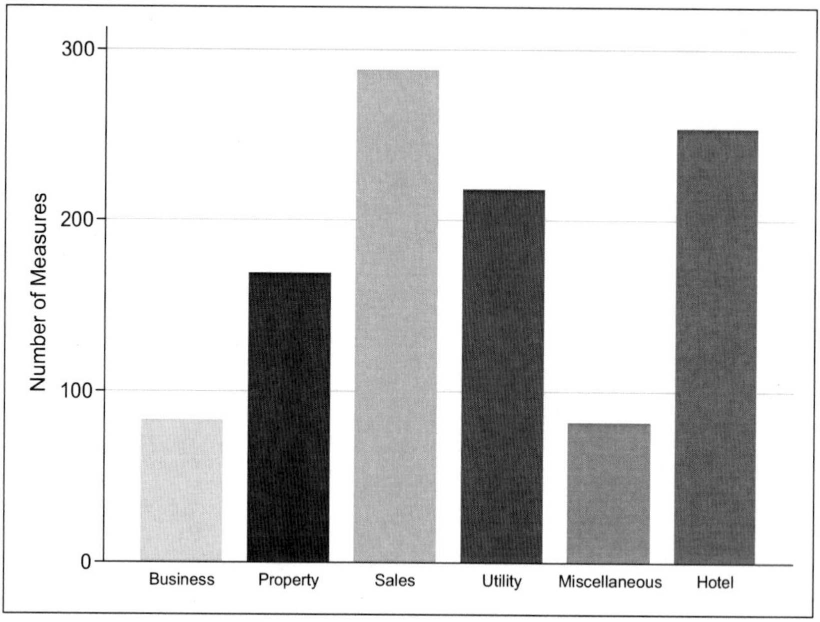

Source: California Elections Data Archive.

the *60 percent approval* rate. This seems counterintuitive given the antitax sentiment that supposedly pervades public discourse. Several types of taxes, including business, utility, and miscellaneous taxes have approval rates near two-thirds or more. The frequently used sales tax passes 56 percent of the time, while the lower approval rate for property taxes of 47 percent indicates its lower popularity and higher vote requirements.

We can also get a better understanding of how local officials prioritize different services they provide by examining the spending targets of special taxes and bonds.[14] Like earmarks at the state level that have been popular in recent decades, these measures dedicate a source of revenue to a specific purpose, but must meet a two-thirds vote threshold. Thus, it behooves local officials to place spending measures on the ballot that enjoy overwhelming public support and

---

[14] We did not include advisory measures in the tally of spending or tax measures. Advisory measures register voters' sentiment for proposed policies, but are not binding on governing bodies. General tax measures are sometimes accompanied on the ballot with these advisory measures in order to recommend where new revenue should be allocated, the so-called a/b strategy. We excluded them here because of their nonbinding nature and their relatively infrequent occurrence.

Figure 8.5. Passage Rates by Type of Tax Measure, 2000–2012

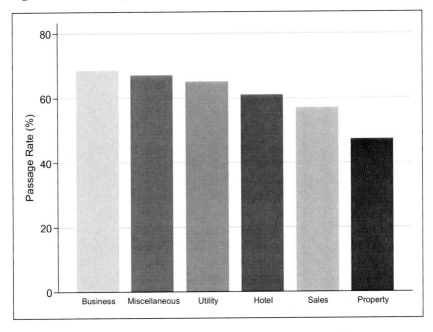

Source: California Elections Data Archive.

reflect the community's priorities. Table 8.2 lists the number and passage rates of proposed special taxes and bonds by function from 2000 to 2012. The most frequent measures are for emergency/medical services. Libraries and transportation are the next two most common measures followed by public safety and parks and recreation. The overall passage rate is 47 percent, which is what we might expect with high vote thresholds. The two most frequent topics also have some of the highest passage rates. This suggests that the relatively higher passage rates may drive the frequency of these topics because local officials may seek to capitalize on voter attitudes. Surprisingly, public safety is ranked fourth on frequency and has the lowest passage rate. This runs counter to the notion that public safety and being "tough on crime" is a preeminent concern of local communities.

Having now examined patterns of local ballot measures, a few observations about local ballot-box budgeting deserve mention. First, earmarking is not as prevalent at the local level probably because of the higher vote thresholds for special taxes and the weaker presence of interest groups. Second, local ballot measure campaigns are not the intense, commercial-driven battles they are at the state level. In many cases, they are one-sided affairs, with elected officials lead-

Table 8.2. County and City Special Tax and Bond Spending Measures By Function, 2000–12.

Function	No. Measures Proposed	Passage Rate (%)
Emergency/medical services	95	60
Libraries	67	54
Transportation	61	43
Public safety (police, fire)	53	34
Parks and recreation	35	46
General Government (solid waste, water, etc.)	26	35
Other	129	56
Totals	466	47

Source: California Elections Data Archive.

Note: Includes all special tax and bond measures for cities and counties and excludes special district measures.

ing the charge against little opposition, particularly in smaller communities. Lastly, tax measures at the local level seem to lack the third-rail stigma normally associated with tax issues at higher levels. Ironically, mandated voter approval of tax increases may serve to defuse the visceral reactions typically stoked by such proposals. Local elected officials can deflect the blame for these unpopular policy actions by letting the voters decide at the same time they are seeking additional resources to maintain or increase the quality of services in their jurisdiction.

The Struggle for Fiscal Autonomy

As discussed above, Proposition 13 set in motion a series of steps that have reduced local government fiscal autonomy. There have been two antagonists responsible for the plight of local government: state policymakers and antitax groups. The latter used the initiative process to constrain local authority over fiscal matters, while the former have employed several policy tools to reconfigure the state-local fiscal relationship, including the budget act, legislation, and the ballot box. A closer review of the policy developments affecting the state-local relationship reveals two distinct patterns (see Table 8.3). First, state policymakers have generally not used the ballot box to take funding sources away from local government. Instead, legislative action has been the preferred method

Table 8.3. Significant Developments in the State-Local Fiscal Relationship

Year	Policy	Description	Source	Type
1978	Prop 13	Imposed statewide 1 percent uniform property tax rate; required voter approval of local taxes; delegated property tax allocation to state	I	CA
1978–79	AB 8/ SB154	Used state surplus to backfill funding for local services; established property tax allocation system	Leg.	S
1979	Prop 4	Established state and local government spending limits and required state to reimburse mandates	I	CA
1986	Prop 47	Guaranteed vehicle license fee (VLF) revenue for cities and counties	Leg.	CA
1988	Prop 98	Earmarked at least 40 percent of general fund for K-12 education and community colleges; established formulas for determining allocation	I	CA
1991	Realign.	Shifted responsibility for certain mental health and other programs from state to counties with funding sources	Leg.	S
1992–94	ERAF	Shifted annual statewide property tax revenue from cities, counties, and special districts to schools to reduce state share of education funding	Leg.	S
1993	Prop 172	Dedicated portion of state sales tax for local law enforcement purposes	Leg.	CA
1996	Prop 218	Further constrained ability of local government to raise taxes	I	CA

1999–2004	Bud	State reduced VLF rate and back-filled with other funding sources	Leg.	S
2004	Prop 1A	Restricts state's authority over local revenue sources for property tax, sales tax, and VLF	I	CA
2009	Bud	Shifted local redevelopment revenue to state and borrowed property tax revenue	Leg.	S
2010	Prop 22	Reduces state's authority over state fuel tax and property tax revenue	I	CA
	Prop 26	Broadens definition of tax to subject more fees to voter approval requirements	I	CA
2011	Bud	Shifted authority for criminal justice programs to counties and offsets costs with state sales and VLF revenue	Leg.	S
	ABX126	Dissolved local redevelopment agencies and redirected property tax revenue to local government and schools	Leg.	S
2012	Prop 30	Guarantees county and city funding for 2011 realignment	I	CA

Source: Legislative Analyst's Office, *Major Milestones: Over Four Decades of the State-Local Fiscal Relationship.*
Note: Bud=budget; I=initiative; Leg.=Legislature; CA=constitutional amendment; S=statute.

for "redirecting" local revenue to meet state funding obligations. The first major raid was the ERAF shift, which "signaled the start of a second, highly contentious stage in the post-Proposition 13 state-local relationship, during which the full measure of Proposition 13's effects came home for local governments."[15] One reason state policymakers have used legislation is the urgency of the situation. Typically, they faced the deadline to pass a budget, or had already

---

[15] Elisa Barbour, *State-Local* Conflicts *in California: From Proposition 13 to Proposition 1A* (San Francisco: Public Policy Institute of California, 2007), 5.

exceeded it, and sought ways to close the state's budget shortfalls in an expeditious manner. Seeking voter approval is a slow process and would have delayed the state's budget even more. Furthermore, had policymakers sought voter approval for these local government raids, they probably would not have been approved since the public has a more positive view of local government than state.

The second pattern in developments of the state-local relationship is that protections for local government revenue sources have been authorized at the ballot box. These revenue protection efforts normally follow a series of funding raids or reallocations that sparked resentment among local officials. For instance, in 2004, after a decade of such funding shifts, and on the heels of a proposed $2.6 billion raid, local government advocacy groups sponsored an initiative (Proposition 65) to limit the state's authority over local revenue sources. Governor Arnold Schwarzenegger (R) later convinced local government advocates to abandon their proposition in favor of a legislative measure (Proposition 1A) that accomplished similar goals. Local governments lost the $2.6 billion, but received constitutional protections against such future raids and Schwarzenegger's endorsement of the measure.[16] "Proposition 1A prevents the state government from using local governments as a fiscal 'shock absorber.'"[17]

Even constitutional protections have not stopped the governor and legislature from shoring up the state's fiscal condition at the expense of local governments. In 2011, Governor Brown and legislators began the process of dissolving local redevelopment agencies, which served as funding sources for economic development projects. In yet another round of realignment, more responsibility for lower-level criminal offenders was also transferred to counties. Governor Brown assured county officials that adequate funding for these additional responsibilities would be protected with the passage of Proposition 30. However, if history is any guide, these funding streams will prove inadequate and the recent reconfiguration of the state-local fiscal relationship will not be the last.

Balancing Local Budgets

Although there is no statutory requirement that counties and cities balance their budgets, it is an accepted norm that permeates the public sector in California, one of more than 20 states that does not have such a requirement.[18] However, according to a 1994 study, all 15 of the largest cities in California had a balanced budget requirement (BBR) in their charters. Across the country, it appears quite common for large cities to have this requirement; 99 out of 100 cities surveyed in the study had them. In contrast, we do not know how common BBRs are for medium and small-sized cities. For cities with these requirements, the

---

[16] Dan Walters, "Local Governments Seek Shield From Sacramento Bandits," *Sacramento Bee*, October 13, 2004.

[17] Barbour, *State-Local Conflicts*, 27.

[18] Carol W. Lewis, "Budgetary Balance: The Norm, Concept, and Practice in Large U.S. Cities," *Public Administration Review* 54, no. 6 (1994): 516.

type varies by jurisdiction. Some cities like Los Angeles must adopt a balanced budget, but do not have a year-end requirement. On the other hand, San Diego and San Jose are prohibited from ending the fiscal year with a deficit.[19] While researchers have studied the effectiveness of BBRs at the state level quite extensively, we know little about their impact at the local level. Of the 15 largest California cities examined in the 1994 study, notably only Stockton fell victim to bankruptcy in the wake of the Great Recession. However, nearly all others encountered significant fiscal stress with some, such as Los Angeles, San Diego, and Fresno, on the brink of bankruptcy.[20]

Another fiscal tool to balance budgets common at the state level that some large California cities have adopted is a rainy-day fund (RDF) or budget stabilization fund (BSF). These savings accounts provide cities with some financial cushion when revenue levels do not keep pace with projected expenditures. According to a 2009 survey, only one (Oakland) of five large California cities (not necessarily the largest) did not have a formal rainy day fund.[21] Long Beach, Los Angeles, Sacramento, and San Diego all had some type of reserve fund for budget shortfalls. Nationally, these seem to be much less popular than BBRs; only 11 of the 27 large U.S. cities surveyed had a rainy-day fund. In studies done of smaller cities in other states, less than half had them.[22] Surprisingly, studies also show that cities typically carry much larger reserve balances than what conventional wisdom usually suggests. On average, these funds exceeded 20 percent of a jurisdiction's revenue. One reason these balances may be so high is that the definition of budget reserves has not been clearly defined. Some restricted funding balances may have made their way into the calculation. In the future, local governments will have to comply with new accounting rules set by the Governmental Accounting Standards Board (GASB) that standardize the reporting of budget reserves. Nevertheless, unlike at the state level, research indicates that rainy-day funds have little impact on stabilizing municipal spending.[23]

Aside from the adoption of formal fiscal rules, two other patterns explain how local governments have sought to strengthen their fiscal health. One tool that cities in particular have employed is zoning and land use. Through *fiscalization of land use*, local officials attempt to increase their revenue from sales tax by attracting retail-intensive businesses to their jurisdiction. These land-use pol-

---

[19] *Ibid.*, 517. San Jose's charter does leave open the possibility of carrying over a deficit.

[20] Of course, bankruptcy is a crude measure of BBR effectiveness. Other measures of fiscal condition, such as year-end deficits and balances, would provide a more comprehensive assessment of their effectiveness. Lewis looks at bond ratings, but finds no link to BBRs.

[21] Justin Marlowe, "Fiscal Slack, Reserves, and Rainy-Day Funds," in *Handbook of Local Government Fiscal Health*, ed. Helisse Levine, Jonathan B. Justice, and Eric A. Scorsone (Burlington, MA: Jones & Bartlett Learning, 2013), 331.

[22] *Ibid.*, 332.

[23] *Ibid*, 334.

icies have sparked controversy in local communities when governing bodies have considered approval for construction of big-box retailers such as Wal-Mart. Small businesses and mom-and-pop stores believe they cannot compete with these retailers and usually oppose their approval. Local elected officials, however, view these retailers as revenue bonanzas that can help maintain programs and services. Thus, fiscalization of land use is one of the few remaining options that local policymakers can use to shore up their finances without voter approval.

Local governments have also found ways to raise revenue by turning to an increasing assortment of fees and charges. Most of these charges do not require voter approval and thus present an easier path to more revenue. However, much of this revenue is usually restricted so it must be used for related purposes. Cities, in particular, have taken advantage of this revenue source. In 1978, fees and charges represented 15 percent of total city revenue; in 2010–11, they were 45 percent. For counties, they only increased from 12 percent in 1978 to 15 percent by fiscal year 2011–12.[24]

None of the fiscal coping mechanisms of local government could prepare them for the enormous economic consequences from the Great Recession. Because of how property and sales taxes are administered, the impact on revenue was somewhat delayed for counties and cities compared to the more immediate effects the recession had on state revenue. In a 2009 survey of local officials, more than a year after the recession began, less than 25 percent regarded their fiscal condition as poor, but nearly all (more than 96 percent) anticipated their ability to provide services would worsen.[25] Once property taxes experienced their first year-over-year decline in 2009–10 in over 15 years and sales tax revenue collections registered the effects of anemic consumer spending, projected budget deficits afflicted many local jurisdictions by 2010. The city of San Diego faced a $120 million deficit, while Sacramento County confronted a $180 million deficit. In Los Angeles, the city encountered a $212 million deficit in 2010 and then another $484 million shortfall in 2011.[26] Crisis budgeting took hold as local governments struggled to keep their finances afloat. Their normal budget calendars were abandoned as governing bodies scrambled to adopt solutions as updated budget estimates only made a bad situation worse. They burned through whatever budget reserves they had and looked for areas to cut. The 2009 survey indicated that spending cuts for services, the elimination of unfilled positions,

---

[24] State Controller, *Annual Report of Financial Transactions Concerning Counties of California* (Sacramento: State Controller, 1977-78); State Controller, *Annual Report of Financial Transactions Concerning Cities of California* (Sacramento: State Controller, 1977–78); *Counties Annual Report, 2011–12*; *Cities Annual Report, 2010–11*.

[25] Baldassare and Hoene, *Local Budgets*, 18.

[26] Christina Plerhoples and Eric A. Scorsone, "Fiscal Stress and Cutback Management among State and Local Governments: What Have We Learned and What Remains to Be Learned," in *Handbook of Local Government Fiscal Health*, ed. Helisse Levine, Jonathan B. Justice, and Eric A. Scorsone (Burlington, MA: Jones & Bartlett Leanring, 2013), 272.

fee increases, hiring freezes, and employee layoffs were among the top actions taken by county and city officials.[27]

As the history of state-local relations might suggest, the state provided no relief for local governments and in fact exacerbated their worsening financial conditions. The biggest blows were a $4 billion shift in redevelopment funds to the state and a $2 billion "loan" of property taxes to cover the state's Proposition 98 education obligation. These hits to local finances made it harder for counties and cities to manage cash flow and, for some, bankruptcy became a real possibility. Unlike states, local governments can file for bankruptcy through federal Chapter 9 bankruptcy protection laws. Local governments rarely use this option because of the stigma and downgrade in bond ratings associated with it. In 2012, however, three California cities, San Bernardino, Stockton, and Mammoth Lakes, all filed for bankruptcy protection.[28] In 19 other states, the state government can intervene in financial crises of local government, but California is among those that take a hands-off approach.[29] In 2011, the state did enact a mediation law that allows labor unions, creditors, and other parties to request a 60-day "neutral evaluation process" whereby a mediator is brought in to reach a settlement. Stockton used the mediator option, but failed to reach a settlement. San Bernardino claimed their situation was too dire and bypassed the option altogether. If more local jurisdictions succumb to bankruptcy, it is likely to put more pressure on the state to establish a monitoring system for county and city finances. The establishment of such a system would further entangle state and local government finances and place local governments even more at the mercy of the state.

Conclusion

The main impetus behind Proposition 13 was excessive property tax burdens levied by local officials. While the initiative cut the burden in half, it also stripped local elected officials of their tax-raising authority, but left state legislators with unilateral authority to raise taxes. Ironically, the general public has a more favorable view of local government than state government even though counties and cities send tax measures to the ballot much more often than the state does. According to a 2012 Public Policy Institute of California (PPIC) poll, 54 percent of the public had a favorable impression of local government, while only 31 percent had one for state government.[30] As such, the public has the most

---

[27] Baldassare and Hoene, *Local Budgets*, 22.

[28] The bankruptcy filing for Mammoth Lakes was later dismissed when the city reached a settlement with its main creditor.

[29] The Pew Charitable Trusts, *The State Role in Local Government Financial Distress* (Washington, DC: The Pew Charitable Trusts, 2013), accessed March 28, 2014, at http://www.pewstates.org/uploadedFiles/PCS_Assets/2013/Pew_State_Role_in_Local_G overnment_Financial_Distress.pdf.

[30] Public Policy Institute of California Statewide Survey, *Californians and their*

confidence in the level of government with the least amount of autonomy—local government.

Despite the generally positive views of local government, at least relative to the state, counties and cities will continue to operate under severe fiscal constraints. Just like at the state level, the pro-growth budgeting era is unlikely to return anytime soon. Property tax revenue is not expected to grow much annually given the capped rate and new regulations governing the real estate industry in the wake of the housing bubble. Likewise, sales tax revenue is unlikely to fuel a local government resurgence, especially because of its outdated tax base. Spending growth may occur in fits and starts in between recessions, but an austerity budgeting environment is likely to continue. Some observers suggest that a "new normal" has set in for local governments across the country. "A protracted period of sorting out may well take place as local governments visit and revisit: what they are legally obligated to do, what they believe they must do, and what they can stop doing."[31] If past is prologue, then state policymakers and voters will undoubtedly play a central role in sorting out which revenue sources and services local government will control.

Review Questions

1. Which developments in the state-local fiscal relationship have most shaped the fiscal authority of local governments?

2. What are the trends in ballot-box budgeting at the local level? How are they different than trends at the state level?

3. What tools do counties and cities have to balance their budgets? What additional tools might help them better cope with fiscal stress?

Additional Resources

The California Local Government Finance Almanac

http://www.californiacityfinance.com/

The website has policy analyses, issue summaries, fiscal data, and other information on finances for all types of local government.

Government (San Francisco: Public Policy Institute of California, October, 2012).
[31] Lawrence L. Martin, Richard Levey, and Jenna Cawley, "The 'New Normal' for Local Government," *State and Local Government Review* 40 (2012): 23S.

California State Association of Counties and League of California Cities

http://www.csac.counties.org/
http://www.cacities.org/

These are the websites for the organizations representing California cities and counties. They contain educational and advocacy materials for member agencies pertaining to fiscal and other matters.

Howard Jarvis Taxpayers Association

http://www.hjta.org/

This website provides information on property tax issues, commentary on fiscal problems, and legislative advocacy tools.

Chapter 9

The Fix—Improving the Budget System

I sent you the Tax Reform Commission's plan in late September, but it seems
to have disappeared somewhere under this dome.
—Governor Arnold Schwarzenegger (R)
2010 State of the State speech

After a tumultuous 2009 in which government leaders stared down a $60 Billion
deficit, passed two separate budget plans, and the state issued IOUs after running out of cash, Governor Arnold Schwarzenegger (R) issued an executive order creating the Commission on the 21st Century Economy to tackle the prickly
issue of tax reform. It was commonly acknowledged by both Democrats and
Republicans alike that the outdated tax system was the root cause of California's
roller coaster budget system. "Here is what we need to accept: our economy is
21st century, but our tax system is 20th century."[1] When the commission released its final report in 2009, many Democrats came out in support of it, including former Assembly Speakers Willie Brown and Robert Hertzberg and former
Governor Gray Davis. The plan "proposed major, radical reforms," including
the introduction of a new business net receipts tax, the elimination of the state
sales tax, and the flattening of income tax rates. As Governor Schwarzenegger
later proclaimed in his State of the State message, "Bold is what we do in California." Democratic leaders in the legislature, however, did not share these
warm feelings and never brought it to a vote.

---

[1] Governor Arnold Schwarzenegger, 2010 State of the State speech.

Only six years earlier, another tax reform commission, the California Commission on Tax Policy in the New Economy, was tasked with "examin[e]ing all aspects of the current and future California economy with special attention to the influence of new technologies, and assess[ing] the impact of the evolving California economy on public revenues." Authorized by SB 1933 in 2000, this commission's report had the unfortunate fate of being released in December 2003, shortly after Governor Davis, who signed the legislation, was removed from office and Schwarzenegger took his place. With a neophyte governor and an enormous budget deficit consuming his time, the recommended tax reforms lacked a forceful advocate to push them through the legislature. By 2009, Governor Schwarzenegger, now acutely aware of the importance of tax reform to budget stability, resurrected a similar commission only to have its recommendations suffer the same fate.

California is often regarded as a model of policy innovation, but as these cases illustrate, budgetary reform efforts produce few results more often than not. The state has seen numerous commissions, committees, and study groups established to overhaul the tax system, improve the budgetary process, or revise the state constitution. In this concluding chapter, we examine California's experience with budgetary reform and analyze potential pathways the state can take to increase budget stability and fiscal sustainability. We focus less in this chapter on specific reforms, although several are discussed, because many have been presented in previous chapters and there is no shortage of them in published material. Instead, we concentrate more on the platforms or policy vehicles for change because the primary obstacle for improving the budgetary system has not been the lack of reform ideas, but the avenues for successful adoption.

Short History of Budgetary Reform

Before embarking on an historical review of budgetary reform, a definition of budgetary reform is warranted. Here budgetary reform means constitutional or statutory changes to the budget process or tax structure, including the mix of taxes, or the adoption or elimination of certain taxes. In political discourse, reform usually refers to a positive change that will make the system better. Reform can be *wholesale* in nature, where a package of changes is presented, or *incremental*, where single changes with significant budgetary implications are proposed or considered one at a time. There is no fine line between these two distinctions, but they are useful for understanding how reforms have unfolded in the state's history.

There have been several different types of vehicles for consideration of budgetary reforms. The first type, and potentially offering the most comprehensive changes, is a constitutional convention or its close cousin, a constitution revision commission. Until 1962, the only way that revisions, or substantial alterations, to the constitution could be proposed was through a convention. Amendments that modified one or more provisions and that were less substantial in nature could be proposed and had been by both the legislature and initiative sponsors.[2] In 1962, Proposition 7 granted authority to the legislature to allow it to establish a commission to recommend to the legislature revisions that could then be placed on the ballot.[3] Conventions and commissions have not typically been established to consider only budgetary matters. They can be if the scope is limited to that topic, but they most often are set up to examine the entire government structure and process, including its budgetary and fiscal system. For instance, the impetus behind the state's second constitutional convention in 1879 was not budgetary matters; generally it was an attempt to loosen the grip of the railroads and business on the legislature. In 1934, voters did authorize a constitutional convention, which, in part, was driven by the changing nature of the economy, but the legislature failed to approve enabling legislation.[4]

Just one year after voters approved revision commissions, the legislature established the first one by appointing a 70-person work group, including three members each from the Assembly and Senate. The first major product placed on the ballot by the legislature was Proposition 1A in 1966, which is considered one of the most significant ballot measures in the state's history. Although the commission considered abolishing the two-thirds vote requirement to pass a budget, it ultimately decided against including such a provision in Proposition 1A. The primary effect of the measure was to professionalize the legislature by making it full-time with longer sessions, higher salaries, and more legislative staff. For budgeting purposes, the longer sessions and full-time pay meant that legislators had less incentive to wrap up budget negotiations to return to their full-time jobs. In fact, Governor Pat Brown (D) initially opposed the ballot measure because of the potential for prolonged budget negotiations and the absence of a majority vote provision for the budget.[5] His concern was prescient as the state encountered its first budget stalemate three years later when Governor Ronald Reagan (R) tussled with legislative Democrats (see Chapter 2).

The success of the first constitution revision commission relieved the pressure on constitutional conventions as the only means of considering major government reform. Following the budget crisis period of the early 1990s, the legislature established a second constitution revision commission and, this time, the budget process was one of the central concerns. In the findings and declarations of the enabling legislation (SB 16, Killea, 1993) it highlighted the dysfunctional budget process:

---

[2] The state Supreme Court distinguished between amendments and revisions in court decisions dating back to 1894. See Amador Valley Joint Union High School District v. State Board of Equalization, 22 Cal. 3d 208 (Cal. 1978).

[3] Eugene C. Lee, "The Revision of California's Constitution," *California Policy Seminar Brief* (Berkeley: University of California, 1991).

[4] *Ibid.*, 3.

[5] *Ibid.*, 5.

(a) California's budget process has become crippled by a complex entanglement of constraints that interfere with an orderly and comprehensive consideration of all fiscal matters. A complete review of the process by an independent citizens' commission would provide the Legislature a basis for considering changes that would result in a more thoughtful and deliberative process.

The final commission report in 1996 issued a number of recommendations concerning the budget process, including moving to a two-year budget cycle, a stronger reserve fund, a balanced budget requirement, and a prohibition against external short-term borrowing. It also made recommendations regarding the state-local structural relationship, K-12 financing, and other major issues. Unlike the first revision commission, the legislature failed to place recommendations of the 1990s' commission on the ballot. By the time the final report was issued in 1996, the state budget situation was benefitting from the rapidly growing economy and dot.com boom. Although budget gridlock was still present, state policymakers argued over how to spend the revenue windfall. The budget crisis of the early 1990s had passed and so too the momentum for any significant changes to the fiscal and budgetary system.

It would take the second crisis budgeting era in the state's history before calls for a constitutional convention gained steam in the late 2000s. Two groups, California Forward, a good government group, and the Bay Area Council, a business advocacy group, organized efforts to authorize a convention, albeit through different routes. The Bay Area Council, under the moniker Repair California, supported a two-step initiative process to first give voters the right to call a constitutional convention and then, on the same ballot, ask them to approve a convention. Around the same time, California Forward first tried to negotiate with the legislature to approve a revision commission and threatened to take their reform proposals to the ballot if one was not authorized. In the end, the campaigns of both groups fizzled for lack of financial support. Once again, a severe fiscal crisis failed to produce any meaningful wholesale budget reform.

Constitutional conventions have not only fallen out of favor with voters in California, but in the rest of nation as well. Since 1990, voters have rejected every call for a state constitutional convention, suggesting that efforts for wholesale government reform may be fruitless for the near future.[6] The political system seems too entrenched to dislodge even in the face of severe crises. In California, perhaps more momentum for a major overhaul could have been built if the state did not begin to emerge from its fiscal crisis in 2012.

Tax Commissions

As noted at the outset of this chapter, a second vehicle for budgetary reforms that the state has employed quite frequently is tax commissions. As their

---

[6] Vladimir Kogan, "Lessons from Recent State Constitutional Conventions," *California Journal of Politics & Policy* 2, no. 2 (2010): 1–13.

name would suggest, these commissions have been focused solely on revamping the tax system by exploring the distribution of the tax burden, the administration and efficiency of certain taxes (e.g., property), and the mix of taxes. These commissions are established either by an executive order or legislation and typically include elected officials, legislative staff, outside experts, and business executives. Similar to a constitution revision commission, the process involves convening a group that produces a set of recommendations for legislative consideration or referral to the ballot. The track record for tax commissions has been poor; numerous commissions through the years have yielded few significant changes to the tax code (see Table 9.1). The most far-reaching overhaul of the tax system resulted from the 1906 tax commission that eventually led to the separation of sources system. It required two attempts at the ballot box before voters approved it in 1910.

Aside from the 1906 commission, the only other commission that was relatively successful was the 1943 Citizens' Tax Committee established by Governor Earl Warren (R). At the time, state coffers were flush with cash thanks to the adoption of the personal income and sales tax in the 1930s and a robust economy fueled by federal defense spending from World War II. The main purpose of this committee was to explore reductions in the income, franchise, and sales tax to return revenue to taxpayers. The legislature later adopted some of its recommendations, including a reduction in the sales tax rate.

Aside from these rare success stories, why have tax commissions generally been unsuccessful? One obvious reason is the procedural hurdle, the two-thirds vote that tax changes must surmount in the legislature, at least since the passage of Proposition 13. With the passage of Proposition 26 in 2010, even revenue neutral changes to the tax code require two-thirds approval. Another reason might have to do with the political environment that each commission operated within. Over the last 60 years, none of the tax commissions established have produced changes that were adopted into law. During this time period, divided government was often present and party polarization has increased significantly. These factors make it difficult for the governor and legislature to agree on recommendations. As alluded to at the beginning of this chapter, the 2003 commission report just happened to be released at an unprecedented time in our state's history (the recall election), while the 2009 report was dead on arrival because of how Democrats viewed the redistribution of the tax burden under the proposed changes.

Yet another factor for the lack of commission success is the antitax sentiment that has pervaded public discourse since the tax revolt in the 1970s. Any voters who view the tax changes as a hit to their pocketbook will not support them. Advocates of proposed changes then must demonstrate to a clear majority of voters that they will not fare worse under the new system.

Table 9.1. Select Major Budget Reform Vehicles and Outcomes

Year	Vehicle	Main Topics	Enacted
1906	Tax Commission	Separation of sources; adoption of public utilities gross receipts tax	Yes
1922	Prop 12 (LM)	Executive budget	Yes
1927	Tax Commission	Separation of sources	No
1933	Prop 1 (LM)	Property taxes; school funding; budget vote requirement (Riley-Stewart plan)	Yes
1943	Citizens' Tax Committee	Personal income taxes; franchise and sales taxes	Yes
1966	Constitution Revision Commission	General government including budget process; budget session; budget submission; legislative budget deadline	Yes
1985	Tax Commission	Split roll for property taxes; sales tax exemptions	No
1996	Constitution Revision Commission	General government including budget process; balanced budget requirement; majority vote for budget passage; reserve fund; deficit borrowing	No
2003	Tax Commission	Sales taxes; flat tax	No
2009	Tax Commission	Revenue volatility; income taxes; business net receipts tax	No

Note: LM=legislative measure; Years represent year final report was issued, if applicable.

Ballot-Box Reforms

The last vehicle for budget reform is ballot measures that arise from the legislature or the initiative process independent of any constitution review or tax commission. These usually represent incremental changes by bill authors or initiative sponsors to improve the efficiency and effectiveness of the budget system, but, on occasion, have been more wholesale in nature. These include propositions that established the executive budget process, an annual budget cycle, or altered the mix of major taxes. It is difficult to quantify the number of budget reforms that have appeared on the ballot because of the ambiguity of defining a reform. Advocates like to label their proposals "reforms" because of the positive connotations associated with that word and its appeal to voters, but it may be questionable as to whether a given change constitutes a reform. As a crude measure, we can use the number of propositions dealing with the budget process. From 1911 to 2012, there were 97 such measures on the ballot and just under half (47 percent) of them were adopted.

The model example of this vehicle for reform is Proposition 12 adopted in 1922, which instituted the executive budget process. It was an initiative sponsored by the Commonwealth Club, a good government group still in existence today. The organization convened a work group to study budget processes in other states before it submitted the petition for signature qualification. It received the backing of nearly all important stakeholders, including the governor, and passed with an overwhelming 71 percent of the vote.

Aside from the reform vehicles mentioned above, a major tax study conducted by the Assembly Revenue and Taxation Committee in the 1960s served as the basis for a number of tax changes that were later enacted. The package of reforms, which included revisions to all major state tax sources, was originally passed by the Assembly in 1965, but encountered a peculiar death in the Senate when a 5 a.m. hearing was purposely scheduled to kill it. Pieces of the package were pealed out and adopted in individual bills in ensuing decades. As David Doerr, a staffer on the study group notes, "Had AB 2270 [package of reforms] passed, it would be recognized today as one of the major developments in California tax history, along with the Separation of Sources plan, the Riley-Stewart Plan, and Proposition 13."[7]

The Need for Reform

The need and urgency for budget reform in California has generally risen and fallen with the boom and bust cycles of state finances. As fiscal conditions have worsened and crisis budgeting mode sets in, discussions about reforming the budget process and tax system have intensified only to dissipate once the budget is adopted or the economy begins to turn around. Despite two tax reform com-

---

[7] David Doerr, *California's Tax Machine, A History of Taxing and Spending in the Golden State*, 2d ed. (Sacramento: California Taxpayers Association, 2008), 642.

missions, a failed attempt at a constitutional convention, and numerous propositions to reform the fiscal system during the last crisis budgeting era, California adopted only a few reforms that directly improved the budget. The switch to a majority vote budget has been the single most important change to the budget process. It immediately curtailed the budget gridlock that had gripped Sacramento for the last five decades and placed decision making in the legislature in the hands of one party, which also improves accountability.

With gridlock and structural deficits in check for the time being, this begs the question of whether budget reform is still necessary. If California hopes to avoid future boom-and-bust cycles and the crisis budgeting that accompanies the latter, then there is more that could be done. The general public seems to think so as well. Despite the relatively strong budget conditions in 2014, 52 percent of Californians still viewed the situation as a "big problem," while 38 percent viewed it as "somewhat of a problem." Regarding the state and local tax system, 51 percent of respondents believed that major changes were necessary, while 30 percent thought minor changes were still necessary.[8]

If reforms are still necessary, which ones would be the most helpful? To address the boom and bust problem, a strong rainy-day fund and tax reform would be the most effective. Both are preventative measures that could blunt the impact of future economic recessions that are inevitable. Rainy-day funds directly address the volatility problem by stashing funds away in higher revenue years so they can be tapped in lower revenue years, but mainly treat the symptom of precipitous revenue downturns rather than the cause. The new rainy-day fund voters adopted in 2014 should ease the bust phase of the cycles, but the reserve is unlikely to be large enough to prevent the need for some major spending reductions. As long-time Sacramento columnist George Skelton put it, "What California should be doing is curing the disease by reforming the tax system, stabilizing it and ridding us of the volatility."[9] Tax reform has the potential to make the revenue system less responsive (elastic) to economic cycles and the potential to produce adequate revenue to meet the state's growing service demands.

Other reforms discussed throughout this book can improve process efficiency and fiscal accountability and are worthy of consideration in their own right, but probably cannot stabilize the state's finances as well as the two above. Lowering the vote requirement to change taxes, restrictions on ballot-box budgeting and either joint Assembly-Senate budget hearings or unicameral review would streamline the process. Restrictions on external short-term borrowing and a stronger balanced budget rule (see Chapter 7) would enhance accountability, prevent overspending, and reduce borrowing costs.

---

[8] Public Policy Institute of California Statewide Survey, *Californians and Their Government* (San Francisco: Public Policy Institute of California, May, 2014). Public Policy Institute of California Statewide Survey, *Californians and Their Government* (San Francisco: Public Policy Institute of California, March 2013).

[9] George Skelton, "The Reason for California's Tax Volatility: We Soak the Rich," *The Los Angeles Times*, May 4, 2014.

Prospects for Reform

Although the subject of which budget reforms to advance is certainly important, the more important factor in the eventual success of reform efforts may be the vehicles for reform that advocates choose, particularly given the fact that failure is more often the fate of these efforts than success. Previous reform efforts in California and other states can shed light on which vehicles may be the most productive avenues for reform.

First, a constitutional convention, while the most comprehensive approach to enact systemwide reforms, is the most unlikely vehicle for significant budgetary reform. Despite fruitless efforts in the late 2000s, state leaders have not seriously considered a convention in several decades, and, judging by the appetite for conventions among voters in other states, the idea is unlikely to appeal to Californians. The uncertainty in the outcomes of such a convention would strike fear in powerful interest groups whose position in a new system would be unpredictable. In a similar vein, the likelihood that a constitution revision commission could produce sweeping reforms, budget-related and otherwise, that would be *adopted* is low as well for similar reasons. However, if the state's financial circumstances took a turn for the worse and disrupted the delivery of state and local services more severely, then the chances for a successful revision commission would increase.

Despite their low rates of success historically, a new tax commission could serve as a successful vehicle for a revamp of the tax code if it had the proper characteristics and mission. First, the composition of the commission is important because commission members would have to know what the legislature and governor could potentially approve. This means that the governor and legislative leaders from both parties would have to serve themselves or appoint representatives who could negotiate directly on their behalf. Second, the mission of reform would have to be narrow in scope and revenue neutral. Wholesale changes (i.e., punctuations) akin to what happened in 1910 with the separation of sources or the adoption of new taxes in the 1930s are unlikely to gain much traction. Instead, a small package of piecemeal reforms would stand a better chance of eventual adoption. Any tax burden increases would have to be offset with lower rates that did not worsen the overall tax burden for middle- and lower-income residents. The goal would be revenue neutrality, and not necessarily more revenue, so that revenue growth could better keep pace with the economy (buoyancy).

Lastly, the approval procedure in the legislature would likely have to be a straight up-or-down vote on the tax reform package, similar to how Congress considered BRAC (Base Realignment and Closure) commission recommendations in the 1980s and '90s. This procedure would forgo the consideration of amendments to the tax package and attempt to depoliticize the approval process, to the extent it can be. The up-or-down stipulation would provide political cover to legislators who may still oppose specific provisions of the package, but agree the overall package is necessary.

Even with these tax commission characteristics, tax reform would be an up-hill battle in the austerity budgeting age. Lav points out that no major tax reforms have been adopted in other states since 1990.[10] In that case in Massachusetts and another in Florida in 1986, both states attempted to extend the sales tax to services and passed legislation to this effect, but it was subsequently repealed because of the political backlash. Attempts in other states since then have been piecemeal and largely failed.

With voters' apparent predisposition against wholesale budget reforms produced by either commissions or conventions, ballot measures are more likely to serve as the primary vehicle. Many significant budget reforms in California have been adopted in this fashion unaffiliated with any commission established for that purpose. This includes the adoption of the executive budget in 1922 and the Riley-Stewart plan in 1933. More recently, these ballot-box reforms have been more incremental in nature, such as the elimination of the two-thirds vote to pass a budget in 2010, the adoption of a balanced budget requirement in 2004, and the approval of a new rainy-day fund in 2014. In 2012, reform group California Forward sponsored a measure that would have made a number of changes to the budget process, including a move to a biennial cycle, and granting more budget authority to local governments, but, perhaps because of its complicated nature, the proposal failed miserably. Future proposed reforms that are incremental and simple to understand are likely to have better results.

Regardless of the vehicle employed to move budget reforms, previous experience in California and other states suggests several ways to increase the chances for success. First, reforms should be thoroughly prepared and vetted before they are pitched to the public. Many that have been adopted have been proposals that were kicked around for years before their adoption. Second, the timing of the proposal is important because there may be a small policy window to advance the reform or package of reforms.[11] Tax reform, in particular, is probably only feasible under either the best or worst fiscal circumstances and not somewhere in between. A budget crisis would provide the urgency to change the system, while strong economic and revenue conditions could ease the transition for taxpayers to a new system. Third, any serious effort at reform would have to be led by the governor, at the very least, and would probably require the support of legislative leaders as well. Lastly, as Lav suggests, significant budget reforms, especially of the tax system, need to be treated like a campaign.[12] Reform proponents need to promote a clear message and rationale for the proposal and embark on a statewide campaign to educate voters on the merits. Even after the adoption of reform, particularly involving controversial issues such as taxes,

---

[10] Iris J. Lav, "Accomplishing State Budget Policy and Process Reforms," in *The Oxford Handbook of State and Local Government Finance*, ed. Robert D. Ebel and John E. Peterson (New York: Oxford University Press, 2012), 871–93.

[11] John Kingdon, *Agendas, Alternatives, and Public Policies* (New York: Harper-Collins, 1996).

[12] Lav, "Accomplishing State Budget."

public education efforts should continue for a year or longer to preempt the losing side from instigating a repeal movement.

Conclusion

Until the 1970s, California voters and policymakers regularly adopted budget reforms by restructuring the tax system or improving the budget process. Several different types of policy vehicles were used to enact these reforms, including tax commissions, a constitution revision commission, and, most frequently, independent ballot measures. Policymakers have frequently turned to tax commissions to reform the tax code, but they have not been successful venues in the last several decades. In a similar vein, wholesale reforms were more common in the first half of the 20th century, while policymakers and voters have favored more incremental changes in recent decades.

Although no major budget reform package was adopted in the recent crisis budgeting era, switching to a majority vote to pass the budget eased much of the gridlock that regularly characterized California's budget process. While not directly related to the budget, other significant changes to the state's political system, such as lengthening term limits and the top-two primary, should help reduce the state's budget problems. Although the new rainy-day fund voters adopted in 2014 should soften the revenue blow during future economic recessions, the boom-and-bust budget cycles are likely to continue without further budgetary reforms, although perhaps to a lesser degree. Other reforms discussed throughout this book and elsewhere can improve the state's fiscal sustainability, but California, and other states, will probably never be fully immune from encounters with crisis budgeting.

Review Questions

1. What are the vehicles for budget reform? Which ones have been more successful and why?

2. Which vehicle for reform is most likely to produce results in the future? What can be done to improve the chances for adoption of budget reforms?

Additional Resources

National Conference of State Legislatures' List of State Tax Commissions

http://www.ncsl.org/research/fiscal-policy/state-tax-study-commissions.aspx

The website provides a link to reports produced by state tax commissions over the past two decades.

California Forward

http://www.cafwd.org/

The mission of California Forward is to work towards "smarter" government. They have sponsored some of the recent efforts to reform the budget process and California government.

About the Author

Jeff Cummins (Ph.D., Claremont Graduate University) is Associate Professor of Political Science at California State University, Fresno. He previously worked for the Legislative Analyst Office (LAO) in Sacramento where he advised the legislature on budgetary and policy issues. He also worked for the California State Auditor, performing audits of various state agencies. He is co-author of *California: The Politics of Diversity* and his publications on state politics and policy have appeared in *State Politics and Policy Quarterly*, *Social Science Quarterly*, and *American Politics Research*. He is a frequent contributor to the news media, where his commentary on California politics can be heard on the radio, including local affiliates of National Public Radio (NPR), and read in newspapers, such as the *Sacramento Bee*, *Los Angeles Times*, and *Fresno Bee*.

Index